D1128202

The Doors
FAQ

Series Editor: Robert Rodriguez

Other titles from the FAQ Series

Beach Boys FAQ: All That's Left to Know About America's Band
Jon Stebbins

Black Sabbath FAQ: All That's Left to Know on the First Name in Metal
Martin Popoff

Fab Four FAQ: Everything Left to Know About the Beatles . . . and More!
Stuart Shea and Robert Rodriguez

Fab Four FAQ 2.0: The Beatles' Solo Years, 1970–1980
Robert Rodriguez

**Led Zeppelin FAQ: All That's Left to Know About the Greatest
Hard Rock Band of All Time**
George Case

**Lucille Ball FAQ: Everything Left to Know About America's
Favorite Redhead**
James Sheridan and Barry Monush

Pink Floyd FAQ: Everything Left to Know . . . and More!
Stuart Shea

**Three Stooges FAQ: Everything Left to Know About the Eye-Poking,
Face-Slapping, Head-Thumping Geniuses**
David J. Hogan

**U2 FAQ: Anything You'd Ever Want to Know About the
Biggest Band in the World . . . and More!**
John D. Luerssen

The Doors
FAQ

All That's Left to Know About the Kings of Acid Rock

Rich Weidman

Backbeat
Books

An Imprint of Hal Leonard Corporation

Copyright © 2011 by Rich Weidman

All rights reserved. No part of this book may be reproduced in any form, without written permission, except by a newspaper or magazine reviewer who wishes to quote brief passages in connection with a review.

Published in 2011 by Backbeat Books
An Imprint of Hal Leonard Corporation
7777 West Bluemound Road
Milwaukee, WI 53213

Trade Book Division Editorial Offices
33 Plymouth St., Montclair, NJ 07042

The FAQ series was conceived by Robert Rodriguez and developed with Stuart Shea.

Book design by Snow Creative Services

Printed in the United States of America

Library of Congress Cataloging-in-Publication Data

Weidman, Rich.
    The Doors FAQ : all that's left to know about the kings of acid rock / Rich Weidman.
        p. cm.
    Includes bibliographical references and index.
    ISBN 978-1-61713-017-5 (alk. paper)
1. Doors (Musical group) 2. Rock musicians–United States–Biography. I. Title.
    ML421.D66W45 2011
    782.42166092'2–dc23
    [B]
                                                            2011033449

www.backbeatbooks.com

For Nadine

Contents

Foreword

The Doors Through a New Lens

We're voyeurs to the Doors story, but we're voyeurs by invitation; that started with the band's first album. We've seen the Doors through their eyes, through the eyes of friends, through the eyes of professional journalists and biographers. Rarely have we seen them through the eyes of fans. In trying to pull all the separate pieces of the Doors puzzle together and make sense of their story, *The Doors FAQ* fills this void.

The Doors were always different—from their beginnings on Venice Beach where Jim Morrison sang "Moonlight Drive" to Ray Manzarek. What was otherwise a poetic song about love has the shocking ending of the lovers drowning. When the Doors graduated to the Sunset Strip, they didn't fit into a mold or anything resembling an "L.A. sound" or a "Sunset Strip sound." Love, which was the biggest band on the strip (and a group the Doors aspired to be as big as, early on) was a folk-rock group, as were the Lovin' Spoonful, and the Byrds; the Doors were trying to blow the other bands off the stage. They were rock 'n' roll.

After they became one of the major groups of the day, they were still different. The Beatles had graduated from treacly love songs to flowery psychedelia. Like Jim Morrison, John Lennon was influenced by Arthur Rimbaud but in a more superficial way. The Beatles' psychedelia was full of light, flowers, and love; the Apollonian, as Morrison or Nietzsche would say. The Rolling Stones may have come the closest with their occasional forays into the darkness such as "Paint it Black" or "Gimme Shelter." As critic Richard Goldstein said, "The Stones are for blowing your minds, the Doors are for after your mind is blown."

Despite the darkness, the Doors' vision wasn't bleak or devoid of hope, especially on their early albums. If the Doors were in the bright midnight, they were still waiting for the sun. In "The Crystal Ship," the narrator of the song is looking for a moment of bliss, and when his love dies, he'd rather fly. Even "The End" isn't an absolute ending. The narrator of the drama is moving on, to a place where others can't follow. As late as *Morrison Hotel*, Morrison was still optimistic about the future. In "Queen of the Highway," he sang "soon to have offspring/ start it all over." Whether or not this was a reference to any particular woman in his life is arguable, but Morrison was looking to the future and the creative possibilities it might offer. It wasn't until *L.A. Woman* that Morrison's world had finally become a city of night where a cold girl will kill you in a darkened room.

The Doors are one of the truly revolutionary groups of rock 'n' roll. Listen to most lyrics by their contemporaries and you'll find fairly traditionally themed songs. It was only long hair and volume that upset the over-thirty crowd. The Doors weren't revolutionary in the political sense. The Doors changed rock 'n' roll. While Morrison embraced some of the familiar tropes of '60s rock music—girls, love, and cars—in his hands those familiar themes become something different, mysterious, and altogether dangerous. Love becomes sex, an active passion, not an idealistic longing. In declarations such as "love me two times/I'm goin' away" or "love me all night long," the meaning becomes apparent. Cars aren't for cruising with your girlfriend or carrying your surfboard; they become vehicles to destinations unknown and possibly dangerous.

The Doors were a literary band. Most people attribute this to Jim Morrison being well read and taking their name from William Blake via Aldous Huxley's *The Doors of Perception*. Ray Manzarek has always said that the Doors were a synthesis of blues, jazz, classical music, and Beat poetry. Over the years Manzarek has ably demonstrated the musical origins of the Doors on CDs and videos. But their literary influences, beyond a few mentions of writers' names or a Doors reading list, is rarely delved into by other books. But has any other rock group worn its literary influences on its sleeve like the Doors? What other band has included the English poetry of William Blake ("some are born to sweet delight/some are born to endless night"), early twentieth-century French novels (*Journey to the End of the Night*), aphorisms ("blood will be born in the birth of a nation/blood is the rose of a mysterious union") to John Rechy and a city of night, and Nietzsche's *Birth of Tragedy*, a veritable blueprint for the Doors.

Literature influenced the Doors lyrically but also personally. Jim Morrison became the personification of Jack Kerouac's hero of *On the Road*, "a sideburned hero of the snowy West" and one of those "mad to live, mad to talk, mad to be saved, desirous of everything at the same time, the ones who never yawn or say a commonplace thing, but burn, burn, burn . . ." Morrison became the rock star's idea of a rock star, leonine looks in a halo of hair and leather pants. Forty-five years later we've seen endless copies and variations on Morrison's model. His stage attitude and slouch make him the progenitor of punk rock. The Doors as a whole became a model for bands to come like the Screaming Trees, Nirvana, and Pearl Jam.

By the late '70s the Doors were facing the obscurity that had overtaken many of their contemporaries. The first flash of '70s resurrection came with *An American Prayer*, Morrison's poems recorded in '69 and '70. Later the surviving Doors added music, but the poetry of Morrison and the music of the Doors wasn't well received in the age of disco. Then came the almost simultaneous hits of *Apocalypse Now* and the Jerry Hopkins, Danny Sugerman biography of Morrison, *No One Here Gets Out Alive,* which defibrillated the Doors' dormant career and brought their music to a new audience that continues to this day, and threatens to classify them as the classical music of the future.

Doors history didn't stop with the death of Jim Morrison. Surviving members Ray Manzarek, John Densmore, and Robby Krieger went on to solo careers and projects, including the usual twists and turns of rock groups when the venue changed from albums, CDs, and concert halls to courtrooms. *The Doors FAQ* author Rich Weidman goes deeper into this post-Morrison second life of the band than other books.

As a longtime Doors fan I was overcome by a sense of discovery as I read *The Doors FAQ* that I haven't experienced in quite some time from Doors literature. I learned of new connections through Weidman's delving below the surface of what's usually told in the Doors story. He stays true to the band's literary roots and takes an unconventional approach to the Doors and the people, places, and events that make up their Doors history. Whether you're a new fan or an older one, you will take a journey of discovery or rediscovery of the Doors and experience them through a new lens.

Jim Cherry

Jim Cherry writes The Doors Examiner. He is the author of the novels *The Last Stage* and *Becoming Angel,* and a book of short stories, *Stranger Souls.* Writing under the influence of rock 'n' roll! www.jymsbooks.com.

Acknowledgments

First of all, I would like to thank my wife, Nadine, and kids, Hailey and Dylan, for their endless encouragement during the writing of *The Doors FAQ*, as well as their patience with me as I toiled away on the book nights and weekends. Without your support, I would never have been able to complete this project and am eternally grateful. I also appreciate the fact that you let me display all of my Doors memorabilia and stacks of Doors books in the den. Love you guys! A special thanks also to my family—Mom, Dad, Boyd, and Tracy and her family—for all your support and enthusiasm.

Thanks to my good friend and website co-conspirator Jack Thompson, who has collaborated with me on many projects over the years (most being of dubious value!) and served as a mentor throughout the writing of this book. Jack provided invaluable advice as we met weekly to discuss my progress at the Blue Martini for happy hour or during pub trivia at Gator's Dockside. It seems like only yesterday that we were hanging out on Pompano Beach and alienating beachgoers by blaring *Waiting for the Sun* every weekend.

I appreciate all of the Doors researchers and collectors who provided me with fascinating images for the book in the form of promotional photos, posters, handbills, tickets, etc., including Kerry Humpherys of www.doors.com, Logan Janzen of www.mildequator.com, Ida Miller of www.idafan.com, Susan Bourdin of www.jimmorrisonsparis.com, as well as Derek Pattison, Mark Smigel, Stev Bauske, and Dan Thiel. I am extremely grateful for your assistance!

Jim Cherry, author of *The Last Stage*, helped greatly in getting the word out about the book. In addition, Jim is the writer of *The Doors Examiner*, which provided me with a great resource on Doors history and the most up-to-date information on all of the activities surrounding all three surviving band members.

Thanks to my boss, Robert Jensen, who allowed me the flexibility to take a lot of time off work with little notice so I could spend a few weeks working exclusively on the book. A special mention goes to the editors at Alternative Reel—Bill Chinaski, Jim Foley, and Art Spackle (as well as Australian correspondent Ben John Smith)—for offering me their wealth of knowledge about Doors trivia and facts.

Robert Rodriguez, creator of the FAQ series, provided me with an amazing selection of Doors images, as well as informative tips on the editorial process. In addition, Bernadette Malavarca of Backbeat Books assisted me greatly throughout the entire editorial procedure. Thanks also to Robert Lecker of the Robert Lecker Agency for his persistence and assistance.

Last but not least, thanks to Tony Fernandez of Peace Frog, whose lively tribute to Jim Morrison and the Doors is helping introduce the music to a whole new generation of fans as they "break on through to the other side."

Introduction

As a teenager in 1980 I got caught up in the first major renaissance of interest in the Doors (since lead singer Jim Morrison died under mysterious circumstances in Paris on July 3, 1971) when I stumbled upon a copy of the phenomenally successful Morrison biography *No One Here Gets Out Alive* (a tattered copy of which remains prominently on my bookshelf). This led to the purchase of *The Doors: Greatest Hits*, the band's all-time bestselling album that sold nearly one million albums in 1980 alone. After watching the riveting, hallucinatory opening sequence in *Apocalypse Now*, which featured chopper blades, napalm, and the haunting ballad "The End," I was totally hooked on this dark, brooding band that sounded to me like the antithesis of 1960s bubblegum pop as exemplified by the Turtles' "Happy Together," a No. 1 hit in February 1967. That was just one month after the Doors released their self-titled first album, now considered one of the best debuts in rock history.

Next, I started reading the works of authors who had influenced Morrison. They include Jack Kerouac and other Beat Generations writers like Allen Ginsberg and William S. Burroughs, French symbolist poet Arthur Rimbaud, German philosopher Friedrich Nietzsche, and French author Louis-Ferdinand Celine, whose 1932 novel *Journey to the End of the Night* inspired the Doors' haunting ballad "End of the Night." As an English major in college, I was fascinated by this rock band that utilized a myriad of literary references in their songs. So it was no surprise when I attended a tribute to Jack Kerouac in the summer of 1988 in his hometown of Lowell, Massachusetts, and discovered that the poetry reading featured Beat legends Allen Ginsberg, Lawrence Ferlinghetti, Gregory Corso, and Michael McClure, as well as none other than Doors keyboardist Ray Manzarek!

Indeed, every ten years or so produces a new wave of Doors fans—sparked by events such as Oliver Stone's heavily fictionalized 1991 film *The Doors*; the controversial formation of the Doors of the 21st Century in 2002; and in 2010 the release of the Grammy Award-winning documentary, *When You're Strange*, and the Florida Clemency Board's pardon of Morrison for two misdemeanor convictions (profanity and indecent exposure) stemming from the notorious Miami concert on March 1, 1969. While other bands of the 1960s have turned into nostalgia acts that play the state fair circuit, the Doors' music remains timeless, always accessible to turn on a new generation of fans.

Instead of another dull, by-the-numbers band biography, *The Doors FAQ* features a dynamic and unorthodox exploration of this remarkable band—a psychedelic collage that delves into their sources of inspiration (both literary and musical); early beginnings (such as Morrison, a UCLA film student, joining Rick and the Ravens onstage at the Turkey Joint West); Los Angeles Doors landmarks; essential recordings; and, last but not least, Morrison's outrageous stage presence. In addition, the book highlights post-Morrison band activities, including the release of two forgotten studio albums, *Other Voices* and *Full Circle*; the spoken-word album *An American Prayer*; Oliver Stone's *The Doors*; the band's 1993 induction into the Rock and Roll Hall of Fame with Eddie Vedder of Pearl Jam filling in for Morrison; and the controversy surrounding the Doors of the 21st Century.

Finally, the book includes a number of eclectic features such as the top ten most notorious Doors concerts, the band's most notable TV performances, common myths about Morrison's death, musicians who have been influenced by the Doors, films that feature Doors songs in their soundtracks, and much more.

Hopefully, everyone from the casual Doors listener to the hardcore fan who believes he or she has read it all will find *The Doors FAQ* a rewarding reading experience. "Is everybody in? The ceremony is about to begin . . ."

Friends I Have Gathered Together

Key Players in the Doors' Saga

In the beginning we were creating our music, ourselves, every night . . . starting with a few outlines, maybe a few words for a song. Sometimes we worked out in Venice, looking at the surf. We were together a lot and it was good times for all of us. Acid, sun, friends, the ocean, and poetry and music.

—*Jim Morrison*

Through a series of unlikely coincidences and good fortune, the Doors somehow formed in Venice Beach, honed their sound in Sunset Strip clubs such as the London Fog and the Whisky A Go Go, and managed to break out and score a contract with Elektra Records, primarily a folk music label founded by Jac Holzman in 1950. Jim Morrison had no musical background, while Ray Manzarek was grounded in classical and blues music, John Densmore desired to be a jazz drummer, and Robby Krieger started out playing flamenco guitar. Producer Paul Rothchild and audio engineer Bruce Botnick worked with these disparate elements to help create *The Doors* (1967), considered today one of the most stunning debut albums in rock history. Other key members of the Doors' circle included Doors manager Bill Siddons, who unwittingly helped perpetuate the "Morrison is still alive" myth by failing to view his body in Paris; Pamela Courson, Morrison's "cosmic mate" who was with him until the end; and Danny Sugerman, super fan and relentless promoter of the Doors' mystique.

Ray Manzarek, Doors Keyboardist

The oldest Door, and the band's cofounder along with Jim Morrison, Ray Manzarek often came off as a kind of bespectacled, perpetually stoned professor, somewhat akin to Donald Sutherland's character, "Dave Jennings," in *Animal House* ("Would anybody like to smoke some pot?"). Onstage, however, with his head flailing wildly and fingers flying maniacally across the keyboard while improvising the bass parts on his Fender Rhodes organ, Manzarek evinced a total psychedelic, blues-driven intensity.

Raymond Daniel Manczarek (he dropped the "c" soon after cofounding the Doors) was born on February 12, 1939, to a working-class family in Chicago, Illinois. His grandparents had immigrated from Poland in the 1890s. Manzarek started practicing piano at an early age, and he eventually studied classical music, including Bach, Rachmaninoff, and Tchaikovsky, at the Chicago Conservatory. However, Manzarek was blown away when he first heard the Chicago blues and eventually fell under the sway of such legends as Muddy Waters (in his official Elektra biography, Manzarek listed Waters along with Belgian singer-songwriter Jacques Brel as influences), Jimmy Reed, John Lee Hooker, and others. He also discovered jazz artists like Miles Davis, John Coltrane, Ahmad Jamal, Ramsey Lewis, and Bill Evans to round out his musical education.

After graduating from the Catholic all-boy St. Rita High School, Manzarek embarked on a conventional career path, earning a bachelor's degree in economics from DePaul University. After briefly attending UCLA law school and serving a two-year stint in the army (where he got the opportunity to smoke some genuine "Thai stick" in Thailand), Manzarek headed back to UCLA, where he majored in cinematography, completed three well-received short films (*Evergreen, Induction,* and *Who and Where I Live*), and met fellow film student Jim Morrison. According to Manzarek in his autobiography, *Light My Fire,* "instead of realizing our parents' dreams, much to their chagrin, we created our own dreams." To help pay for tuition, Manzarek took the stage as "Screamin' Ray Daniels" on weekends at a total dive called the Turkey Joint West with his brothers, Rick (guitar) and Jim (harmonica), in a local surf/blues band called Rick and the Ravens. Manzarek would frequently coax fellow film students, including Morrison, to join him onstage and help him belt out such classics as "Louie, Louie," in front of the crowd of blitzed college students. In the summer of 1965, Manzarek and Morrison cofounded the Doors after a chance meeting on the beach in Venice. Soon later, at a Transcendental Meditation session, Manzarek recruited a drummer, John Densmore, who in turn brought guitarist Robby Krieger into the Doors.

Post-Doors, Manzarek recorded two solo albums, *The Golden Scarab* (which was billed as "a busy fusion of Jazz, Exotica, Rock, Rumba and Salsa") and *The Whole Thing Started with Rock 'n' Roll.* He also performed in several bands (including Nite City), recorded a rock adaptation of Carl Orff's *Carmina Burana* with Philip Glass, produced four albums with influential Los Angeles punk band X (*Los Angeles; Wild Gift; Under the Big, Black Sun;* and *More Fun in the New World*), backed Beat poet Michael McClure's poetry readings, and collaborated with poet Michael C. Ford. In 1996, Manzarek recorded *The Doors Myth and Reality: The Spoken Word History.* Manzarek's autobiography, *Light My Fire: My Life with the Doors,* was published in 1998. In 2001, Manzarek published his first novel, *The Poet in Exile,* which explored the myth that Jim Morrison had faked his death. In 2002, Manzarek organized the highly controversial group the Doors of the 21st Century with Robby Krieger that later morphed into Riders on the Storm and today is simply known as Manzarek-Krieger. In 2006, Ray Manzarek published a second novel, *Snake Moon*, an "erotic ghost story" set during the Civil War that was a reinterpretation of the Japanese film *Ugetsu* (directed by Kenji Mizoguchi). Manzarek and his wife, Dorothy, live in Napa County, California. They have one son, Pablo, who is also a musician. Manzarek and Krieger still occasionally tour as Manzarek-Krieger.

Jim Morrison, Doors Lead Singer/Songwriter

With no musical background whatsoever, Morrison evolved into one of rock 'n' roll's most recognizable icons as he morphed into a variety of roles during the brief, five-year span of the Doors—including the "Lizard King," Dionysus reincarnate, the "King of Orgasmic Rock," shaman, "Erotic Politician," poet-genius, and legendary boozer hell-bent on self-destruction. In the end Morrison was both tragic and pathetic, but, ironically, his death at the age of twenty-seven helped seal his immortality as a rock legend.

James Douglas Morrison was born in Melbourne, Florida, on December 8, 1943, to George Stephen Morrison and Clara Clarke Morrison. He had a sister, Anne, and a brother, Andy. Typical of military families, the Morrisons moved frequently during Jim's early years. Morrison composed his first poem, "The Pony Express," at the age of ten. He reportedly had an IQ of 149. His early influences included German philosopher Friedrich Nietzsche (*The Birth of Tragedy from the Spirit of Music*); French Symbolist poet Arthur Rimbaud (*A Season in Hell*); Charles Baudelaire (*The Flowers of Evil*); Antonin Artaud (*The Theatre and Its Double*); William Blake (*The Marriage of Heaven and Hell*); Louis-Ferdinand Celine (*Journey to the End of the Night*); and Beat Generation writers such as Jack Kerouac (*On the Road*), Allen Ginsberg ("Howl"), and William S. Burroughs (*Naked Lunch*). Indeed, Morrison encapsulated traits of both the wild-eyed, maniacal Dean Moriarty and the shy, introspective Sal Paradise from *On the Road*.

In June 1961, Morrison graduated from George Washington High School in Alexandria, Virginia. His parents then enrolled him at St. Petersburg Junior College, and he went to live with his paternal grandparents in Clearwater, Florida. In 1962, Morrison transferred to Florida State University (FSU) in Tallahassee, where he appeared in a college recruitment film. While attending FSU, Morrison was arrested for a prank en route to a home football game. In January 1964, he moved to Los Angeles to study film at the UCLA Theater Arts Department. One of his courses on Antonin Artaud was taught by Jack Hirschman in the Comparative Literature program with UCLA's English Department. In 1965, the *Artaud Anthology*, which Hirschman edited and assigned to Morrison's class, was published by City Lights Books in San Francisco. Morrison received his bachelor's degree in cinematography from UCLA in 1965.

After graduation, Morrison led a bohemian lifestyle in Venice Beach, living on his friend Dennis Jakob's rooftop, dropping acid, and writing song lyrics. After a chance meeting with Ray Manzarek on the beach, the two agreed to form the Doors. Morrison suggested the band's unique name from the title of

The Doors had their rather unlikely origins at the UCLA Film School, the beach in laid-back Venice, and the Third Street Meditation Center in Los Angeles.

Courtesy of Robert Rodriguez

Aldous Huxley's *The Doors of Perception*, which itself was taken from a quote from William Blake's *The Marriage of Heaven and Hell*: "If the doors of perception were cleansed everything would appear to man as it is, infinite." In his official Elektra biography, Morrison famously wrote, "I am interested in anything about revolt, disorder, chaos—especially activity that seems to have no meaning. It seems to me to be the road toward freedom—external revolt is a way to bring about internal freedom." Under "Family Info" Morrison simply wrote "dead." For musical influences he listed the Beach Boys, Kinks, Love, Frank Sinatra, and Elvis Presley. As far as "Plans/Ambitions," he answered "make films."

Morrison was known for his outrageous stage antics, which included getting arrested onstage during an infamous performance at the New Haven Arena in 1967 and encouraging fans to riot as he did at the Singer Bowl concert in New York City and the Cleveland Public Auditorium, both in 1968. Manzarek compared Morrison's onstage persona to that of Marlon Brando in *The Fugitive Kind*. In *Light My Fire*, Manzarek remarked, "Jim was a combination of Brando's character in *The Fugitive Kind* and James Dean's in *Rebel Without a Cause*."

During one fateful night in Miami at the Dinner Key Auditorium on March 1, 1969, a heavily inebriated Morrison (adapting the radical ideas from Julian Beck's experimental Living Theater) succeeded in killing off his "Lizard King" stage persona through a series of drunken exploits that led to an arrest warrant for lewd and lascivious behavior, indecent exposure, open profanity, and drunkenness. Morrison then tried to move away and explore his other interests: poetry and film. In 1969, he realized a dream by self-publishing two volumes of his poetry, *The Lords/Notes on Vision* and *The New Creatures*. He was also part of a film project called *HWY: An American Pastoral*. On his twenty-seventh birthday on December 8, 1970, Morrison recorded some of his poetry in a sound studio. The recordings would later end up on the posthumous spoken-word album *An American Prayer*, which was released in 1978.

Disillusioned with his rock star image, Morrison and his girlfriend, Pamela Courson, headed to Paris in March 1971. Four months later, on July 3, 1971, he died under mysterious circumstances. He is buried in the Pere Lachaise Cemetery, and his gravestone reads: KATA TON DAIMONA EAYTOY (Greek meaning "true to his own spirit"). After Morrison's death, Jac Holzman, president of Elektra Records, released a statement, saying that Morrison "possessed special insight into people, their lives and into the dark corners of human existence."

John Densmore, Doors Drummer

John Paul Densmore was born on December 1, 1944, in Santa Monica, California. A prototypical band geek, Densmore started playing the drums in junior high school and joined the marching band in high school. He became interested in jazz at University High School (also attended by Robby Krieger) and used a fake ID to get into Shelly's Manne-Hole in North Hollywood to watch the performances of his favorite jazz musicians. Densmore's main influence was Elvin Jones, a renowned drummer with the John Coltrane Quartet. He also admired Dave Brubeck, Les McCann, Miles Davis, and John Coltrane. Densmore attended Santa Monica City College as a music major and Cal. State-Northridge, changing his major to sociology and then anthropology. He later ended up at UCLA and dropped out when he was only a year away from getting his bachelor of arts degree in anthropology.

Densmore joined a group called Terry Driscoll and the Twilighters before forming another short-lived band with Robby Krieger called the Psychedelic Rangers. After a chance meeting with Ray Manzarek during a Transcendental Meditation course in the summer of 1965, Densmore became the third member to join the Doors. In his official Elektra biography, Densmore cited the Beatles, Van Morrison, and Jimmy Reed among his musical influences. As the jazz player in the Doors, Densmore "kept perfect time for Jim," according to Doors manager Bill Siddons in *Follow the Music*. Densmore left the band several times over the years in response to Morrison's drunken antics onstage. In *Light My Fire*, Manzarek caused controversy by claiming that early on in the band's career, Morrison told Manzarek he wanted the band to get rid of Densmore and find a drummer because he couldn't "stand him as a human being." Manzarek convinced Morrison to keep the drummer.

Densmore married Julia Brose in 1970 (the two divorced in 1972). After the Doors disbanded in 1973, Densmore formed the reggae-influenced Butts Band with Robby Krieger. The band folded in 1975 after just two albums. During the 1980s, Densmore turned to acting and appeared in a one-act play he had written called *Skins*. In 1985, he won the Los Angeles Weekly Theater Award for music with *Methusalem*, which was directed by Tim Robbins. Densmore published his autobiography, *Riders on the Storm*, in 1990. It was the first Doors autobiography written by a band member. During the 1990s, Densmore had several acting jobs, including a cameo as a recording engineer in Oliver Stone's *The Doors* and an episode of *Coach* where he portrayed a Harley-Davidson salesman with a goatee. Today, Densmore is married to documentary filmmaker Leslie Neale and lives in his hometown of Santa Monica. He has spent the past decade or so filing legal injunctions to prevent the other Doors members to tour using the "Doors" name. Densmore is reportedly going to publish *The Doors Unhinged: Rock 'n' Roll Goes on Trial* in 2011; however, a dispute with the publisher has left the book's publication in doubt.

Robby Krieger, Doors Guitarist/Songwriter

The youngest Door, Robert Alan "Robby" Krieger was born on January 8, 1946, in Los Angeles, one of nonidentical twins. The son of an aeronautical engineer, Krieger was a laid-back surfer who didn't pick up a guitar until the age of seventeen. He purchased a Mexican flamenco guitar a year later and took flamenco lessons for a few months. He also became interested in Indian music, studying the sitar and sarod. Krieger attended U.C. Santa Barbara and then transferred to UCLA, where he studied psychology briefly. In college Krieger played in a jug band called the Back Bay Chamberpot Terriers. However, after seeing Chuck Berry in concert at the Santa Monica Auditorium, he traded in his classical guitar for a Gibson SG.

Krieger, who played with Densmore in a band called the Psychedelic Rangers, was the last member to join the Doors (in fact, he did not participate in recording the Doors' demo in September 1965). After rehearsing "Moonlight Drive" with the band, Krieger was sold on the Doors' potential and promptly signed on. In his official Elektra biography, Krieger listed Fats Domino, Elvis Presley, the Paul Butterfield Blues Band, Van Morrison, Jimmy Reed, James Brown, and the Platters as his musical influences. Krieger wrote several of the Doors' biggest hits, including their first No. 1 hit, "Light My Fire" (which was the first song he ever wrote!), as well as "Love Me Two Times" (the second song he ever wrote), "Touch Me," and "Love Her Madly." In addition, Krieger can be heard singing "Runnin' Blue," the Otis Redding tribute he wrote for the Doors' fourth album, *The Soft Parade*. Krieger shared lead vocal duties with Manzarek on the Doors' final two albums, *Other Voices* and *Full Circle*. In *Follow the Music*, Doors manager Bill Siddons compared Krieger to Jackson Pollock, calling him "the abstract artist in the group."

In 1972, Krieger married Lynn Veres (who had briefly dated Morrison years before). He teamed with Densmore to form the Butts Band and later released several solo albums, including *Versions* (1983), which featured a memorable instrumental version of "The Crystal Ship." Krieger is listed No. 91 on Rolling Stone's list of the "100 Greatest Guitarists of All Time." At the 2007 Grammy Awards, the Doors received a Lifetime Achievement Award, which was accepted by Krieger along with Manzarek's brother, Rick, and Morrison's sister, Anne (Densmore appeared via a video "thank you"). Krieger thanked his bandmates for inviting him to join the Doors since he had "only been playing guitar for three months at the time, but I didn't tell them that." In addition, Krieger related some early advice his father had given him when he first joined the band: "The first time my Dad met Jim Morrison, he looked at me and Ray and John and said, 'Boys, I think we better invest in a good criminal attorney.' And we did." In 2010, Krieger's solo album, *Singularity*, was nominated for a Grammy Award in the category of Best Pop Instrumental Album.

Paul Rothchild, Doors Producer

Often referred to as the "fifth Door," Paul A. Rothchild was born on April 18, 1935, in Brooklyn, New York, grew up in Teaneck, New Jersey, and began his career as a producer on the Boston folk scene. In 1963, he become a producer for Elektra Records and soon relocated to Los Angeles. In his autobiography, Manzarek referred to Rothchild as the "coolest, hippest, most intelligent producer on the planet." According to Manzarek, Rothchild was both streetwise and college smart, knowing his "Bach, Mingus and Monk, Sabicas, Jim Kweskin Jug Band, Arthur Rimbaud and Federico Fellini." The fact that Rothchild had been busted for drugs simply enhanced his "street cred" among the Doors.

Holzman hired Rothchild to Elektra Records with the intention of bringing "street music to this company." One of Rothchild's first independent signings was the Paul Butterfield Blues Band. Rothchild attended the 1965 Newport Folk Festival on July 25, 1965, the historic night Dylan (backed by the Paul Butterfield Blues Band) went "electric": "I was at the console, mixing the set, the only one there who had ever recorded electric music. I could barely hear Dylan because of the furor . . . To me, that night at Newport was as clear as crystal. It's the end of one era and the beginning of another."

Rothchild produced the first five Doors albums: *The Doors, Strange Days, Waiting for the Sun, The Soft Parade*, and *Morrison Hotel*—all of which achieved gold record status. However, he quit as Doors producer during the recording of *L.A. Woman*, bored by what he perceived as "cocktail music" (his least favorite song being the Robby Krieger-penned "Love Her Madly"). Over his storied career, Rothchild also produced LPs and singles by John Sebastian, Joni Mitchell, Neil Young, Tom Paxton, Fred Neil, Tom Rush, the Paul Butterfield Blues Band, the Lovin' Spoonful, Tim Buckley, Love, Clear Light, Rhinoceros, and Janis Joplin (including her final album *Pearl*, which featured her only No. 1 single, "Me and Bobby McGee").

During the 1970s, Rothchild produced the Outlaws' self-titled debut album, as well as the soundtrack album for the Bette Midler film *The Rose*, which was very loosely based on the life of Joplin. In 1991, Rothchild produced the soundtrack to Oliver Stone's *The Doors*. Rothchild died of lung cancer in Los Angeles in 1995 at the age of fifty-nine. Legendary record producer Rick Rubin in *Canyon of Dreams* praised Rothchild's skills, stating that his "records feel immediate and lively, like you're there. He's a real light hand as a producer."

Bruce Botnick, Doors Audio Engineer/Producer

Known as the "boy wonder" of Sunset Sound Recording Studio and the "sixth Door," Botnick served as the Doors' audio engineer and record producer. Botnick started his career directly out of high school, first at Liberty Records' recording studio and then moving in 1963 to Sunset Sound Recorders, where the Doors would eventually record their first two studio albums—*The Doors* and *Strange Days*. During the early years, Botnick basically lived at the studio, working on commercials and children's albums for Sunset Sound's legendary founder, Tutti Camarata, who had served as Walt Disney's director of recording during the 1950s. Camarata later credited Botnick as being instrumental in establishing Sunset Sound's early rock credentials. Botnick engineered Love's first two albums and coproduced their third album, the band's masterpiece, *Forever Changes*, along with eccentric singer-songwriter Arthur Lee. Botnick, who also engineered albums for Buffalo Springfield, Neil Young, and Tim Buckley, was "the *perfect* engineer" for the Doors, according to Ray Manzarek, a "good and decent man with ears of gold." In an interview with Paul Williams of *Crawdaddy!* magazine, Doors producer Paul Rothchild referred to Sunset Sound Recorders as "the best studio in the country right now, mainly because of Bruce Botnick . . . one of the grooviest engineers I can conceive of, extraordinarily creative and very pleasant to work with."

Botnick was totally unfazed by Morrison's frequent drunken and/or stoned antics in the recording studio. He has also disputed one of the most popular Doors legends—that Morrison threw a television through the control room window after he caught Botnick watching a baseball game during a recording session. In *Temples of Sound: Inside the Great Recording Studios*, Botnick remarked, "It was my TV. It was tuned to a Dodgers game, and it was facing into the control room and he bumped up against it, and it fell on the floor. But it still works. I still have it." Botnick took over production of the Doors' sixth studio album, *L.A. Woman*, after Rothchild quit in disgust over what he perceived as a lack of quality songs and apathy among the band members. Post-Doors, Botnick produced Manzarek's first solo effort, *The Golden Scarab*; served as an assistant on the Rolling Stones' *Let It Bleed* album; and produced Eddie Money's first two albums,

Eddie Money in 1977 and *Life for the Taking* in 1978. He has also engineered scores for films by Steven Spielberg and James Cameron.

Bill Siddons, Doors Manager

A teenage roadie for the Doors, Siddons was born in 1949 and grew up in Redondo Beach, California. In high school, he briefly dated Lynette "Squeaky" Fromme, who would later become a member of the notorious Manson Family. Siddons served as the Doors' manager from 1968 to 1973. Once asked for his first impression of Morrison, Siddons replied, "He scared me to death." Manzarek gave Siddons a rather mixed review in *Light My Fire*, referring to him as "our roadie and we promoted him to phone answerer, but . . . it went to his head. He became arrogant . . . But what the hell, he was trustworthy."

After Jim Morrison died in Paris on July 3, 1971, it was Siddons who flew to Paris and helped arrange the funeral and burial. However, controversy ensued since Siddons never bothered to look at Morrison's body, lending to the "faked his death" conspiracy theory as outlined in the 1980 Jim Morrison biography, *No One Here Gets Out Alive*. Post-Doors, Siddons managed or co-managed a variety of popular bands and artists such as Crosby, Stills, and Nash; Poco; America; Van Morrison; Pat Benatar; Jerry Cantrell; Robert Palmer; and John Klemmer. The cofounder of Core Entertainment, a professional management firm, Siddons is married to comedian Elayne Boosler.

Jac Holzman, Founder of Elektra Records

In his fascinating history of Elektra Records, *Follow the Music: The Life and Times of Elektra Records in the Great Years of American Pop Culture*, Jac Holzman stated, "The Doors embodied—incarnated—a major upheaval in popular culture. Their music was of the times and it shaped the times." Born in 1931, Holzman was the founder and chief executive officer of both Elektra Records and Nonesuch Records. He founded Elektra Records (named after a Greek demi-goddess) at the age of nineteen while attending St. John's College in 1950 and initially ran the label out of his dorm room with an operating budget of $600. Primarily a folk label in the early days (the first folk record they put out was *Jean Ritchie Singing Traditional Songs of Her Kentucky Mountain Family*), Elektra signed such legendary acts as Tom Paxton, Phil Ochs, Love, Paul Butterfield Blues Band, the Doors, Judy Collins, Carly Simon, MC5, the Stooges, Harry Chapin, Bread, and Queen. In 1964, Holzman founded Nonesuch Records, the world's first budget classical music label.

In the liner notes to *Journey to Love: Rare and Early Elektra Classics*, Holzman stated, "I worked with my artists as if I were a patron. Artists liked that, that you could talk to them about what interests them most, which is what they do, and over time they begin to trust you and your judgment." According to Billy James (who "discovered" the Doors in 1965 and signed them to their first contract with Columbia Records), "Jac was in a class by himself because of his technical sense, his respect for and knowledge of engineering and acoustical properties, which was something he had been interested in as a child." Holzman ran Elektra until 1973. He continued with Warner Communications as Chief Technologist. In 1982, he became chairman of Panavision, Inc., and in 1986 he created FirstMedia. In 1991, he established the Discovery family of labels, which later became part of the Sire Records Group, a unit of Time Warner. In 2011, Holzman received the NARAS Trustee Grammy for Lifetime Achievement. Holzman is the father of jazz-rock keyboardist Adam Holzman.

Pamela Courson, Morrison's "Cosmic Mate"

Courson shared a tumultuous but enduring relationship with "the Lizard King." According to Manzarek, "There were always girls along the line but none of them was like Pamela . . . They were destined for each other." Three years younger than Morrison, Courson was born on December 22, 1946, in Weed, California, a short distance from Mount Shasta. Her father had been a bombardier navy pilot and was now a commander in the U.S. Naval Reserve and high school principal. Contrary to Oliver Stone's romantic Hollywood version of the first meeting between Courson and Morrison, she most likely met him for the first time at either the London Fog or Gazzarri's while studying art at Los Angeles City College. She was just nineteen years old.

According to Manzarek, it was Densmore who first tried to make a move on Courson, "the first one to be hooked by her cinnamon bait," but he struck out miserably and Morrison immediately stepped up to the plate. According to legend, Neil Young wrote "Cinnamon Girl" about the red-haired beauty. Morrison's buddy Frank Lisciandro called Courson Morrison's "soulmate, refuge and friend." Although they both had multiple flings on the side, they always ended up together during their five-year relationship. Several classic Doors songs were reportedly inspired by Courson such as "Roadhouse Blues," "Queen of the Highway," "Love Street," "Blue Sunday," and "You Make Me Real," among others. Morrison bought Courson a trendy boutique called Themis that was never profitable. Courson lived with Morrison in Paris during the spring and summer of 1971 and was the last known person to see him before he died mysteriously in the apartment they shared. In a will signed on February 12, 1969, Morrison left his entire estate to Courson, who followed him to the grave after overdosing on heroin in her Los Angeles apartment on April 25, 1974. She is buried under the name "Pamela Susan Morrison" at Fairhaven Memorial Park in Santa Ana, California. Her death certificate listed her occupation as "women's apparel." Courson's parents, Columbus and Penny Courson, inherited Morrison's fortune, which included his 25 percent share of the Doors' recording and publishing concerns. After Morrison's parents entered the fray, the estate went back into court for another five years until 1979, when the singer's quarter-share was divided between the Coursons and Morrison's parents.

Danny Sugerman, Doors Biographer, Co-Manager

Daniel Stephen "Danny" Sugerman did as much as anyone to further the Doors' mystique after Jim Morrison's death in Paris in 1971. He was just twelve years old when he attended his first Doors concert at the California State Gymnasium in Los Angeles on October 6, 1967. In his autobiography, *Wonderland Avenue*, Sugerman details his first impression of Morrison onstage: "Nothing in my life prepared me for the arrival of Jim Morrison . . . I heard a scream, long, pained, thick and husky: loud enough and strong enough to wake me up. In his black leather, with long brown hair and angelic features, the singer was a phantom, staggering across the stage, about to fall but somehow keeping his balance, bellowing a long-winded series of screams and grunts . . . He dropped back, then leapt forward, throwing his face at ours, his eyes agog, terrorized, tearing at the microphone, hands a blur, on the verge of insanity, and he screamed again, the sound of a thousand curtains torn." Astonished by Jim Morrison's intense performance that night, which culminated when the lead singer collapsed "in a lifeless heap" on the stage during "When the Music's Over," Sugerman remarked, "It was the end. It was the end of the world as I had known it. Nothing would ever again be the same for me."

Sugerman, who was born on October 11, 1954, and grew up in Beverly Hills, began hanging out at the Doors office and eventually started answering fan mail and compiling a comprehensive scrapbook of the band that would later evolve into *The Doors: The Illustrated History*, which was published in 1983. Sugerman cowrote *No One Here Gets Out Alive*, the first biography about Jim Morrison and an instrumental part of the "Doors resurrection" of the early 1980s. According to coauthor Jerry Hopkins, "It was [Sugerman's] devotion and dedication that moved *No One Here Gets Out Alive* from my closet of unpublished manuscripts to the public eye." Sugerman inspired the song "Wild Child," which appeared on the Doors' fourth album, *The Soft Parade*, according to Manzarek. Sugerman also managed Iggy Pop briefly, and wrote an autobiography, *Wonderland Avenue* (Sugerman lived at 8632 Wonderland Avenue in Laurel Canyon), and a biography, *Appetite for Destruction: The Days of Guns N' Roses* (which is as much about Jim Morrison as it is about Axl Rose!) in 1991. That same year, Sugerman married Fawn Hall, Oliver North's secretary of Iran-Contra infamy. He eventually became the co-manager of the Doors' musical and business interests. A recovering heroin addict, Sugerman died of lung cancer at the age of fifty on January 5, 2005. He is buried at Westwood Village Park Cemetery in Los Angeles. His epitaph reads, "There are things known and things unknown and in between are the doors." *The Doors by the Doors*, an official biography of the band published in 2006, was dedicated to Sugerman.

2

Tell Me Where Your Freedom Lies

Jim Morrison's Earliest Influences

A real theatrical experience shakes the calm of the senses, liberates the compressed unconscious and drives towards a kind of potential revolt.

—Antonin Artaud

Unique among rock 'n' roll songwriters, Jim Morrison composed lyrics that referenced visions of the French symbolism of Arthur Rimbaud, the stream-of-consciousness methods of James Joyce, the spontaneous prose of the Beat Generation, and the "Theatre of Cruelty" techniques of Antonin Artaud. In fact, rock critics often used such verbiage as "Artaud Rock" and "Joycean pop" when reviewing the Doors. Morrison was fortunate to discover literature before he became interested in music and carried an old box of books wherever he went full of such titles as *On the Road*, *A Season in Hell*, *Ulysses*, *Journey to the End of the Night*, and *The Birth of Tragedy from the Spirit of Music*. All of these early influences would make their way into his lyrics and poetry in one form or another over the brief history of the Doors.

Charles Baudelaire (1821–67)

In a famous letter written in 1862, French poet, essayist, and art critic Charles Baudelaire declared, "I have cultivated my hysteria with delight and terror . . . I have felt the wind of the wing of madness pass over me." One of the major innovators in French literature, Baudelaire was born in Paris on April 9, 1821. His father died when he was six years old, and he developed a strong bond with his mother. As a teen, Baudelaire attended a military boarding school but was soon kicked out for his rebellious ways. He later received a large inheritance and lived the life of a dandy, wearing outlandish outfits and experimenting with hashish and opium.

In 1857, Baudelaire published his first and most famous volume of poems, *Les Fleurs du mal* (*The Flowers of Evil*), which contains the lines "O man, dear disinherited! to you I sing/This song full of light and brotherhood/From my prison of glass with its scarlet wax seals." The scandalous subject matter of the poems led to Baudelaire's prosecution but he was fined rather than imprisoned. The young French symbolist poet Arthur Rimbaud praised Baudelaire in a letter as "the king of poets, a true God." Baudelaire also translated the work of his idol, Edgar Allan Poe, whom he referred to as a "twin soul."

Published in 1862, Baudelaire's *Le Spleen de Paris* contains the lines, "What matters an eternity of damnation to someone who has found in one second the infinity of joy?" In 1866, Baudelaire suffered a massive stroke that left him in a semiparalyzed state. He died a year later at the age of forty-six and many of his works were published posthumously. In his autobiography, *Wonderland Avenue*, Danny Sugerman called Baudelaire "the first real rock star" because he smoked dope, stayed up all night, frequented whorehouses, and proceeded to "fuck around so much he finally got syphilis and ultimately died insane and mad, brilliant as he was tragic."

Friedrich Nietzsche (1844–1900)

In *Riders on the Storm*, John Densmore quipped, "Nietzsche killed Jim Morrison, I had once said rather melodramatically to some startled friends in Berkeley. Morrison the Superman, the Dionysian madman, the Birth of Tragedy himself." Densmore claimed he once picked up a copy of Nietzsche's *The Birth of Tragedy*, but "couldn't figure out why anyone would want to read a whole book of such double-talk."

While still in high school, Morrison devoured Friedrich Nietzsche's works, including *On the Genealogy of Morals* and *Beyond Good and Evil*, in which the philosopher stated, "In music the passions enjoy themselves." Morrison was especially fascinated by Nietzsche's views on the Apollonian-Dionysian duality as outlined in *The Birth of Tragedy from the Spirit of Music*:

> Even under the influence of the narcotic draught, of which songs of all primitive men and peoples speak, or with the potent coming of spring that penetrates all nature with joy, these Dionysian emotions awake, and as they grow in intensity everything subjective vanishes into complete self-forgetfulness. In the German Middle Ages, too, singing and dancing crowds, ever increasing in number, whirled themselves from place to place under this same Dionysian impulse . . . There are some who, from obtuseness or lack of experience, turn away from such phenomena as from "folk-diseases," with contempt of pity born of consciousness of their own 'healthy-mindedness.' But of course such poor wretches have no idea how corpselike and ghostly their so-called 'healthy-mindedness' looks when the glowing life of Dionysian revelers roars past them.

Few philosophers in history have been as misunderstood as Nietzsche, a German philosopher who was born on October 15, 1844. A child prodigy, Nietzsche later studied theology and classical philology at the University of

Bonn. However, he abandoned his theological studies after just one semester. At the age of twenty-four, Nietzsche was appointed to the Chair of Classical Philology at the University of Basel. During the Franco-Prussian War of 1870–71, Nietzsche served as a medical orderly in the Prussian forces. He developed a friendship with the composer Richard Wagner and published his first book, *The Birth of Tragedy*, in 1872. A succession of brilliant works followed, including *Human, All Too Human, Thus Spoke Zarathustra,* and *On the Genealogy of Morals,* which contains the line: "While every noble morality develops from a triumphant affirmation of itself, slave morality from the outset says No to what is 'outside,' what is 'different,' what is 'not itself'; and this No is its creative deed." Nietzsche went totally insane in 1889 and spent his remaining years under the care of his mother and sister until his death on August 25, 1900.

In "The Shaman as Superstar," a profile of Morrison that appeared in *New York* magazine, writer Richard Goldstein remarked that the Doors singer "suggests you read Nietzsche on the nature of tragedy to understand where he is really at. His eyes glow as he launches into a discussion of the Apollonian-Dionysian struggle for the control of life. No need to guess which side he's on."

Arthur Rimbaud (1854–91)

The visionary poetry and self-destructive genius of Arthur Rimbaud deeply influenced Morrison, who adopted one of his phrases, "I alone have the key to this savage sideshow." In a famous letter to Paul Demeny in May 1871, Rimbaud defined the role of the poet as visionary: "A poet makes himself a visionary through a long, boundless, and systemized *disorganization* of *all the senses*. All forms of love, of suffering, of madness: he searches himself, he exhausts within himself all poisons and pressures their quintessences. Unspeakable torment, where he will need the greatest faith, a superhuman strength, where he becomes among all men the great invalid, the great accursed—and the Supreme Scientist! For he attains the unknown! So what if he is destroyed in his ecstatic flight through things unheard of, unnameable . . ."

A child prodigy, Jean Nicolas Arthur Rimbaud was born on October 20, 1854. His father, a career military officer, deserted the family when he was just seven years old. As a teenager, the self-destructive Rimbaud sought out experience and embraced anarchism, alcohol, drugs, and violence. A close reading of Charles Baudelaire led to Rimbaud's literary career, which lasted just four years. Rimbaud corresponded with symbolist poet Paul Verlaine, and the two embarked on a short affair that ended abruptly after Verlaine shot Rimbaud in the left wrist and was sentenced to two years in prison. At the age of nineteen, Rimbaud completed his farewell to literature, *Une saison en enfer* (*A Season in Hell*), in which he wrote, "Boredom is no longer my love. Rage, debauchery, madness—I know all their aspirations and disasters—all my burden is laid aside." He then embarked on a reckless career as a trader and gun runner in Africa. In 1891, Rimbaud died in the Hospital of the Immaculate Conception in Marseille at the age of thirty-seven. His gravestone reads, "Priez pour lui" ("Pray for him"). Rimbaud's poetry influenced the Symbolist, Dadaist, and Surrealist movements. Albert Camus called him "the poet of revolt, and the greatest."

Wallace Fowlie, James B. Duke Professor of French Literature at Duke University, published *Rimbaud and Morrison: The Rebel as Poet*, in 1993. The scholarly treatise analyzed both the poetry and self-destructive nature of both poets with Fowlie commenting, "The parallels between the French poet and the American singer-poet are striking: the rebellion, the absence of a father . . . the themes of violence and pathos in both poets."

James Joyce (1882–1941)

One of the lines in James Joyce's masterpiece, *Ulysses*, reads, "Every life is many days, day after day. We walk through ourselves, meeting robbers, ghosts, giants, old men, young men, wives, widows, brothers-in-love. But always meeting ourselves." One of the most influential writers of the twentieth century, Irish novelist and poet James Augustine Aloysius Joyce was born in Dublin on February 2, 1882. Joyce's major works include the short-story collection *Dubliners* (1914), as well as the novels *A Portrait of the Artist as a Young Man* (1916), *Ulysses* (1922), and *Finnegans Wake* (1939). Joyce died on January 13, 1941. His last words were "Does nobody understand?" He is buried in the Fluntern Cemetery in Zurich, Switzerland. Joyce was a major influence on writers such as Samuel Beckett, Jorge Luis Borges, Flann O'Brien, and many others. In 1998, the Modern Library ranked *Ulysses* No. 1 on its list of the "100 Best English-Language Novels of the 20th Century."

Morrison first encountered the writings of James Joyce while still in high school, reading *Ulysses* the summer before his senior year. A modern retelling of *The Odyssey*, *Ulysses* takes place during a single day—June 16, 1904. According to fellow classmates, Morrison's teacher believed he was the only student in the class who actually understood the novel. Morrison also read Joyce's highly unconventional and difficult last novel, *Finnegans Wake*. Joyce's influence can be found in Morrison's stream-of-conscious lyrics, most notably in "The End." In fact, influential rock critic Richard Goldstein echoed this relationship in his article "The Doors Open Wide," for *New York* magazine: "'The End' is eleven and one-half minutes of solid song . . . Anyone who disputes the concept of rock literature had better listen long and hard to this song. This is Joycean pop, with a stream-of-consciousness lyric in which images are strung together by association. 'The End' builds to a realization of mood rather than a sequence of events."

Franz Kafka (1883–1924)

As a teenager, Morrison enjoyed the works of Franz Kafka and owned his *Diary 1910–1923*. One of the most influential writers of the twentieth century, Kafka tackled many of the same themes of anxiety and alienation that later show up in Jim Morrison's song lyrics and poetry. Kafka was born on July 3, 1883, in Prague, Bohemia, and grew up in a middle-class Jewish family with a domineering father. After he received a law degree in 1906, Kafka was employed at the Worker's Accident Insurance Institute. Kafka's major works include short stories such as "The Metamorphosis" (1915) and "In the Penal Colony" (1914), and posthumous novels *The Trial* (1925), *The Castle* (1926), and *Amerika* (1927). In *The Trial*, Kafka wrote, "It is often safer to be in chains than to be free."

Kafka, who suffered from tuberculosis, spent much of his time after 1917 in sanatoriums and health resorts. He died on June 3, 1924, virtually unknown since none of his novels was printed during his lifetime. Although Kafka had demanded that all his manuscripts be destroyed on his death, his friend Max Brod fortunately paid no heed to the request. Kafka was buried in the New Jewish Cemetery in Prague-Zizhov.

Antonin Artaud (1896–1948)

Antonin Artaud once remarked, "If there is still one hellish, truly accursed thing in our time, it is our artistic dallying with forms, instead of being like victims burnt at the stake, signaling through the flames." An early article about the Doors in the UCLA *Daily Bruin* by Bill Kerby was titled "Artaud Rock: Dark Logic of The Doors": "The founder of the Theatre of Cruelty, Antonin Artaud, poet-actor, described one of his infrequent scenarios thus: 'eroticism, savagery, blood-lust, a thirst for violence, an obsession with horror, collapse of moral values, social hypocrisy, lies, sadism, perjury, depravity, etc.' To anyone who has ever listened to The Doors at any length, this will appear to be a catalog of their material, but that's just a part of the whole."

Artaud desired to revolutionize theater by stripping away masks to reveal the truth to the audience: "If the theatre is not just play, if it is a genuine reality, by what means can we give it that status of reality, make each performance a kind of event? . . . It is not to the mind or the senses of our audience that we address ourselves, but to their whole existence. Theirs and ours. So that ultimately the audience will go to the theatre as they go to the surgeon or the dentist, with a sense of dread but also of necessity."

A playwright, poet, actor, and theater director, Antonin Artaud was born Antoine Marie Joseph Artaud on September 4, 1896, in Marseille, France. Artaud was influenced by Arthur Rimbaud, Charles Baudelaire, and Edgar Allan Poe. In the 1920s, Artaud joined the surrealist movement. He also acted in several classic silent movies, including Abel Gance's *Napoleon* as Jean-Paul Marat and Carl Theodor Dreyer's *The Passion of Joan of Arc* as the monk Massieu. In 1926–28, Artaud ran the Alfred Jarry Theatre, along with Roger Vitrac.

In 1931, Artaud's "First Manifesto for a Theatre of Cruelty" was published in *La Nouvelle Revue Francaise*. Artaud's best-known work, *The Theatre and Its Double*, a collection of essays, was published in 1938. In *Van Gogh, the Man Suicided by Society*, Artaud remarked, "There is in every madman a misunderstood genius whose idea, shining in his head, frightened people, and for whom delirium was the only solution to the strangulation that life had prepared for him." Artaud died in Paris on March 4, 1948.

In a review of *Strange Days* that appeared in the *L.A. Free Press*, Gene Youngblood called the Doors' second album "a landmark in rock music" that "ventures beyond the conventional realm of musical expression: It has become theater. The cruel theater of Artaud, and of *Marat/Sade*."

Louis-Ferdinand Celine (1894–1961)

The haunting "End of the Night," one of the Doors' earliest songs that appears on the band's debut album, was inspired by French writer Louis-Ferdinand Celine's autobiographical *Journey to the End of the Night*. The novel follows the absurd, picaresque adventures of the antihero Bardamu, who evinces a "scabrous nihilism," and admits that "Truth is a never-ending agony. The truth of this world is death. One must choose—die or lie. I've never been able to kill myself." In the preface to the 1952 edition of *Journey to the End of the Night*, Celine wrote, "Everything gets taken the wrong way. I've been the cause of too much evil . . . Of all my books it's the only really vicious one." *Journey to the End of the Night* greatly influenced such writers as Jean-Paul Sartre, Samuel Beckett, Henry Miller, Jean Genet, Jack Kerouac, William S. Burroughs, Ken Kesey, Charles Bukowski, Joseph Heller, and Kurt Vonnegut.

Born Louis-Ferdinand Destouches on May 27, 1894, Celine (he took the pen name from his grandmother's first name) joined the French army in 1912 and served in World War I, wounding his arm in 1914. He received a medical degree in the early 1920s and in 1925 embarked on a journey that would take him to Switzerland, England, the Cameroons, Canada, the United States, and Cuba— travels that would serve as the basis of *Voyage au bout de la nuit* (*Journey to the End of the Night*). He subsequently published *Mort a credit* (*Death on the Installment Plan*), another autobiographical novel, in 1936. Celine, who once remarked, "The more one is hated, the happier one is," was a Nazi apologist during World War II. He died on July 1, 1961, one day before the death of Ernest Hemingway.

Mad Magazine

Growing up in a strict household within a stifling atmosphere of conformity, Morrison sought escape in the anarchic humor of *Mad* magazine. Founded by William Gaines and Harvey Kurtzman in August 1952, *Mad* began as a comic book published by EC Comics. After *Mad* converted to magazine form in 1955 and soon hired a new editor, Al Feldstein, the magazine's creative staff added a slew of legendary artists such as Dave Berg, Antonio Prohias, Frank Jacobs, Mort Drucker, and Don Martin. With its groundbreaking parodies and gap-toothed mascot, Alfred E. Neuman ("What, me worry?"), *Mad* skewered everything sacred in mainstream culture. Morrison loved the satiric humor he found in *Mad* and

Unique for a rock star, Jim Morrison drew inspiration for his lyrics from such "literary anarchists" as Charles Baudelaire, Arthur Rimbaud, Antonin Artaud, Louis-Ferdinand Celine, and the writers of the Beat Generation.   *Courtesy of Kerry Humpherys/doors.com*

enjoyed pulling outrageous pranks in school. According to *No One Here Gets Out Alive*, Morrison also adopted several catchphrases from the magazine as his own, saying he was "crackers to slip the rozzer the dropsy in snide."

Comics historian Tom Spurgeon remarked, "At the height of its influence, *Mad* was *The Simpsons*, *The Daily Show* and *The Onion* combined." Poet and singer Patti Smith once claimed, "After *Mad*, drugs were nothing." *Mad* magazine has spawned many imitators over the years, most notably *Cracked* (founded in 1958), *Sick* (1960–80), and *Crazy Magazine* (1973–83).

Beat Generation

In *Light My Fire*, Ray Manzarek stated that "if Jack Kerouac had never written *On the Road*, the Doors would never have existed. It opened the floodgates . . . That sense of freedom, spirituality, and intellectuality in *On the Road*—that's what I wanted in my work." Both Manzarek and Morrison devoured the works of Beat Generation writers such as Kerouac, Allen Ginsberg, and William S. Burroughs during the late 1950s. Manzarek later remarked, "Jim and I originally conceived the band to be a merging of poetry and Rock & Roll, just as the beats a decade before us married poetry and Jazz."

Disillusioned with the repression and conformity encompassing post-World War II life in the United States, the Beats actively sought more creative alternatives to the mind-numbing banality of modern culture. Beat Generation writers were no strangers to controversy: Both Ginsberg's prophetic, Blakean poem "Howl" (1956) and Burroughs' novel *Naked Lunch* (1959) led to obscenity trials, while *On the Road* (1957) was blamed by the establishment for corrupting the nation's youth. "Howl" itself helped define a generation with its powerful opening lines: "I saw the best minds of my generation/destroyed by madness, starving hysterical naked." During the mid-1950s, the Beat scene moved from New York City to San Francisco. The so-called San Francisco Renaissance was driven by such talented poets as Gary Snyder, Lawrence Ferlinghetti (owner of the legendary City Lights Bookstore, which Morrison discovered at an early age while living in nearby Alameda), Philip Whalen, Lew Welch, Kirby Doyle, Harold Norse, and Michael McClure (who later befriended Morrison).

Morrison, who would later share Kerouac's affinity for both writing *and* booze, copied his favorite quotes from *On the Road* into his notebooks. He was particularly drawn to the novel's hero, the wild-eyed, maniacal Dean Moriarty, based on Kerouac's friend Neal Cassady, "a young jailkid all hung-up on the wonderful possibilities of becoming a real intellectual." Moriarty represented one of the "mad ones, the ones who are mad to live, mad to talk, mad to be saved, desirous of everything at the same time, the ones who never yawn or say a commonplace thing, but burn, burn, burn, burn, like fabulous yellow roman candles exploding like spiders across the stars and in the middle you see the blue centerlight pop and everybody goes 'Awww!'" In *On the Road*, Moriarty and Kerouac's alter ego, the quiet, introspective Sal Paradise, embarked on a reckless odyssey of self-discovery—fueled by alcohol, drugs, jazz, and whores—across the wasteland of post-World War II America.

Cassady, who served a stint in San Quentin State Prison for marijuana possession in the late 1950s, would later provide a bridge between the Beat Generation and the 1960s counterculture when he served as the bus driver (nicknamed "Speed Limit") for Ken Kesey and his Merry Pranksters as they made their way across the United States during the summer of 1964, promoting the use of psychedelic drugs. The bus, known as "Further," was painted in wild psychedelic colors. In 1968, totally burnt out and exhausted, Cassady died beside a railroad track in Mexico, just four days shy of his forty-second birthday. According to legend (Kesey's short story "The Day After Superman Died" features a vivid depiction of Cassady's final hours), a drug-fueled Cassady had decided to count the nails in the railroad ties between towns. His last words were "sixty-four thousand nine hundred and twenty-eight."

Kerouac (real name: Jean-Louis Lebris de Kerouac) was born to working-class Catholic, French-Canadian parents on March 12, 1922, in Lowell, Massachusetts. He received a football scholarship to Columbia University, where he met Ginsberg. Kerouac published his first novel, *The Town and the City*, in 1950. The conventional, semi-autobiographical work was strongly influenced by Thomas Wolfe (*Look Homeward, Angel*). Like Morrison, Kerouac was inspired by William Blake, Charles Baudelaire, and Edgar Allan Poe. According to legend, Kerouac next wrote *On the Road*, which detailed his travels across the country between 1947-50, on a 120-foot roll of teletype paper without margins or page breaks during three Benzedrine-fueled weeks in 1951. In addition to Dean Moriarty and Sal Paradise, the thinly disguised characters in *On the Road* included Old Bull Lee (Burroughs) and Carlo Marx (Ginsberg).

Kerouac believed in a theory of spontaneous prose, where the novelist wrote whatever comes to mind, "all first-person, fast, mad, confessional," much like the improvisation evident in jazz music. Some critics attacked this writing style, most notoriously Truman Capote, who remarked, "That isn't writing at all; it's typing." Kerouac's life work, known as "The Legend of Duluoz," encompassed all of his individual books, which also included *Visions of Gerard, Doctor Sax, Maggie Cassidy, Vanity of Duluoz, The Subterraneans, Tristessa, The Dharma Bums, Desolation Angels, Big Sur*, and *Satori in Paris*. During the 1960s, Kerouac, who was a political conservative, sought to distance himself from the so-called beatniks who cropped up everywhere after the publication of *On the Road*, remarking "I want to make this very clear. I mean, here I am, a guy who was a railroad brakeman, and a cowboy, and a football player—just a lot of things ordinary guys do. And I wasn't trying to create any kind of consciousness or anything like that. We didn't have a whole lot of heavy abstract thoughts. We were just a bunch of guys who were out trying to get laid."

Most observers were shocked at how quickly Kerouac transformed from the free spirit of *On the Road* to the hard-drinking curmudgeon of his later years, but Burroughs noted: "[H]e didn't change that much . . . first there was a young guy sitting in front of the television in a tee shirt drinking beer with his mother, then there was an older, fatter person sitting in front of the television drinking beer with his mother." On October 21, 1969, Kerouac died at the age of forty-seven of a severe hemorrhage brought on by a mixture of Johnny Walker Red and Dexedrine pills while watching *The Galloping Gourmet* at his house in St. Petersburg, Florida. Kerouac is buried in the Edson Cemetery in Lowell, Massachusetts. His epitaph reads: "He Honored Life."

According to Burroughs, it was Kerouac who suggested the title for *Naked Lunch*: "[A] frozen moment when everyone sees what is on the end of every fork." Critics over the years have variously described this groundbreaking novel, which documents an unrepentant drug addict's Boschian descent into a personal hell, as "brutal," "obscene," "disgusting," and "immoral." *Naked Lunch* was banned for obscenity by Boston courts in 1962, but the Massachusetts Supreme Judicial Court reversed the decision in 1966. Known variously as the "Elvis of American Letters," "Cosmonaut of Inner Space," and "Godfather of Punk," Burroughs, a longtime heroin addict, once described himself as "an unaffiliated conservative anarchist." A countercultural icon, he appeared on the cover of the Beatles' *Sgt. Pepper's Lonely Hearts Club Band* and also performed "Is Everybody In?" on *Stoned Immaculate*, a Doors tribute album released in 2000. Burroughs himself was a fan of Morrison's poetry, stating in the album's liner notes that his poems "are very much in the tradition, not necessarily imitated, of Rimbaud and Saint Jean-Perse particularly. It's very pure poetry."

French New Wave Cinema

Morrison once remarked, "I'm interested in film because, to me, it's the closest approximation in art that we have to the actual flow of consciousness." At UCLA, Morrison studied the French New Wave, film theory, auteurism, and avant-garde films. The New Wave (La Nouvelle Vague) consisted of a loosely knit group of innovative French filmmakers during the 1950s and 1960s who were influenced by classical Hollywood cinema and Italian Neorealism. Many of the prominent members of the group, such as Francois Truffaut, Jean-Luc Godard, Eric Rohmer, Claude Chabrol, and Jacques Rivette, started out as critics for the influential film magazine *Cahiers du cinema*, which was founded in 1951 by Andre Bazin, Jacques Doniol-Valcroze, and Joseph-Marie Lo Duca. Morrison especially enjoyed the films of Truffaut such as *The 400 Blows* (1959) and *Shoot the Piano Player* (1960). Other major figures in French New Wave Cinema included Jacques Demy and his wife, Agnes Varda, who later befriended Morrison.

The French New Wave heavily influenced American film directors such as Arthur Penn (*Bonnie and Clyde*), Robert Altman (*M*A*S*H*), Francis Ford Coppola (*The Godfather*), Brian De Palma (*Scarface*), and Martin Scorsese (*Taxi Driver*). In addition, director Bob Rafelson (*Five Easy Pieces*) claimed that his vision for the TV series *The Monkees* was influenced by the Marx Brothers and the French New Wave. More recently, director Quentin Tarantino has been strongly influenced by the French New Wave, and his 1992 film *Reservoir Dogs* was dedicated to Godard.

3

A Place for Me to Hide

How the Lizard King's Upbringing Affected His Anti-Authority Stance

When you make your peace with authority, you become authority.
—Jim Morrison

M orrison's upbringing as the son of a naval officer and future admiral contributed to his rebellious nature, outsider status, and frequently outrageous stage persona. In fact, the family lived a gypsy-like existence, moving frequently, and Morrison's father was away from them for long periods of time. Between Morrison's grammar school through high school years, the family lived in nearly a dozen different cities. His parents utilized a quasi-military-style of discipline on their children that provided the basis for the future rock star's early rebellion. Morrison hinted at his troubled childhood later in an interview with Lizze James for *CREEM* magazine (Autumn 1969) when he commented, "Some people surrender their freedom willingly—but others are forced to surrender it. Imprisonment begins with birth. Society, parents—they refuse to allow you to keep the freedom you are born with."

Melbourne, Florida

Morrison's father, George Stephen "Steve" Morrison was born in Rome, Georgia, in 1919 and raised in Leesburg, Florida. A career Navy man, he graduated from the Naval Academy at Annapolis in February 1941. He met his future wife, Clara Clarke, that same year on a blind date while he was stationed in Hawaii. In April 1942, George and Clara got married. Shortly after the attack on Pearl Harbor, he applied for flight training and received orders to Pensacola, Florida, and then Melbourne, Florida, where James Douglas Morrison was born at Brevard Hospital on December 8, 1943. Jim was given the middle name Douglas after General Douglas MacArthur. In the summer of 1944, Steve Morrison left for the South Pacific and Clara and Jim went to live with Steve's parents in Clearwater,

Florida. It was the beginning of a nomadic existence for the family. Jim had a sister, Anne, born in 1947, and a brother, Andy, born in 1949.

Albuquerque, New Mexico

The Morrison family moved to Albuquerque, New Mexico, in 1947, where Steve Morrison was stationed at the Los Alamos testing ground. It was here that a traumatic experience had a significant impact on four-year-old Jim Morrison. He was driving with his parents and grandparents along a desert highway between Albuquerque and Santa Fe at dawn when the family came upon a horrible traffic accident—a truckload of Native American workers had overturned on the road and "there were Indians scattered all over the highway, bleeding to death," according to Jim, who said "It was the first time I discovered death . . ." In the posthumous spoken-word album, *An American Prayer*, Morrison remarked, "The reaction I get now thinking about it, looking back—is that the souls of the ghosts of those dead Indians . . . maybe one or two of 'em . . . were just running around freaking out, and just leaped into my soul. And they're still there." Morrison later commemorated this mystical experience in the song "Peace Frog" from *Morrison Hotel*: "Indians scattered on dawn's highway bleeding/Ghosts crowd the young child's fragile egg-shell mind."

Alameda, California

Around the time the Morrisons moved to Alameda (a small island community in the San Francisco Bay that was home to the Naval Air Station Alameda) in the fall of 1957, Jack Kerouac published *On the Road*, the seminal work of the Beat Generation. Morrison devoured the book, reading it over and over and copying his favorite passages in a notebook. On weekends, he and his best friend, Fud Ford, wandered to the legendary City Lights Bookshop (a sign on the window read "Banned Books"), owned by poet Lawrence Ferlinghetti. Morrison enjoyed reading the poetry of Ferlinghetti, as well as Allen Ginsberg and Kenneth Rexroth. Around this time, Morrison also started drinking, sneaking his father's gin and replacing the amount he drank with water. He spent his freshman year and first half of his sophomore year at Alameda High School.

Alexandria, Virginia

In 1958, Steve Morrison was promoted to captain and relocated to the Pentagon, so the family moved to Alexandria, Virginia (located just six miles southwest of Washington, D.C.), residing at a home at 310 Woodland Terrace in the Jefferson Park area of the city. Starting in the second semester of his sophomore year, Morrison attended George Washington High School, where Cass Elliott, later of the Mamas and the Papas, attended school briefly. At George Washington, Morrison met Tandy Martin, his first girlfriend, who he reportedly tormented

A strict upbringing in a military family combined with a nomadic lifestyle led Jim Morrison to develop an "outsider" persona fueled by rebellion against all authority and a strong desire to destroy conventional boundaries.   *Courtesy of Kerry Humpherys/doors.com*

repeatedly with his unpredictable and often outrageous behavior. For instance, sometimes he would take her via bus to Washington, D.C., and then simply run off, telling her to "find your own way home." According to his friends, Morrison enjoyed making others feel uncomfortable just so he could see their reactions.

An avid reader, Morrison also retreated to his basement room (where a previous occupant had reportedly committed suicide). The room had its own exit, so Morrison could come and go as he pleased. With his own radio, record player, bookshelves, and small refrigerator, Morrison enjoyed independence from the strict discipline of his parents for the first time in his life. During this period, Morrison devoured the works of such authors as Arthur Rimbaud (*A Season in Hell*), James Joyce (*Ulysses*), and Friedrich Nietzsche (*The Birth of Tragedy from the Spirit of Music*). In addition, he started to copy quotes and write poetry in notebooks. On weekends, he scoured the used bookstores in Washington, D.C., and spent hours reading in the Alexandria Library.

In high school, Morrison carried a B+ average and scored 1,158 on the SAT. The 1961 George Washington High School yearbook features a photo of a rather dour-looking Morrison and only one senior statistic listed: "James Morrison: Honor Roll (2)." He didn't bother to attend the graduation ceremony, much to the chagrin of his parents. Before heading to Clearwater, Morrison apparently had a falling out with Martin, appearing at her house the night before he left and taunting her that he was free of her and would never even think of her again.

On August 18, 1967, Morrison returned to Alexandria when the Doors performed at the Alexandria Roller Rink Arena, which was located just two miles from Morrison's former home on Woodland Terrace. According to several eyewitness reports, Morrison ended the concert by yelling "Hey Alexandria" and then flipping off the crowd. A year after Morrison's death, Andy donated his brother's vast book collection to the Alexandria Library. Mark Opsasnick's 2006 biography *The Lizard King Was Here: The Life and Times of Jim Morrison in Alexandria, Virginia* serves as the definitive account of Morrison's Alexandria years.

Clearwater, Florida

In August 1961, Morrison moved back to Clearwater to live with his grandparents, Caroline and Paul Morrison, and enrolled in St. Petersburg Junior College. Here he dated Mary Werbelow, a sixteen-year-old Clearwater High School student, who would later follow him to Los Angeles. Morrison's grades during his first semester were one A, two Bs, one C, and one D. However, he still read avidly and would often challenge friends to pick out a book among the hundreds in his collection and read a passage—then he could tell them the name of the book and the author nearly every time. Morrison's favorite hangout was the bohemian-style Renaissance Gallery and Coffeehouse, which featured poetry readings and folk singing. Completely free of his parents for the first time in his life, Morrison started drinking heavily and frequently returned drunk late at night to his grandparent's house. He also enjoyed leaving empty wine bottles all over the house for his grandparents to discover.

Tallahassee, Florida

After completing his freshman year at St. Petersburg Junior College, Morrison transferred to Florida State University (FSU) in Tallahassee. According to Morrison, he went to FSU "mainly because I couldn't think of anything else to do." At FSU, he took one course in the philosophies of protest and another on collective behavior, the psychology of crowds. He also took a role in a college production of Harold Pinter's absurdist play *The Dumbwaiter*. It was also at FSU that a heavily inebriated Morrison got arrested for the first time on his way to a Seminole football game. He reportedly stole a helmet from a police car and was charged with petty larceny, disturbing the peace, resisting arrest, and public drunkenness. Morrison would often hitchhike back and forth between Tallahassee and Clearwater. At FSU, Morrison also became obsessed with Elvis Presley.

Los Angeles, California

In January 1964, Morrison moved to Los Angeles and transferred to UCLA. Before classes started, he visited his father aboard the aircraft carrier he captained, *Bon Homme Richard*. Once aboard, his father made him get a haircut at the ship's barber. When they returned home, Morrison thought it was ironic that his mother yelled at his father to take out the garbage. Admiral Morrison commanded the *Bon Homme Richard* during the Gulf of Tonkin incident.

Soon thereafter, Morrison and his father had a total falling out, presumably because Morrison had expressed his desire to pursue a career in rock music that his father found ludicrous since the younger Morrison had never shown any inclination toward music growing up. Under "Family Info" in his official Elektra biography, Morrison simply wrote "dead." Even after the Doors became successful, Morrison continued his transient lifestyle with few possessions. According to *No One Here Gets Out Alive* author Jerry Hopkins, "Even when Morrison's band was the most successful in the U.S.—'the American Rolling Stones'—the lead singer continued to live in a $10-a-night motel room and owned only a couple of leather suits (which he never had cleaned), an American-made car (frequently destroyed as the consequence of his indulgences) and a couple of boxes of books."

4

Let's Swim to the Moon

Early Incarnations of the Band

I said, well let's get together and have a rehearsal and we rehearsed and I think the first song we played was "Moonlight Drive" and the magic was there. It was incredible.

—*Ray Manzarek*

The unlikely origins of the Doors can be traced to UCLA Film School, where Ray Manzarek first met Jim Morrison; a dive bar called the Turkey Joint West, where a mediocre surf/blues band called Rick and the Ravens performed on weekends; Venice Beach, where Morrison first started writing his acid-influenced song lyrics; and the Third Street Meditation Center in Los Angeles, where three of the four Doors attended classes. All of these disparate elements somehow came into alignment, and within just two years of establishing the Doors they would have a No. 1 hit on the charts, "Light My Fire."

Rick and the Ravens

The Doors had rather inauspicious beginnings as an outgrowth of a band called Rick and the Ravens that seemed at the time to be destined for oblivion. Known as "Screamin' Ray Daniels" or "the Bearded Blues Shouter," Ray Manczarek (he would soon drop the "c" from his name) joined his brothers Rick (guitar) and Jim (organ/harmonica) in this surf/blues band. They played numerous weekend gigs at the Turkey Joint West, a nightclub "for swingin' young people" located just two blocks from the beach at Second Street and Broadway in Santa Monica that catered to the college crowd. Each of the band members—which also included at one time or the other Patrick Stonner (saxophone), Roland Biscaluz (bass), and Vince Thomas (drums)—would take home about $5 per night.

On occasion, Morrison and other UCLA film students would join Manzarek onstage at the Turkey Joint West (later known as the Brass Bell and operated since 1974 as Ye Olde King's Head British Pub) to help out with the chorus to "Louie, Louie" or "Gloria." Manzarek would really ham it up, announcing:

"Ladies and gentlemen, we've got a special treat for you tonight. Direct from UCLA film school, we've got Jim Morrison!" During Turkey Joint West gigs, Rick and the Ravens also enjoyed covering such hits as "Hoochie Coochie Man," "Money," "I'm Your Doctor, I Know What You Need," "King Bee," and "Close to You" (for an idea of the Rick and the Ravens sound, listen to Ray Manzarek singing "Close to You" on the Doors' live album, *Absolutely Live*).

Rick and the Ravens recorded three rather unremarkable promotional singles for Aura Records, a subsidiary of World Pacific Records: "Soul Train"/"Geraldine," "Henrietta"/"Just for You," and "Big Bucket T"/"Rampage." However, with no hits and few prospects, Rick and the Ravens was on the fast track to nowhere by the early summer of 1965.

UCLA Film School

While moonlighting in Rick and the Ravens, Manzarek attended UCLA Film School, where he met Jim Morrison (Francis Ford Coppola, who later used the Doors' "The End" so effectively in his Vietnam War epic *Apocalypse Now*, was also a film student there at the time). Manzarek created a couple of well-received student films, both of which featured his future wife, Dorothy, during this period: *Evergreen* and *Induction* (in which Morrison briefly appears in a party scene). Both of these films are included on *The Doors Collection DVD* (1999).

Morrison's unnamed student film project, which unfortunately has been lost to history, was considerably less successful. He later called it "less a film than an essay on film," and in essence it was a series of unrelated images amateurishly spliced together. However, at least one fellow student, Manzarek, was impressed with the final product, which he called "cinematic poetry," later remarking, "Jim just put a lot of things he liked into a film. It didn't have anything to do with anything. Everybody hated it at UCLA. It was really quite good." Morrison, who carried a B+ average in film school, received a "D" for his first and last student film, which included a juxtaposition of him smoking a "monster hit" off a huge joint along with a clip of an atomic bomb explosion. By most accounts, Morrison was extremely upset by the almost universal rejection of his student film.

One highlight of the UCLA Film School was that both Manzarek and Morrison got the opportunity to take a course led by famous German director Josef von Sternberg, who directed Marlene Dietrich in such classic expressionistic films as *The Blue Angel, Shanghai Express, Morocco, Blonde Venus, The Scarlet Empress,* and *The Devil Is a Woman.* Morrison would later claim that his favorite film was *Anatahan*, von Sternberg's last film, shot in 1954 in Japan. In an interview with Digby Diehl that appeared in the article "Love and the Demonic Psyche," in *Eye* magazine, Morrison commented, "For me, films have to be either very artificial and surreal or very real and documentary. The more extreme in either tendency, the better."

Legendary French director Jean Renoir (*The Rules of the Game*) was another professor at the UCLA Film School during this period. The film students at

UCLA were also exposed to the works of such influential French New Wave directors as Jean-Luc Godard (*Breathless*), Francois Truffaut (*The 400 Blows*), and Robert Bresson (*Pickpocket*), as well as Akira Kurosawa, Ingmar Bergman, Satyajit Ray, Federico Fellini, and others.

According to Manzarek, the two future Doors' stint in film school had an immense effect on the band's development, and reviewers would often comment on the "cinematic" nature of the Doors' music. For example, Gene Youngblood of the *L.A. Free Press* remarked, "The music of the Doors is the music of total abandon. If the Beatles find their cinematic equivalent in Fellini ('For the Benefit of Mr. Kite') or Antonioni ('A Day in the Life'), The Doors conjure up the eyeball-slashing of Luis Bunuel (*Un Chien Andalou*) and the baroque orgies of Anger's *Inauguration of the Pleasure Dome.*" In addition, Eric Van Lustbader of *Circus* magazine stated that "Listening to *Strange Days* is like watching Fellini's *Satyricon.* Morrison's words are so cinematic that each song begins to form pictures in the mind."

A lasting legacy of Morrison's stint at the UCLA Film School was the establishment of the Jim Morrison Award, which started in 1972 with a donation by Elektra Records president Jac Holzman and was supplemented by donations from Morrison's estate. The endowment funds two substantial annual awards for film directing.

Morrison's First Gig

In late May 1965, Morrison and Manzarek both graduated from UCLA; Morrison with a bachelor's degree and Manzarek with a master's degree, both in cinematography. In June 1965, Manzarek hired Morrison for his first music gig,

RICK & THE RAVENS
Featuring The Voice of
R A Y   D A N I E L S

PROMOTIONAL PRODUCTIONS
Artists' Management
P.O. Box 1371
Manhattan Beach, Calif.
772-5739 — 372-8923
"Star Stature Stomp Band"

Billed as a "Star Stature Stomp Band," Rick and the Ravens featured "Screamin' Ray Daniels" (Ray Manzarek) and his brothers Rick and Jim. A surf/blues band, they frequently performed at a dive called the Turkey Joint West where occasionally Jim Morrison and other UCLA film students would join them onstage for raucous versions of "Louie, Louie."

Courtesy of Kerry Humpherys/doors.com

paying him $25 to stand with Rick and the Ravens after one of the band members quit and pretend to play electric guitar at a high school dance headlined by Sonny and Cher, whose hit song, "I Got You Babe" would reach the top of the charts that August.

At it turned out, Sonny and Cher never showed up for the gig, so Rick and the Ravens performed the entire set. According to Manzarek, Morrison "had the time of his life" at the gig. And Morrison later joked that it was the easiest money he ever made. He informed Manzarek that he intended to make his way to New York City and absorb the avant-garde film culture there. Meanwhile, Manzarek desired to stay in Hollywood in order to break into the film business, but he was totally broke and had no connections.

The Doors: Opened and Closed

After spending fifteen years in school, Morrison felt free for the first time in his life, so he put off his New York City plans and intended to enjoy the summer in California before deciding on his future. He ended up making his way to funky and laid-back Venice, a vibrant artistic community and favorite haunt of the Beat Generation during the 1950s. There he lived on the rooftop of a decrepit office building at the corner of Speedway and Westminster just one block from the beach. Morrison and his UCLA buddy Dennis Jakob, who Manzarek later referred to as a "notorious UCLA Film School, Nietzschean madman," even discussed starting a band called the Doors: Opened and Closed (inspired by Aldous Huxley's *The Doors of Perception*), but the idea went nowhere.

With total freedom for once in his life, Morrison grew his hair long, basically stopped eating (dropping to about 135 pounds), started taking huge quantities of acid, threw away all of his old high school notebooks and journals, and began writing lyrics to such songs as "Hello, I Love You," "Moonlight Drive," "My Eyes Have Seen You," and "End of the Night." He later remarked in a *Rolling Stone* interview: "Those first five or six songs I wrote, I was just taking notes at a fantastic rock concert that was going on inside my head. And once I had written the songs, I had to sing them."

Meeting on Venice Beach

One summer afternoon in 1965 a week or so after Fourth of July weekend, Manzarek was sitting on the beach in Venice, pondering what to do with his life, when he ran into Morrison purely by accident (although some Doors biographers believe that Morrison was actually seeking Manzarek out, knowing he was in a band). Surprised to see Morrison since he thought he was in New York, Manzarek asked Morrison what he had been up to. Morrison told him he had been writing some songs. Manzarek encouraged Morrison to sing one of his songs, and after quite a bit of coaxing Morrison broke into "Moonlight Drive." The first lines—"Let's swim to the moon, let's climb through the tide/Penetrate the evening that the city sleeps to hide"—totally blew Manzarek away. Morrison then sang the lyrics to "My Eyes Have Seen You" and "Summer's Almost Gone" in a "Chet Baker voice," according to Manzarek, who enthusiastically suggested that the two form a band and "make a million dollars." Morrison recommended they name themselves the Doors after the William Blake line that inspired Huxley: "If the doors of perception were cleansed, everything would appear to man as it truly is, infinite."

Manzarek quickly persuaded Morrison to move into the Ocean Park apartment that he shared with his girlfriend, Dorothy Fujikawa, and set about creating a band. At the time, songs such as "(I Can't Get No) Satisfaction" by the Rolling Stones and "Mr. Tambourine Man" by the Byrds dominated the U.S. charts. In *Riders on the Storm,* John Densmore remarked, "I dug the Byrds' lyrics, but their arrangements conjured up images of bodies with nothing below the waist. No balls."

Transcendental Meditation

In an interview that appeared in the March 6, 2008, issue of *Rolling Stone* magazine, John Densmore remarked, "There wouldn't be any Doors without Maharishi." During the summer of 1965, Maharishi Mahesh Yogi opened the Third Street Meditation Center in Los Angeles, and Transcendental Meditation (TM) soon became the rage. The head of World Pacific Records, Dick Bock, who had signed Rick and the Ravens to the label's rock subsidiary, Aura Records, recommended that Manzarek look into TM as an alternative to dropping acid. Manzarek told Bock that he "was in the throes of a bad acid meltdown after having blissful experiences of oneness on the chemical. I wanted that bliss back. Instead, I was lost in the paranoid darkness of ego trip."

Manzarek decided to sign up for meditation (which cost $35), where he met Densmore, who later claimed that the lanky keyboardist stood out in the class by constantly raising his hand, proclaiming "no bliss, no bliss" over and over. Manzarek needed a drummer and eventually invited Densmore to join the band. Robby Krieger was also in the meditation class, which consisted of approximately twenty people and, somewhat miraculously, three-fourths of the Doors. According to Krieger in an interview in the June 2007 issue of *MOJO* magazine, "By the time I was in The Doors I was cutting down on my acid use. That's why I was doing meditation classes—I had to come back to earth."

The Psychedelic Rangers

Densmore had briefly played in a band with guitarist Robby Krieger during the spring of 1965 called the Psychedelic Rangers (notable as the first known instance of a rock band referring to themselves as "psychedelic"). Another high school friend of Densmore's, Grant Johnson, played piano in the band, while Krieger's friend Bill Wolff played guitar. Wolff actually auditioned for the

Doors before Krieger was hired by the band. The Psychedelic Rangers wrote a folk-rock song called "Paranoia," but had few actual gigs. They spent most of the time jamming on blues songs and dropping acid together. In addition to jamming with the Psychedelic Rangers, Krieger also briefly belonged to a band called the Clouds.

World Pacific Studios

As cofounder of Pacific Jazz Records (with drummer Roy Harte), which later morphed into World Pacific Records, Dick Bock (1927–88) had "brought the cool jazz West Coast sound to America," according to Manzarek. Over the years, Bock recorded such jazz legends as Chet Baker, Gerry Mulligan, Shorty Rogers, Paul Desmond, Joe Pass, Gerald Wilson, Chico Hamilton, Shelly Manne, and many others. It turns out that Rick and the Ravens owed Bock one more single to fulfill their obligation with the label. However, Manzarek negotiated a deal with Bock to trade the single for a demo session.

On September 2, 1965, an early incarnation of the Doors, including remnants of Rick and the Ravens and minus Krieger, recorded a demo at World Pacific Studios of Morrison's early arsenal of songs, including "Moonlight Drive," "My Eyes Have Seen You," "Summer's Almost Gone," "Hello, I Love You," "Go Insane," and "End of the Night." After the demo failed to generate any interest whatsoever, Manzarek's brothers both quit the band and Krieger, a fellow attendee of the meditation class, joined the Doors. In an interview that appeared in the Summer 2007 issue of *Classic Rock* magazine, Manzarek remarked, "We were full of vitality, full of LSD, full of love for our fellow man . . . and we wanted to change the world through our music."

5

I Was Turning Keys

How the Doors Got Their Name

We are The Doors, because you go into a strange town, you check into a hotel. Then after you've played your gig, you go back to your room down an endless corridor lined with doors until you get to your own. But when you open the door, you find people inside and you wonder: Am I in the wrong room? Or is this some kind of party?

—Jim Morrison

As Jim Morrison and Ray Manzarek sat on Venice Beach in July 1965 and discussed the possibility of forming a band, they jokingly suggested a few names such as "Morrison and Manzarek," "Jim and Ray," and "Two Guys from Venice," according to Manzarek in *Light My Fire.* Then Morrison threw out "the Doors," tapping into a rich literary tradition that stretched all the way back to English writer William Blake's *The Marriage of Heaven and Hell* by way of Aldous Huxley's *The Doors of Perception.* Morrison would often say, "There are things known and things unknown and in between are the Doors."

William Blake

The Doors took their name indirectly from eighteenth-century English poet, painter, printmaker, and mystic William Blake (1757–1827), who wrote in the "A Memorable Fancy" section of *The Marriage of Heaven and Hell,* "When the doors of perception are cleansed, things will appear as they truly are, infinite. For man has closed himself up, till he sees all things through narrow chinks of his cavern." Utilizing prose, poetry, and illustrations, *The Marriage of Heaven and Hell* was written in imitation of biblical books of prophecy and featured powerful lines that Morrison loved to quote such as "The road of excess leads to the palace of wisdom."

Born in London on November 28, 1757, Blake, who once wrote, "Those who restrain desire, do so because theirs is weak enough to be restrained," strongly influenced Beat Generation poets such as Allen Ginsberg and musicians such as Morrison and Bob Dylan. A true visionary, Blake was misunderstood by his contemporaries, who believed he was insane for his idiosyncratic views. Blake published a number of classic works during his lifetime such as *Songs of Innocence*

(1789), *Songs of Experience* (1794), and *Jerusalem* (1820), which was his longest single work. Also known for his apocalyptic illustrations, Blake was painting watercolors for an edition of Dante's *Divine Comedy* that he worked on up to the day of his death. Blake was buried in an unmarked grave at Bunhill Fields in London. In 1957, a memorial was erected for Blake and his wife, Catherine, in the Poet's Corner of Westminster Abbey.

Aldous Huxley

Blake in turn had inspired English writer Aldous Huxley (1894–1963), who detailed his experiences while taking mescaline (the principal agent of the psychedelic cactus peyote) in *The Doors of Perception*, which was published in 1954. Huxley came from a famous family that included his grandfather, Thomas, a biologist and close friend of Charles Darwin, who was known as "Darwin's Bulldog" for his defense of the theory of evolution. At the age of sixteen, Huxley lost most of his eyesight due to an eye infection. According to legend, it was actually notorious English occultist Aleister Crowley ("Do what thou wilt shall be the whole of the Law") who first introduced Huxley to peyote in the early 1930s. Huxley relocated to California in 1937 and soon embarked on a study of Eastern religions, which led to some experimentation with mescaline. By the mid-1950s, he had turned to LSD.

In *The Doors of Perception*, Huxley wrote, "That humanity at large will ever be able to dispense with Artificial Paradise seems very unlikely. Most men and women lead lives at the worst so painful, at the best so monotonous, poor, and limited, that the urge to escape, the longing to transcend themselves if only for a few moments, is and has always been, one of the principal appetites of the soul. Art and religion, carnivals and saturnalia, dancing and music—all these have served, in the H. G. Wells phrase, as Doors in the Walls." In the last paragraph of *The Doors of Perception*, Huxley stated, the individual "who comes back through the Door in the Wall will never be quite the same" as the one who went out: "He will be wiser but less cocksure, happier but less self-satisfied, humbler in acknowledging his ignorance yet better equipped to understand the relationship of words to things, of systematic reasoning to the unfathomable Mystery which it tries forever vainly, to comprehend."

According to Manzarek in an interview that appeared in the June 2007 issue of *MOJO* magazine, "Philosophically, Aldous Huxley's *The Doors of Perception* was obviously important, that's where we got the band name. LSD opened the doors of perception for us." Huxley died of throat cancer at the age of sixty-nine on November 22, 1963, the day JFK was assassinated in Dallas, Texas. British author C. S. Lewis (*The Chronicles of Narnia*) also died on that day. On his deathbed, Huxley had requested that his wife administer him 100 micrograms of LSD. A cultural icon, Huxley appeared on the famous cover of the Beatles' 1967 album *Sgt. Pepper's Lonely Hearts Club Band*, along with Crowley, William S. Burroughs and many others.

The Doors took their name from English writer Aldous Huxley's 1954 book *The Doors of Perception*, which in turn had been inspired by William Blake's line, "When the doors of perception are cleansed, things will appear as they truly are, infinite."

Courtesy of Kerry Humpherys/doors.com

The Outsider

A voracious reader who started collecting boxes of books from a young age, Morrison most likely first encountered both Blake and Huxley in prolific British writer Colin Wilson's influential *The Outsider*, which was published in 1956 when the author was just twenty-four years old. Wilson defined "the Outsider" as a creative force who "wants to express himself so he can better understand himself. He sees a way out via intensity, extremes of experience." Wilson wrote that the exploration of oneself is "usually also an exploration of the world at large, of other writers, a process of comparison with oneself with others, discoveries of kinships, gradual illumination of one's own potentialities."

Billed as "the seminal work on alienation, creativity, and the modern mind-set," *The Outsider* focuses on the works and lives of various artists such as Friedrich Nietzsche, Feodor Dostoyevski, Franz Kafka, Albert Camus, T. S. Eliot, Ernest Hemingway, Hermann Hesse, D. H. Lawrence, and George Bernard Shaw, among others. According to Wilson, "The Outsider's case against society is very clear. All men and women have these dangerous, unnameable impulses, yet they keep up a pretence, to themselves, to others; their respectability, their philosophy, their religion, are all attempts to gloss over, to make look civilized and rational something that is savage, unorganized, irrational. He is an Outsider because he stands for truth."

In addition to *The Outsider*, Wilson has published a rather eclectic selection of books over the years such as *Origins of the Sexual Impulse* (1963), *Rasputin and the Fall of the Romanovs* (1964), *The Mind Parasites* (1967), *The Occult: A History* (1971), *Wilhelm Reich* (1974), *The Space Vampires* (1976), and *Encyclopedia of Modern Murder* (1983), among many others.

"I Don't Get It! What Door?"

The band's name was constantly misunderstood in the early years. For example, in the fall of 1965 when they tried to drop off their demo at Capitol Records, the label's receptionist was totally confused. When Manzarek said they were a rock band called the Doors, she had a puzzled look on her face and remarked, "I don't get it. What door?" Densmore tried to explain that it was a "door in your mind." She replied, "I don't have a door in my mind." Manzarek felt like he had "entered an Ionesco play by mistake."

In addition, Ed Sullivan and his minions made a mockery of the band's name during the Doors' first and last appearance on the show on September 17, 1967, by crowding the set with doors of different colors and sizes. The tacky stage set was one of the reasons the band aimed a collective "fuck you" at the show by defying the producer's insistence that the band change the word "higher" in the hit song "Light My Fire." Needless to say, they were never invited back to the show.

6

Stumbling in the Neon Groves

The Circumstances Surrounding the Band's First Demo

It's incredible they got a deal off the first demo, because they almost sounded incompetent. The female bass player is like a full beat behind on everything.
—*Bill Siddons*

By the summer of 1965, Rick and the Ravens had released three promotional singles that generated little or no interest. The band still owed Aura Records a single, but Ray Manzarek talked Dick Bock into letting the "Doors" obtain some studio time to record a demo of the songs Morrison had recited to Manzarek on the beach in Venice instead of Rick and the Ravens' last single.

Recording Session

On September 2, 1965, the Ravens/Doors lineup of Jim Morrison (vocals), Ray Manzarek (piano/background vocals), his two brothers Rick (guitar) and Jim (harmonica), John Densmore (drums), and an "unknown female bass player" (later identified as Patricia "Pat" Sullivan of Patty and the Esquires) recorded the demo at World Pacific Jazz Studios on Third Street in downtown Los Angeles. Robby Krieger was not yet a member of the band.

The recording session lasted just three hours. The band recorded extremely raw, crude versions of "Moonlight Drive" (the song that started it all on Venice Beach), "Hello, I Love You" (which would later become the Doors' second No. 1 hit), "Summer's Almost Gone" (which Manzarek has described as a song "about the loss of innocence"), "My Eyes Have Seen You" ("Jim's most erotic lyric," according to Densmore), "End of the Night," and "Go Insane (A Little Game)," the song that convinced Densmore that Morrison was crazy. With Morrison's undeveloped voice, Manzarek on piano instead of an organ, the inclusion of Manzarek's brother on the harp and no Krieger, the demo does not sound

An early incarnation of "the Doors" (sans Robby Krieger) recorded a raw demo at World Pacific Jazz Studios that included versions of future classics such as "Moonlight Drive" and "Hello, I Love You." *Courtesy of Robert Rodriguez*

like the Doors at all. Rather, it is more akin to a typical garage band of the mid-1960s such as the Seeds or Question Mark and the Mysterians, who had a No. 1 hit in 1966 with "96 Tears."

Shopping the Demo

According to Manzarek in *Light My Fire*, "We hit . . . all the labels in L.A.—and got rejected by everyone. Capitol, RCA, Liberty, Dunhill, Decca, Reprise . . . I was shocked! It was a damn good demo . . . A bit raw and undeveloped . . . but good." An executive at Liberty Records threw Manzarek out of his office after hearing "Go Insane," declaring it a "sick" song. Lou Adler of Dunhill Records placed the disc on a turntable and played each cut for ten seconds before rejecting them all.

Disappointed in the lack of response to the demo, Manzarek's brothers, Jim and Rick, both decided to quit the band and return to school. Approximately a month after recording the demo, the band—which now consisted of just Manzarek, Morrison, and Densmore—officially changed its name to the Doors and hired a new guitarist, Robby Krieger, on Densmore's recommendation. Densmore had been in a band called the Psychedelic Rangers with Krieger, who was also in the same Transcendental Meditation course as both Densmore and Manzarek. According to Krieger, the demo was "rough," but he appreciated Morrison's powerful lyrics and was sold on the band's potential. With the arrival of Krieger, the Doors' lineup was now complete. According to Densmore in a June 2007 interview with *MOJO* magazine, "It was a real melting pot, just like America. Robby was into flamenco and folk, Ray and I were into jazz and classical, and Jim had read every book on the planet."

Signing with Columbia Records

After several more rejections from record labels, the Doors finally attracted the interest of Billy James, a talent scout for Columbia Records. James signed the band to a six-month provisional contract with the record company in October 1965. Founded in 1888, Columbia Records had released Bob Dylan's self-titled debut album in 1962 and later signed the Byrds, Paul Revere and the Raiders, Janis Joplin, Simon & Garfunkel, and Barbra Streisand.

According to James in *Follow the Music*, "[The Doors'] music was different. It had an insidious quality, not just moody, almost threatening, a quality of implied danger." Most importantly, James even let the band pick out some Vox equipment. According to Manzarek in *Canyon of Dreams*, "Without Billy James . . . The Doors would have never made it. Oh my God. I got my Vox Continental courtesy of Billy James. He heard The Doors' original rough demo and said, 'You guys got something. You're going all the way.'" However, frustrated with the lack of initiative at Columbia Records, the Doors opted out of their contact after just five months even though they would have received $1,000 if they had waited another month. James soon left Columbia to join Elektra, the Doors' future record label.

The Demo's Legacy

"End of the Night," which revealed the influence of both Louis-Ferdinand Celine and William Blake ("some are born to sweet delight/some are born to the endless night") on Morrison's lyrics, was the only song from the demo to appear on the Doors' self-titled debut album, which was released in January 1967. "Moonlight Drive" and "My Eyes Have Seen You" appeared as tracks on their second album, *Strange Days*. In addition, the group didn't even bother recording "Summer's Almost Gone" or "Hello, I Love You" until their third album, *Waiting for the Sun*, and only then because they desperately needed to fill one side of the album after the failure to record Morrison's epic poem, "The Celebration of the Lizard." Ironically, "Hello, I Love You" became the Doors' second single to reach No. 1 on the charts in August 1968. "Go Insane" was part of the "Celebration of the Lizard," later included on the first Doors' live album, *Absolutely Live*. The demo can be heard in its entirety on *The Doors Box Set*, which was released in 1997.

7

Heavenly in Its Brilliance

Musical Acts That Influenced the Doors

The image is one thing and a human being is another . . . It's very hard to live up to an image, put it that way.

—*Elvis Presley*

The Doors claimed a wide range of influences such as blues legends Jimmy Reed, Willie Dixon, and Muddy Waters, as well as early rockers Little Richard, Fats Domino, and Chuck Berry. In addition, Jim Morrison greatly admired the crooning abilities of his two favorite singers: Frank Sinatra and Elvis Presley. The Doors were also heavily influenced by Love, one of the first bands to enjoy huge early success along the Sunset Strip, and Them (featuring Van Morrison), who the Doors got the opportunity to jam with during their stint as house band at the Whisky A Go Go in 1966.

In *Light My Fire*, Ray Manzarek claimed that early blues masters like Waters and Reed "unlocked the door for us," while rockers like Berry and Little Richard "ripped it off its hinges." In an interview that appeared in *Rolling Stone* magazine in 1969, Jim Morrison remarked, "The birth of rock and roll coincided with my adolescence, my coming into awareness . . . It was a real turn-on, although at the time, I could never allow myself to rationally fantasize about ever doing it myself. I guess all that time I was unconsciously accumulating information and listening. So when it finally happened my subconscious had prepared the whole thing."

Muddy Waters (1913–83)

Born McKinley Morganfield in Rolling Fork, Mississippi, Muddy Waters was heavily influenced by Delta blues legends such as Charley Patton, Son House, and Robert Johnson. A migrant worker from Stovall's plantation in nearby Clarksdale, Waters bought his first guitar at the age of thirteen. He first attracted attention in 1941 when folklorist Alan Lomax, heading up a field recording team for the Library of Congress, came to Clarksdale searching for Johnson, unaware he had been dead for nearly three years. Lomax ended up recording Waters performing several songs. Waters headed to Chicago in 1943 with his guitar and a suitcase full of clothes. The following year, he purchased an electric guitar and set about merging his Delta blues influences with the amplified urban sound to become one of the leading proponents of Chicago-style blues. Waters was signed to Aristocrat Records (later known as Chess) in 1946 and in 1948 released his first single, "Rollin' Stone," which would later give the Rolling Stones, as well as *Rolling Stone* magazine, their name.

Waters's band at one time or another included such legends as Little Walter, Otis Spann, Junior Wells, James Cotton, Buddy Guy, Leroy "Baby-Face" Foster, and Willie Dixon, who wrote the Howlin' Wolf hit and future Doors cover "Back Door Man." A slew of blues hits followed such as "Honey Bee," "She Moves Me," "Hoochie Coochie," "I Just Want to Make Love to You," "I'm Ready," "Rollin' and Tumblin'," "Got My Mojo Working," and "Mannish Boy," among others. In 1959, Manzarek caught a performance of Muddy Waters at Pepper's Lounge at Forty-Seventh and Racine in Chicago. Manzarek later cited Waters as one of his favorite singers in his original Elektra Records biography. Waters appeared in the 1978 documentary *The Last Waltz.* He died of a heart attack on April 30, 1983, at the age of sixty-eight. Waters is buried in Chicago's Restvale Cemetery. His epitaph reads, "THE MOJO IS GONE, THE MASTER HAS WON . . ."

Willie Dixon (1915–92)

The Doors featured Willie Dixon's "Back Door Man" on their self-titled album debut and frequently performed the crowd favorite in concert. Krieger discovered "Back Door Man" on an album by John Hammond Jr., and it was one of the mainstay songs when the band performed at bars such as the London Fog and Whisky A Go Go. In addition, the Willie Dixon-penned "(You Need Meat) Don't Go No Further" served as the B-side for "Love Her Madly" (with Manzarek on vocals!).

Dixon, who was born on July 1, 1915, in Vicksburg, Mississippi, and moved to Chicago in 1927, was a major figure in the development of the Chicago blues scene along with Muddy Waters and Howlin' Wolf. Discussing his songwriting techniques in an interview that appeared in *Give My Poor Heart Ease: Voices of the Mississippi Blues* by William Ferris, Dixon commented, "I began to take apart life and put it together in words. I would try to find the right tone to emphasize the facts of life. I found out that things from the past it fitted a lot of people in the present and also the hopes of the future."

In addition to "Back Door Man," Dixon wrote a slew of blues classics (many of which boasted sexually suggestive lyrics) such as "I Just Wanna Make Love to You," "Little Red Rooster," "Wang Dang Doodle," "You Shook Me," "Spoonful," "I'm Your Hoochie Coochie Man," "I Ain't Superstitious," and "I Can't Quit

You." These songs and others were later covered by the likes of Howlin' Wolf, Muddy Waters, Bo Diddley, Little Walter, Otis Rush, Sam Cooke, the Rolling Stones, Cream, the Doors, and Led Zeppelin, against whom Dixon won a lengthy copyright battle. Dixon, who wrote an autobiography called *I Am the Blues*, died of heart failure on January 29, 1992, at the age of eighty-six and was survived by eleven children and thirty grandchildren. He is buried in Burr Oak Cemetery in Chicago.

Frank Sinatra (1915–98)

In *Follow the Music*, Doors producer Paul Rothchild remarked, "[Morrison] talked about being a crooner. He admired Sinatra's phrasing enormously . . . But he was really an accidental musician. He couldn't play an instrument." Ironically, back in 1957, Sinatra had called rock 'n' roll "phony and false, and it's sung, written and played for the most part by cretinous goons." He also referred to rock as "the most brutal, ugly, desperate, vicious form of expression it has been my misfortune to hear."

Born in Hoboken, New Jersey, Francis Albert Sinatra was discovered in 1939 while singing at a roadhouse and soon joined the Tommy Dorsey Orchestra. As a solo artist, Sinatra churned out a handful of classic albums such as *In the Wee Small Hours, Songs for Swingin' Lovers, Come Fly with Me, Only the Lonely, Nice 'n' Easy*, and *September of My Years*, among others. After his career stalled in the early 1950s, his fortunes changed with his portrayal of "Private Angelo Maggio" in the critically acclaimed 1955 film *From Here to Eternity*, earning him an Academy Award for Best Supporting Actor. He also acted in several other classic films over the years such as *On the Town, Guys and Dolls, High Society, The Man with the Golden Arm*, and *The Manchurian Candidate*, among others.

During the 1960s, Sinatra was a founding member of the so-called "Rat Pack" along with Dean Martin, Sammy Davis Jr., Peter Lawford, and Joey Bishop. At the age of fifty in 1965, Sinatra recorded the retrospective album *September of My Years*, which contained the hit singles "Strangers in the Night" and "My Way." Over the course of his brilliant musical career, Sinatra earned eleven Grammy Awards, including the Grammy Legend Award and the Grammy Lifetime Achievement Award. He was also awarded the Presidential Medal of Freedom by Ronald Reagan and the Congressional Gold Medal in 1997.

In the liner notes for *Strange Days* in the *Perception Box Set*, Doors engineer Bruce Botnick related the story of how he chose a Telefunken U47 microphone for Morrison: "The significance of the U47 wasn't lost on him, since he was a big fan of Frank Sinatra and Elvis Presley. The first time Jim stepped up in front of the microphone, he immediately recognized it from *Sinatra's Swingin' Session* album cover and was flattered to be sonically linked to one of his idols!"

Jimmy Reed (1925–76)

In their original Elektra Records biographies, both Robby Krieger and John Densmore cited blues musician and songwriter Jimmy Reed among their musical influences. Known as "the Bossman of the Blues," Mathis James "Jimmy" Reed was born in Dunleith, Mississippi, and raised on the Delta blues. He journeyed to Chicago in 1953 and quickly got involved in the blues scene there. Reed eventually scored twenty-two chart-topping hits, including "You Don't Have to Go," "Ain't That Lovin' You Baby," "Honest I Do," "Baby What You Want Me to Do," "Big Boss Man," "Bright Lights, Big City," and "Shame, Shame, Shame."

Reed died of respiratory failure in 1976, just eight days shy of his fifty-first birthday. In 1991, he was posthumously inducted into the Rock and Roll Hall of Fame. Reed's influence extends to the Doors, Elvis Presley (who scored a 1967 hit with a cover of "Big Boss Man"), the Rolling Stones (who performed Reed's "The Sun Is Shining" at the notorious Altamont concert in 1969), the Yardbirds, Neil Young, and the Grateful Dead (who often played "Big Boss Man" in their concerts). The influence of Reed's "You Got Me Runnin'" ("You got me run, hide, hide, run") can be heard in "Break on Through" ("Tried to run/Tried to hide"). "Big Boss Man" and "Bright Lights, Big City" were both voted onto the list of the Rock and Roll Hall of Fame's "500 Songs that Shaped Rock and Roll."

Chuck Berry (1926–)

Chuck Berry once remarked, "It used to be called boogie-woogie, it used to be called blues, used to be called rhythm and blues . . . It's called rock now." A native of St. Louis and a high school dropout who graduated from beauty school with a degree in hairdressing and cosmetology, Berry was working as a beautician in St. Louis when he traveled to Chicago and met his idol Muddy Waters, who encouraged him to contact Leonard Chess of Chess Records. To Berry, who soon signed with Chess, Waters "was the godfather of the blues. He was perhaps the greatest inspiration in the launching of my career."

Berry recorded his first hit, "Maybellene," followed by such early rock 'n' roll classics as "Roll Over Beethoven (Dig These Rhythm and Blues)," "School Days," "Rock and Roll Music," "Sweet Little Sixteen," "Johnny Be Goode," and "Rockin' & Rollin'." Ironically, Berry's only No. 1 hit was "My Ding-A-Ling," a throwaway novelty song about masturbation that overtook Michael Jackson's "Ben" to top the charts on October 2, 1972.

After watching Chuck Berry perform at a Santa Monica concert in the early 1960s, Krieger went out and traded his classical guitar for a Gibson SG. At the inaugural Rock and Roll Hall of Fame induction ceremonies on January 23, 1986, Rolling Stone Keith Richards remarked, "It's hard for me to induct Chuck Berry, because I lifted every lick he ever played!"

Fats Domino (1928–)

Piano rocker Antoine "Fats" Domino was a fixture on the New Orleans music scene, learning the ropes from such legends as Fats Waller and Professor Longhair. Domino's first hit, "Ain't That a Shame," was released in 1955 and reached No. 10 on the charts. He followed with such classics as "Blueberry Hill," which skyrocketed to No. 2 on the charts and "I'm Walkin'," which charted at No. 4. Domino, who strongly influenced the Beatles (Paul McCartney reportedly wrote "Lady Madonna" in an emulation of Domino's style), was inducted into the Rock and Roll Hall of Fame in 1986 as part of its inaugural class. He was awarded a Grammy Lifetime Achievement Award the following year.

Little Richard (1932–)

In Little Richard's 1984 biography, *The Life and Times of Little Richard*, the flamboyant rocker exclaimed, "My music made your liver quiver, your bladder splatter, and your knees freeze. And your big toe shoot right up in your boot!"

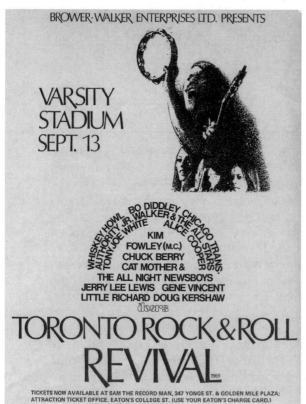

Never dull and always influential, Little Richard was born Richard Penniman in Macon, Georgia, on December 5, 1932. As a youth, Penniman (one of twelve children) sang with his family's gospel troupe, the Penniman Family. Tragically, his father, the owner of a bar called the Tip In Inn, was shot and killed under mysterious circumstances in 1952.

Once described as a "wild-eyed, pompadoured madman," Little Richard broke out in the mid-1950s, unleashing such early rock 'n' roll classics as "Tutti Frutti," "Long Tall Sally," "Rip It Up," "Ready Teddy," "The Girl Can't Help It," "Good Golly Miss Molly," "Jenny, Jenny," "Keep a Knockin'," and "Lucille." Known for his outrageous

At the Toronto Rock & Roll Revival Concert on September 13, 1969, the Doors got the rare opportunity to perform with some of their earliest musical influences, including Chuck Berry and Little Richard.   *Courtesy of Kerry Humpherys/doors.com* stage antics, Little Richard and his band, the Upsetters, wore pancake makeup and eye shadow and sported piled-high hair. Ironically, Little Richard never enjoyed a chart-topping hit, his most successful song, "Long Tall Sally," reaching No. 6 on the charts in 1956. Little Richard also appeared in such cult film classics as *The Girl Can't Help It* and *Don't Knock the Rock.*

In 1957, Little Richard quit rock and became a minister of the Seventh Day Adventist Church. He would not perform again until 1964. Little Richard performed at the Toronto Rock & Roll Revival Concert on September 13, 1969, along with other rock legends such as Chuck Berry, Jerry Lee Lewis, and Gene Vincent, as well as the Doors and John Lennon (with his Plastic Ono Band in his first performance without the Beatles).

In 1986, Little Richard was inducted into the Rock and Roll Hall of Fame as part of its inaugural class. In addition, his "Tutti Frutti" was recognized by *MOJO* magazine (June 2007) as No. 1 on its list of the "100 Records That Changed the World," a song that "smashed down the doors of culture and ushered in an attitude we still call rock 'n' roll." In *The Doors by the Doors*, Robby Krieger remarked, "That guy, for raw rock 'n' roll power, you can't beat him."

Elvis Presley (1935–77)

In his original Elektra Records biography, Morrison cited "the King of Rock 'n' Roll" as one of his favorite singers, along with Frank Sinatra. Morrison later convinced rock critic Jerry Hopkins to write his first biography about Presley (Hopkins had originally intended to write about Frank Zappa). Hopkins in turn dedicated the book to Morrison. Manzarek also discovered Elvis as a teenager and commented in *Light My Fire* that he leapt out of his chair when he first heard Presley sing "Blue Suede Shoes" on TV: "What a killer! He just blew me away. Finally, a white guy doing it. Doing the blues." Morrison was often compared both favorably and unfavorably to Elvis over the years. For instance, a review of a Doors concert in Madison Square ("Ooo, They Lit the Garden's Fire!") that appeared in the New York *Daily News* stated, "The Doors, for the benefit of any squares who read this, are the new Beatles led by an Elvis Presley type named Jim Morrison, who cranks up kids effectively as a shot of LSD." In a *New York Times* article by Michael Lydon titled "The Doors: Can They Still 'Light My Fire'?," Morrison remarked, "I'm not a new Elvis, though he's my second favorite singer—Frank Sinatra is first."

Elvis Aaron Presley, who once referred to rock 'n' roll as "a combination of folk or hillbilly music and gospel singing," was born in Tupelo, Mississippi, on January 8, 1935, to Gladys Love Smith Presley and Vernon Presley. His twin, Jesse Garon, died at birth. The Presley family was dirt poor and lived in a shotgun shack. Presley grew up listening to B. B. King, Chester "Howlin' Wolf" Burnett, Arthur "Big Boy" Crudup, Big Bill Broonzy, and other blues legends. After finishing second in a talent show at the Mississippi-Alabama State Fair, Presley received a $12.98 guitar from his mother as a birthday present. After graduating from

L. C. Humes High School, Presley worked as a truck driver for Crown Electric. During a lunch break one summer day in 1953, Presley stopped by the Memphis Recording Service and paid $3.98 to record the Ink Spots' "My Happiness" as a gift for his mother. He soon scored a recording deal with Sun Records.

RCA bought out Presley's Sun Records contract in 1955, and he achieved his first No. 1 hit with "Heartbreak Hotel" in 1956, quickly turning into a national phenomenon in the process. "Heartbreak Hotel" was quickly followed by such No. 1 hits as "I Want You, I Need You, I Love You" (July 1956), "Don't Be Cruel"/"Hound Dog" (August 1956), "Love Me Tender" (November 1956), "Too Much" (February 1957), "All Shook Up" (April 1957), "(Let Me Be Your) Teddy Bear" (July 1957), and "Jailhouse Rock"/"Treat Me Nice" (October 1957). Presley eventually scored seventeen No. 1 hits in the United States, a feat surpassed only by the Beatles. In 1956, he also appeared in the first of his thirty-three movies, *Love Me Tender*. Heavily addicted to prescription drugs, Presley died of a drug-induced heart attack on August 16, 1977. In 1986, he was inducted into the Rock and Roll Hall of Fame as part of its inaugural class.

In an interview called "Elvis Influenced Doors' Jim" that appeared in the September 21, 1968, issue of *New Musical Express* magazine, Morrison commented, "Along with many of the early rock singers, Little Richard, Fats Domino, Jerry Lee Lewis, Gene Vincent, [Elvis] had an influence on me because of the music and the fact that I heard them at an early age when I was kinda ready for an influence. It was a strong influence and they just seemed to open up a whole new world to me." Morrison was later ecstatic when Elvis's bassist Jerry Scheff agreed to play on the Doors' sixth studio album, *L.A. Woman*.

Love

For a brief period, Los Angeles-based Love was the hottest rock group on the Sunset Strip and envied by all up-and-coming bands, including the Doors. "I dreamed that if someday I could just be in a band like Love, I'd be happy," remarked John Densmore in his 1990 autobiography, *Riders on the Storm*. "After experiencing Love, I knew I had a ways to go before being hip." In his official Elektra Records biography, Jim Morrison cited Love as one of his favorite groups, along with the Beach Boys and the Kinks (who would later accuse the Doors of plagiarizing the melody of their song "All Day and All of the Night" for "Hello, I Love You").

One of the first racially mixed rock bands, Love, which was led by singer-songwriter Arthur Lee, skillfully blended garage rock, folk, and psychedelia. The original lineup also included Johnny Echols (lead guitar), Bryan Maclean (rhythm guitar), Ken Forssi (bass), and Alban "Snoopy" Pfisterer (drums). Performing at Hollywood nightclubs such as Brave New World, Bido Lito's, and the Hullabaloo Club, Love (originally known as the Grass Roots) soon caught the attention of Elektra Records president Jac Holzman, who promptly signed them. According to Holzman, "Love was one of the great underground rock acts of L.A.—in fact, the only good unsigned act when I began foraging for new groups on behalf of Elektra in the mid-'60s."

The group's self-titled debut album was released in 1965 and sold more than 100,000 copies, turning folk label Elektra into a rock 'n' roll player. Love's subsequent album, *Da Capo*, released in 1967, was also successful, especially in England, and scored the group a Top 40 hit with "7 and 7 Is." Widely regarded today as Love's masterpiece, the mesmerizing, psychedelic album *Forever Changes* was released in November 1967 and promptly stalled out, peaking at a dismal No. 154 on the charts. Robert Plant of Led Zeppelin later acknowledged *Forever Changes*, which was coproduced by the "sixth Door," Bruce Botnick, as one of his all-time favorite albums.

According to Lee, "Jim Morrison used to sit outside my door when I lived in Laurel Canyon, wanting to hang out with me. I just let him sit there." Unfortunately, due to Lee's unpredictability and steadfast refusal to perform outside of Los Angeles, Love never developed a wider audience. The band retreated to Bela Lugosi's former Hollywood Hills mansion (known as "The Castle") and consumed mind-numbing quantities of acid and heroin. According to Botnick, Lee "was on acid twenty-four hours a day, or smoking hemp—something. But he was so high all the time that he wasn't high. He had achieved what they call clear light."

By the time "Light My Fire" hit No. 1 on the charts in July 1967, the Doors had left Love in their dust forever. Although Holzman referred to Lee as "one of the smartest, most intelligent, and finest musicians I have ever met in my entire career of making records," he acknowledged that Lee's preference for isolation and "not doing what was necessary to bring his music to the audience" were destructive to the band and "cost him a career." Indeed, over the next few years Love totally fell apart. According to Lee, "After we started making money, the more we made the less we worked, the less we were a unit and Love deteriorated."

Love would re-form under various incarnations over the coming years, but it was never the same. Some of the gigs included opening for Doors tribute bands such as Wild Child at the Whisky a Go Go in the early 1990s. After various encounters with the law, including arrests for drug possession and illegal possession of a firearm, Lee fell victim to California's three strikes law in 1996 and spent a few years in prison. After his release, Lee toured the world as "Arthur Lee and Love." He died of leukemia in 2006.

Them

In their original Elektra Records biographies, both John Densmore and Robby Krieger cited Them among their favorite groups. According to Krieger, "We played with a lot of groups at the Whisky and the most exciting one, I think, was Them. They were always our favorite."

Known today for the garage rock hit "Gloria" and for launching the career of Van Morrison (born George Ivan Morrison), Them was a Northern Irish rock band formed in Belfast in 1964. Morrison grew up listening to American rhythm & blues such as Muddy Waters and John Lee Hooker. He dropped out of school at the age of fifteen to join a band called the Monarchs, which performed at the R&B Club in Belfast. In 1965, Van Morrison formed Them, which charted with the songs "Baby, Please Don't Go" and "Here Comes the Night." Featuring Van Morrison (vocals), Wric Wrixon (keyboards), Alan Henderson (bass), Raymond Sweetman (bass), and Ronnie Millings (drums), Them made their way to Los Angeles and performed between May 30 and June 18, 1966, at the famous Whisky A Go Go, where the Doors were employed as house band.

"We were definitely influenced by British Invasion bands like The Animals and Them," according to Krieger. "Their set-up was similar to ours: the organ and a certain type of lead singer. When we played with Them at the Whisky it was a real highlight. Van used to get really wasted and break mikestands almost every night. He reminded me a lot of Jim. He became a total other person when he was drunk. The dark side of our music came from Jim and his inner demons." According to Doors producer Paul Rothchild in *Follow the Music*, "The thing that was so interesting to me was to learn how much chaos there was inside the group Them. It's almost as if Jim studied their chaos and brought it into the Doors."

On the final night of their residency at the Whisky, Them jammed together with the Doors for a legendary set that included spirited renditions of "Gloria" and "In the Midnight Hour." According to Manzarek in *Light My Fire*, "we all became friends, and the last night of our too-brief week's engagement with the Irish crazies saw us all in a monster jam session. The Doors and Them onstage together. Jim Morrison and Van Morrison onstage at the same time! And singing, 'Gloria'! What a fucking night. The Morrisons were amazing."

Although "Gloria" hardly made a dent in the charts, its influence cannot be understated since thousands of garage bands in the United States tried to emulate the song's sound in the 1960s. In 2007, "Gloria" was inducted into the Grammy Hall of Fame.

8

Just Got into Town

Los Angeles Area Landmarks Associated with the Doors

In L.A. there were two places: one was the beach, where we were conceived, and the other was Laurel Canyon, where you got in touch with the earth and sky.
—Ray Manzarek

The Doors' mystique emerged from rather humble beginnings at the UCLA film school and Venice Beach in the spring and summer of 1965. Many of Jim Morrison's first songs such as "Moonlight Drive," "Hello, I Love You," and "Soul Kitchen" can be traced to area landmarks in and around Venice Beach. Soon the Doors migrated to the Sunset Strip and Laurel Canyon, inspiring such classics as "Love Street" and "People Are Strange." The Doors Office on Santa Monica Boulevard provided the ideal locale for Jim Morrison to enjoy his favorite haunts such as the Alta Cienega Motel, Barney's Beanery, and a strip bar called the Phone Booth.

Venice Beach

Known as the "birthplace" of the Doors, funky and laid-back Venice, which lies just fourteen miles west of Los Angeles, was a favorite haunt of the Beat Generation during the 1950s. John Densmore wrote about his first impressions of Venice in his autobiography, *Riders on the Storm*: "This ain't no surfer territory. This is beatnik vibes with artists and musicians."

Founded as a beach resort by Abbot Kinney in 1905 and featuring sixteen miles of manmade canals as well as beachfront homes and shops, Venice never evolved into the upscale paradise envisioned by its founder and became known instead as the "Coney Island of the Pacific" for its plethora of amusement attractions. By the mid-1960s, Venice had become totally rundown, but offered the enticement of older housing with low rents and cheap eateries—the perfect locale for unemployed film school graduates like Jim Morrison and Ray Manzarek, as well as various artists, hippies, and runaways. After graduating from UCLA with a bachelor's degree in cinematography and little thought for the future, Morrison made his way to Venice during the summer of 1965. He lived on the rooftop of a decrepit office building just blocks from the beach at the corner of Speedway and Westminster where his college buddy, Dennis Jakob, worked as a janitor.

It was in Venice where Morrison started dropping acid and composing song lyrics, one of which, "My Eyes Have Seen You," is about all the TV antennas visible from the roof overlooking Venice: "My eyes have seen you free from disguise/Gazing on a city under television skies." After watching a beautiful black chick stroll across the beach, Morrison composed "Hello, I Love You," which later appeared on the Doors' third album, *Waiting for the Sun*, and reached No. 1 on the charts in the summer of 1968: "Do you hope to make her see you, fool?/ Do you hope to pluck this dusky jewel?" In addition, "Soul Kitchen" was inspired by a local soul food eatery in Venice called Olivia's Place. LSD was still legal at the time, and Morrison scored his acid easily at the neighborhood head shop.

A chance encounter with fellow UCLA film graduate Ray Manzarek on the beach in Venice in July 1965 led to the creation of the Doors. After Morrison told Manzarek he had composed some song lyrics, he sang "Moonlight Drive," and the two friends agreed to start a band. At the time, Manzarek and his future wife, Dorothy, were living in a one-bedroom apartment overlooking the rooftops of Venice for $75 a month. Portions of Manzarek's student film *Evergreen* were shot there. Morrison soon grabbed his meager possessions (basically some clothes and a box of books that included works by Jack Kerouac, Arthur Rimbaud, Friedrich Nietzsche, and others) from the rooftop and moved in with the couple. Manzarek had his first acid trip while residing in Venice and described it as "absolutely stunning."

Manzarek soon found the apartment of his dreams at Northstar and Speedway directly on Venice Beach, where the Doors rehearsed their early songs (it was here that the Doors' signature song, "Light My Fire," took shape). When the group scored their first permanent gig at the London Fog in early 1966, the marquee highlighted their roots, reading, "Doors—Band from Venice." The Doors also performed at a nearby nightclub called the Cheetah, which was located at the end of the Santa Monica Pier, where Morrison unintentionally accomplished the first documented "stage dive." Later, Venice Beach served as a film locale for the Doors' short film of "The Unknown Soldier," in which Morrison is tied to a post and summarily executed, spewing blood in the process.

Today, visitors to Venice can view the famous Jim Morrison mural, which was painted by Rip Cronk, at 1811 Speedway. Venice is also known as the "birthplace of modern progressive skateboarding" as chronicled in the 2001 documentary *Dogtown and Z-Boys*, which spawned the 2005 movie *The Lords of Dogtown*. Prominent residents of Venice over the years have included Anjelica Huston, Julia Roberts, Nicolas Cage, Dennis Hopper, Viggo Mortensen, Robert Downey Jr., Elijah Wood, Fiona Apple, Perry Farrell of Jane's Addiction, and John Frusciante of the Red Hot Chili Peppers, among others. In addition, Arnold Schwarzenegger embarked on his acting career after becoming a regular bodybuilder at Venice's famous Gold's Gym, the self-described "Mecca of Bodybuilding." Oliver Stone filmed portions of his 1991 movie *The Doors* on location in Venice.

Lucky U Cafe

In the early days of the band, all four Doors could often be found enjoying tacos and burritos, and sharing pitchers of beer at their favorite hangout, the Lucky U Cafe. A Mexican American restaurant located at 1660 South Sepulveda Boulevard near the UCLA Film School, the Lucky U offered breakfast all day and was open from 6 a.m. to 2 a.m. According to Manzarek, all the "hip students" hung out at the Lucky U, the type of place where they could nurse their "meager change into a divine meal." Manzarek thought the Lucky U's chef, Rosario Carillo, was "a genius."

The place also drew its share of "lowlifes" and "cripples" from the nearby Veterans Hospital, reminding Morrison of a Nelson Algren story. In addition, the Lucky U served as a film locale for Manzarek's second student film, *Induction*, where Manzarek and his future wife, Dorothy Fujikawa, can be seen at the restaurant's counter eating burritos and drinking beer. Over the years, the Doors would continue to frequent the Lucky U after recording sessions for their six studio albums. In addition, Morrison and a group of friends that included engineer John Haeny, Frank and Kathy Lisciandro, and Florentine Pabst headed there during a break from his birthday poetry recordings on December 8, 1970. The Lucky U Cafe was later torn down and replaced by a gas station.

Olivia's Place

A Southern-style diner located at the corner of Ocean Park and Main near the Venice arcade, Olivia's inspired "Soul Kitchen," which appeared on the Doors' 1967 self-titled debut album. According to John Densmore in *Riders on the Storm*, the diner, which catered to UCLA film students, looked like an "Amtrak dining car that got stranded at the beach."

Morrison filled the bluesy "Soul Kitchen" with sexually suggestive lyrics such as "Let me sleep all night in your soul kitchen/Warm my mind near your gentle stove." Paul Williams, editor and founder of *Crawdaddy!* magazine, referred to "Soul Kitchen" as "a nice little song about desire." Doors producer Paul Rothchild claimed that the key to understanding the song was the refrain, "Learn to forget," to him meaning "learn to forget the bullshit, the alien concepts, get back to reality, sleep in the soul kitchen."

"Soul Kitchen" was later covered by the influential Los Angeles punk band X on their 1980 debut album, *Los Angeles*, which was produced by Ray Manzarek. In addition, punk poet and Morrison disciple Patti Smith recorded the song. "Soul Kitchen" can also be heard during the Vietnam sequence in the 1994

Academy Award-winning film *Forrest Gump*. Today the California Heritage Museum occupies the former site of Olivia's Place.

Alta Cienega Motel

During the late 1960s, Jim Morrison frequently crashed in room 32 on the second floor of the Alta Cienega Motel, a bland, nondescript, and anonymous building located at 1005 North La Cienega Boulevard in West Hollywood, just across the street from the Doors Office and right down the street from the Elektra Records office at 962 North La Cienega. Morrison's favorite bars, Barney's Beanery, the Palms, and the Phone Booth, as well as Monaco Liquors, were all within walking distance of the Alta Cienega Motel.

Manzarek referred to the Alta Cienega Motel as Morrison's "escape hatch," where he could spend time "alone with his thoughts." According to Morrison's friend Frank Lisciandro in his memoir, *Jim Morrison: An Hour for Magic*, Morrison "preferred the anonymity of cheap motels or big hotels, an impersonal room where no one he knew could find him. Perhaps he found in these rooms a quiet, unhurried place to write, or simply a refuge from his demanding fame."

Several scenes from Morrison's experimental film, *HWY*, were shot at the Alta Cienega Motel, which advertised rooms from $10 per night. Mick Jagger visited Morrison at the motel on the afternoon before the Doors' Hollywood Bowl concert on July 5, 1968, and the two rock stars discussed the challenges of performing before stadium-size audiences.

Today, room 32 has evolved into a veritable shrine to the "Lizard King" with graffiti and poetry scrawled all over the walls. Doors fans can book the room (well in advance) at just $84 per night. According to the motel's website: "Alta Cienega Motel has a long and vivid history. World famous legendary rock singer Jim Morrison lived at our motel in Room 32 from 1968-1970. The room is still decorated with Jim's portrait and personal belongings to this day."

Laurel Canyon

This quirky neighborhood of Los Angeles rapidly evolved as a center of the counterculture during the mid-1960s with famous residents such as the Doors, Frank Zappa, Crosby, Stills, and Nash; the Mamas and the Papas; Love; the Turtles; the Byrds; Buffalo Springfield; and Joni Mitchell (the Laurel Canyon home that Mitchell shared with Graham Nash was immortalized in his classic song, "Our House"). Needless to say, drugs and free love were plentiful in the Canyon. In his foreword to Harvey Kubernik's *Canyon of Dreams*, Ray Manzarek writes of Laurel Canyon, "That deep green crease that runs through the Hollywood Hills from the Sunset Strip to the San Fernando Valley. That curving, twisting boulevard of hipness and psychedelia; of movie stars and mystics and jazz and folk and rock; of Harry Houdini, Clark Gable, Shelly Manne, and Joni Mitchell, Frank Zappa, and The Doors."

Ironically, Manzarek never lived in Laurel Canyon, but the three other Doors resided there at one time or another. Morrison lived with Pamela Courson in a rundown boardinghouse at 1812 Rothdell Trail in Laurel Canyon, inspiring him to write the song "Love Street." According to legend, Clark Gable had conducted many trysts at the same locale years earlier. The centrally located Canyon Country Store at 2108 Laurel Canyon Boulevard was "the store where the creatures meet." Once the site of the Bungalow Inn Lodge, which burned down in 1929, the Canyon Country Store became a regular hangout for Morrison and other musicians such as Zappa and Mitchell who would sometime gather on the front patio for impromptu jam sessions.

Morrison wrote many songs in Laurel Canyon that would end up on the Doors albums *Strange Days* and *Waiting for the Sun*, such as "People Are Strange," which Densmore claimed Morrison wrote on a matchbook. It was also here that Morrison and Courson engaged in some of their most legendary fights, which would often spill into the streets with Morrison's clothes and books often flying out of windows. According to legend, Morrison preserved some of his songs and poetry behind the wall of a shower in his Rothdell Trail apartment.

In addition, Densmore and Krieger shared an apartment on Lookout Mountain Drive in Laurel Canyon. During one of his most notorious acid trips, Morrison broke into their apartment, trashed the place, and pissed all over Densmore's bed. Doors producer Paul Rothchild, who was known as the "fifth Door," also bought twenty acres of land in Laurel Canyon. In addition, Danny Sugerman, the coauthor of *No One Here Gets Out Alive* and later Doors co-manager, lived in a two-story bungalow at 8632 Wonderland Avenue in the Canyon. Sugerman titled his 1989 autobiography *Wonderland Avenue*.

During the early 1980s, Laurel Canyon earned notoriety as the site of the so-called Wonderland Murders involving the late porn star John Holmes (a.k.a. "Johnny Wadd"). The film *Boogie Nights* features a fictionalized version of the events surrounding the murders. Morrison's former residence on Rothdell Trail was later renovated into a three-bedroom bungalow that went on the market for $1.199 million in 2010. Narrated by legendary rock photographer Henry Diltz, (who photographed the Doors' *Morrison Hotel* album cover), the 2010 documentary *Legends of the Canyon* highlights the "music and magic of 1960's Laurel Canyon" and includes interviews with David Crosby, Stephen Stills, and Graham Nash.

Chateau Marmont

Movie studio boss Harry Cohn used to tell Hollywood hopefuls, "If you must get into trouble, do it at the Chateau Marmont." Built in the late 1920s, the legendary hotel, located along the world-famous Sunset Strip at 8221 Sunset Boulevard, is perhaps best known today as the notorious locale where John Belushi met his demise in 1982 of a speed-ball drug overdose in Bungalow #3 at the age of thirty-three.

However, the hotel boasts a rich history catering to Hollywood elite such as Greta Garbo, Errol Flynn, Marilyn Monroe, and Montgomery Clift, as well as author F. Scott Fitzgerald (who had a heart attack here). During the 1960s, famous musicians discovered the charms of the Chateau Marmont such as Bob Dylan, Mick Jagger, Ringo Starr, Gram Parsons, Led Zeppelin (who once rode their motorcycles through the lobby), and Jim Morrison, who resided here off and on in 1970 and 1971.

In one incident, Morrison fell off one of the balconies while he was trying to swing from the roof via a drain pipe into the window of his room, later claiming he had used up the "eighth" of his nine lives. In his autobiography, *Wonderland Avenue*, Danny Sugerman related how Morrison took him to the hotel to warn him of the horrors of drug addiction by visiting singer/songwriter, heroin addict, and resident burnout Tim Hardin ("If I Were A Carpenter"). According to Sugerman, Hardin "was horribly thin, naked to the waist, his ribs poking out." During the visit, Hardin begged Morrison for money to feed his habit and then shit his pants. Hardin, who performed at Woodstock, died of a heroin overdose in 1980 at the age of thirty-nine.

Legendary photographer Helmut Newton died at the Chateau Marmont in 2004 after losing control of his car in the driveway and crashing into a wall.

Barney's Beanery

A legendary drinking hole at 8447 Santa Monica Boulevard in West Hollywood, Barney's Beanery was founded in 1920 by John "Barney" Anthony and once catered to Hollywood royalty (along with many legendary Hollywood drunks!) such as John Barrymore, Clara Bow, Errol Flynn, Clark Gable, Judy Garland, Bette Davis, and Lou Costello. Barney's evolved into a popular beatnik hangout during the 1950s.

During the mid-1960s, both Janis Joplin and Jim Morrison became regulars at Barney's Beanery, which was just a short distance from the Doors Office and down the street from the Alta Cienega Motel. According to legend, Joplin even bashed Morrison over the head with a full bottle of Southern Comfort here one drunken night (although this same incident has been reported as happening elsewhere). Rumor has it that Morrison's favorite meal at Barney's was chicken liver with onions. One night, after a typical bout of heavy drinking, Morrison stood up, whipped it out, urinated on the bar at Barney's, and was promptly kicked out. The bar later commemorated the event with a memorial plaque.

On October 4, 1970, Joplin sat down at her favorite booth (#34) and guzzled two screwdrivers before heading down to the Landmark Hotel, where she over-dosed on heroin early the next morning. Other famous Barney's patrons over the years include actors Marlon Brando, Jack Nicholson, and Dennis Hopper; artist Ed Kienholz; author and legendary boozer Charles Bukowski (the "poet laureate of skid row"); and band members from the Blasters, Jane's Addiction, and the Red Hot Chili Peppers.

No stranger to controversy, Barney's once featured a sign over the bar that read "FAGOTS [*sic*]—STAY OUT." Protestors picketed Barney's in 1970; however, the offending sign wasn't removed until the mid-1970s. A scene from the 1991 film *The Doors* was shot here. Director Quentin Tarantino wrote most of the script for his 1994 film *Pulp Fiction* while sitting in his favorite booth at Barney's Beanery.

The Phone Booth

Morrison regularly frequented this topless joint at the Southwest corner of La Cienega and Santa Monica Boulevard in West Hollywood next to the Doors Office at 8512 Santa Monica Boulevard. According to *No One Here Gets Out Alive* author Jerry Hopkins, the Phone Booth was Morrison's favorite bar, and "I don't think Morrison was happier anywhere else, not even on a stage with tens of thousands of adoring fans."

Morrison often demanded that interviewers ask him questions over beers at the Phone Booth, and Hopkins remembers that "'Love Me Two Times' magically fell onto the jukebox turntable" when Morrison walked in and "one of the dancers would come over and shake her Two Times in his face." Doors publicist Diane Gardiner claimed Morrison "was interested in topless dancers and how they felt. He had a real empathy for them." The Phone Booth was briefly featured in Morrison's film *HWY*. Today, a Fatburger restaurant occupies the former Phone Booth site.

Doors Office

A total dump with unpainted walls and dirty carpets, the two-story Doors Office (also known as "The Doors Workshop") at 8512 Santa Monica Boulevard was where the band recorded *L.A. Woman*, their final studio album with Morrison. They also rehearsed most of their albums on the ground floor of the building, while Doors manager Bill Siddons conducted business in the office upstairs. In *Follow the Music*, Siddons described the building as "a ramshackle, rundown duplex."

Morrison enjoyed the office's ideal location, which was next door to the Phone Booth and down the street from the Alta Cienega Motel. According to Danny Sugerman in his autobiography, *Wonderland Avenue*, several totally insane Doors groupies lurked about the Doors Office over the years such as "Crazy Nancy," who believed she had been married to Morrison in a previous life, and "Cigar Pain," who actually had "burnt his vocal cords with a lit cigar" in order to sound like Morrison.

After producer Paul Rothchild bailed on the *L.A. Woman* recording sessions, the Doors, along with engineer Bruce Botnick, decided to record the album at the Doors Office. According to Manzarek in *Light My Fire*, "We knew the sound of the room. We felt comfortable there. The vibrations were well tuned through years of rehearsal, laughter, drinking, philosophizing and pot smoking. This was home for us."

In 1972, a year after Morrison's death, the Doors moved out of the office in 1972, and the building became the Upside Down Studio and later, the Benvenuto Cafe. Rumors spread that Morrison was haunting the restroom at the Doors Office's most recent incarnation, the since-closed Mexico Restaurante. Morrison had actually used the bathroom area to record his vocals for *L.A. Woman*, and patrons reported such weird occurrences as lights switching on and off on their own and the bathroom door handle jiggling by itself.

Duke's Coffee Shop/Tropicana Motel

A regular haunt of the Doors, Janis Joplin, Van Morrison, Tom Waits, and John Belushi, Duke's Coffee Shop was founded in 1968 as part of the Tropicana Motel on Santa Monica Boulevard. Duke's served quality, inexpensive food and was a favorite haunt of the Doors after recording sessions.

Before moving to the slightly more appealing Alta Cienega Motel, Morrison was a regular at the rundown Tropicana, which was once owned by base-

ball legend Sandy Koufax. One of Morrison's favorite bars, the Palms, was located across the street. Jay S. Jacobs, the author of *Wild Years: The Music and Myth of Tom Waits*, described the Tropicana Motel as "a funky little fleabag" and "rock-and-roll landmark" where "music-world banditos rubbed shoulders with groupies, rock-star wannabes, hard-luck cases, and drunken traveling salesmen." The Tropicana had its share of orgies, suicides, overdoses, murders, and drunken brawls during its storied history. The motel's kidney-bean-shaped pool was painted black and occasionally full of floating syringes.

The Doors took the stage at the legendary Hollywood Bowl on July 5, 1968, highlighted by a mesmerizing performance of "The End." On September 10, 1972, the three surviving band members returned to the Hollywood Bowl for their final performance as the Doors.
Courtesy of Mark Smigel/mildequator.com

It was at the Tropicana that the other band members retrieved Morrison, who had consumed a copious amount of acid, and returned him to the Whisky A Go Go on August 21, 1966, for a set that infamously included the Oedipal lyrics to "The End." The Doors were promptly fired from their gig as house band at the Whisky.

Other celebrities who stayed at the Tropicana Motel at one time or another included the Byrds, Frank Zappa, Iggy Pop, the Sex Pistols, the Clash, Blondie, the Ramones, Lou Reed, William S. Burroughs, and Bruce Springsteen. The Tropicana also served as the locale for the Andy Warhol films *Heat* and *Trash*. In *Follow the Music*, Doors manager Bill Siddons called the Tropicana "the flop house of the music business, the new rock generation and the hippies."

In *Riders on the Storm*, John Densmore related how the band took a dinner break from recording *L.A. Woman* and headed to Duke's, where he ordered a "Sandy's favorite," which he described as "a mound of scrambled eggs with onions and stuff."

In 1987, Duke's moved to its current location at 8909 Sunset Boulevard and is known today as Duke's West Hollywood. Sadly, the Tropicana Motel was torn down in 1988 and replaced with a Ramada Inn.

9

We Chased Our Pleasures Here

The Doors' Earliest Venues

I just remember that some of the best musical trips we took were in clubs.
—*Jim Morrison*

In 1964–66, the Los Angeles music scene exploded as the fabled Sunset Strip became populated with a myriad of new rock clubs such as the Trip, Bido Lito's, the Sea Witch, Ciro's, Galaxy, Pandora's Box, Brave New World, and the legendary Whisky A Go Go. Love, led by Arthur Lee, reigned supreme along the Strip in 1966 before fading into oblivion a couple of years later. Other up-and-coming bands fighting for prominence on the Strip included the Byrds, Buffalo Springfield, the Turtles, the Mothers of Invention, and the Seeds. The Doors migrated from Venice Beach and played just about every one of the Sunset Strip clubs at one time or another before scoring big as the house band at Whisky A Go Go and attracting the attention of Elektra Records. The band then traveled to San Francisco and gained new fans at the Fillmore and the Matrix before heading to New York City and conquering the East Coast at such clubs as Ondine and Steve Paul's the Scene.

In a 1970 interview, Robby Krieger remarked, "I really liked it more when we were on the way up, at clubs like the Whisky, and Ondine's and The Scene in New York . . . Once we started the big concerts, it was more show time, and I didn't like that as much."

London Fog

In late February or early March 1966, the Doors scored their first steady gig at the London Fog, a total dive nestled between the Hamburger Hamlet and the Galaxy nightclub at 8919 Sunset Boulevard. The rundown joint was frequented by drunks, prostitutes, and other assorted lowlifes and sleazy characters. In *Riders on the Storm*, John Densmore described the London Fog as "a funky club with nautical decor" that featured "a crow's-nest-size stage." According to author Jerry Hopkins, the club "smelled of spilled beer and ashtrays."

Previously known as the Unicorn, the London Fog was owned by the appropriately named Jesse James, who claimed he was the great-grandson of the legendary outlaw. However, the Doors were elated to be performing on the Sunset Strip just down the street from the legendary Whisky A Go Go. The marquee read "Doors - Band from Venice" and below that in smaller print, "Rhonda Lane Exotic Dancer." The band received $5 each per night for four to five sets and performed on a small stage that was actually a modified go-go platform. Extremely uncomfortable in front of a live audience, Morrison frequently sang with his back toward the crowd.

The London Fog allowed Morrison to gain confidence, while the Doors honed the material that would appear on their first two albums, *The Doors* and *Strange Days*, such as "Light My Fire," "The End" and "When the Music's Over," as well as an "obscene version" of Them's "Gloria." In the liner notes to *The Doors Myth and Reality: The Spoken Word History*, Ray Manzarek remarked that at the London Fog, the Doors "became this collective entity, this unit of oneness. We played some Them, a little bit of Rolling Stones, a little Otis Redding. Some James Brown. But 75% of what we played were Doors' songs. And that is where the magic began to happen."

In order to fill sets, the Doors started stretching songs such as "The End," which began as a simple goodbye song to Morrison's ex-girlfriend Mary Werbelow, and "Light My Fire," with instrumental solos and stream-of-consciousness poetry improvisations. It was at the London Fog that Morrison most likely met his "cosmic mate," Pamela Courson, for the first time.

The Doors performed for the last time at the London Fog on May 7, 1966. The former site of the London Fog is now occupied by Melody Nail & Beauty Salon. In Oliver Stone's 1991 film, *The Doors*, a bar called the Central (which also appeared in *Valley Girl* in the scene featuring the Plimsouls) was used to represent the London Fog. In 1993, Johnny Depp turned the Central into the Viper Room, and on Halloween morning of that year, actor River Phoenix overdosed there at the age of twenty-three.

Brave New World

In the spring of 1966, the Doors opened for Love (at the time one of the hottest bands in Los Angeles) at Brave New World, one of the first psychedelic clubs, which was located at 7207 Melrose. Love had started performing at Brave New World a year earlier as the Grass Roots and briefly became the house band there. Frank Zappa and the Mothers of Invention also performed at the club.

The Doors would later perform several more gigs at Brave New World (ironically the same name of *The Doors of Perception* author Aldous Huxley's 1932 dystopian novel). They once shared billing with a long-forgotten band called the Lost Souls for a four-day stint here (making $2 each per night!).

Brave New World was "a very IN sort of late-teen spot," according to Zappa's Freak Out map, which highlighted the hippest Los Angeles nightspots at the

del-bar productions

TICKETS   SHERMAN-CLAY: 2135 Broadway, Oakland 444-8440; ASUC BOX OFFICE;
Student Union, University of Calif., Ext. 3125; DISCOUNT RECORDS; 2309
Telegraph, Berkeley 849-3332; SAN FRANCISCO STATE Box Office;
MUSIC TOWN: Broadway Shopping Center, Walnut Creek 934-5280

SUNDAY, OCTOBER 15 * TWO SHOWS * 3 PM-7:30 PM

Less than a month after their second album, *Strange Days*, was released, the Doors took the stage at Berkeley Community Theater on October 15, 1967, in a concert that was marred by a blown amplifier and a sedate, apathetic audience.
Courtesy of Kerry Humpherys/doors.com

time. Domenic Priore, the author of *Riot on Sunset Strip*, described Brave New World as "Low key with no signage and off the beaten path—two blocks west of La Brea on Melrose—this was an underground club in the truest sense of the word."

Gazzarri's

Owned and operated by the cigar-chomping Bill Gazzarri, the "Godfather of Rock and Roll," Gazzarri's was originally located at 319 North La Cienega and hosted such musical acts as the Standells, Johnny Rivers (who would soon become a fixture at the Whisky A Go Go), Jackie DeShannon, and the McCoys.

On February 21, 1967, the Doors played at the grand opening of Gazzarri's new location at 9039 Sunset Boulevard on the Sunset Strip in West Hollywood along with the Enemys and the Quirks. Morrison's former girlfriend Mary Werbelow was at one time a "Gazzarri's Go-Go Girl." Tom Baker, who was later arrested with Morrison on a flight to Phoenix on November 11, 1969, caught a

Doors performance at Gazzarri's: "Jim was high on LSD and staggering drunk. His performance was unspectacular, except for one moment—while stumbling through a song early in the set, he suddenly let out a deep-throated, blood-curdling scream." In her review for the *Los Angeles Times*, "Vibrant Jazz-Rock Group at Gazzarri's," Francine Grace referred to the Doors as "four long-haired Venice boys" who "weld a rock 'n' roll beat with continuous jazz improvisation to produce an intense, highly emotional sound."

Other bands that took the stage at Gazzarri's over the years included Buffalo Springfield, Van Halen, Ratt, Cinderella, Quiet Riot, Mötley Crüe, Poison, Warrant, and Guns N' Roses (Slash first heard Axl Rose onstage at Gazzarri's in the early 1980s and proclaimed him "the best singer in Los Angeles at the time"). Gazzarri himself can be seen organizing a "sexy rock and roll" dance contest in the heavy metal documentary *The Decline of Western Civilization, Part 2: The Metal Years*. In 1991, Gazzarri died, and the club closed in 1993.

Whisky A Go Go

Once a hangout for the Hollywood crowd, the Whisky evolved into the hub for psychedelic rock 'n' roll in Los Angeles and possibly the entire West Coast. The concept of "go-go girls" was born at the Whisky (Patty Brockhurst was America's first go-go dancer), which opened on January 16, 1964, at 8901 Sunset Boulevard in West Hollywood. Such Hollywood heavyweights as Cary Grant, Johnny Carson, Steve McQueen, Ann-Margret, Sandra Dee, James Mason, and Gina Lollobrigida hung out at the club in the early days. Manzarek, who used a shot of the Whisky in his UCLA student film *Evergreen*, referred to the Whisky's inaugural year as "the antithesis of everything artistic that you could imagine. It was slick and Hollywood—a rock 'n' roll version of the Rat Pack."

Almost overnight, the Whisky changed. Out went the Hollywood crowd, and in drifted psychedelia. In the spring of 1966, Whisky talent agent Ronnie Haran caught the Doors' act at the London Fog, became totally smitten with Morrison, and invited the band to audition. In Digby Diehl's *Eye* magazine article "The Doors' Story," Haran remarked, "I knew that Jim Morrison had star quality the minute he started singing . . . They needed more polish, but the sound was there."

Hired as the Whisky's house band, the Doors began their stint on May 23, 1966, and eventually opened for such bands as the Byrds, Frank Zappa and the Mothers of Invention, Buffalo Springfield, the Turtles, Captain Beefheart and the Magic Band, the Chambers Brothers, and Them (featuring Van Morrison), as well as more obscure bands such as the No. 1 band from Mexico, the Locos. "The general idea was to blow the headliners off the stage," according to John Densmore in *Riders on the Storm*.

Meanwhile, the Doors continued to refine their material in front of a live audience and filled the rest of the set with blues covers. A typical Doors set at the Whisky consisted of many of the songs that would appear on the band's first album such as "Light My Fire," "Break on Through (to the Other Side)," "Take It as It Comes," "Soul Kitchen," and "The End." In a notorious review of the Doors at the Whisky, Pete Johnson of the *Los Angeles Times* called the band "a hungry-looking quartet" with "what is possibly the worst stage appearance of any rock 'n' roll group in captivity. Their lead singer emotes with his eyes closed, the electric pianist hunches over his instrument as if reading mysteries from the keyboard, the guitarist drifts about the stage randomly, and the drummer seems lost in a separate world." The Doors took Johnson's words as a compliment.

Cindy Williams of *Laverne and Shirley* remarked in an interview that the best time of her life was when she worked as a waitress at the Whisky A Go Go. Her first customer was Jim Morrison. On August 3, 1966, the night Lenny Bruce died, David Crosby was physically assaulted by an LSD-saturated Morrison at the Whisky for no apparent reason. According to Whisky co-owner Mario Maglieri, "I saw that guy Morrison two or three times a week . . . He was always fucked up. Drugs and booze. He drank Jack Daniels like it was going out of style. You know, just a pathetic guy. But Jim was a good kid."

One of the highlights of the Doors' stint at the Whisky was the night of June 18, 1966, when they joined Them onstage for a jam session that included Wilson Pickett's "In the Midnight Hour" and "Gloria," which had already evolved into a garage band standard.

Arthur Lee of Love had encouraged Elektra Records president Jac Holzman to catch the Doors at the Whisky. According to Holzman in *Follow the Music*, "Morrison made no impression whatsoever. I was more drawn to the classical figurings of keyboardist Ray Manzarek and was attracted to the leanness of the music. The lead singer seemed reclusive and tentative, as if preserving himself. There was nothing that tagged him as special." After catching the band four nights in a row, however, Holzman finally realized their potential and signed

As house band at the Whisky A Go Go in 1966, the Doors got the chance to open for such acts as Love, Buffalo Springfield, Captain Beefheart, and Them (featuring Van Morrison).

Courtesy of Dan Thiel/mildequator.com

them for an advance of $5,000 and an initial commitment to release three albums.

On August 21, 1966, the Doors were unceremoniously fired from the Whisky after Morrison launched into an acid-induced version of "The End" that contained the Oedipal-inspired lyrics, which the rest of the band had never heard before: "The killer awoke before dawn . . . Father, I want to kill you! Mother, I want to fuck you!" After the notorious set, Whisky co-owner Phil Tanzani stormed up to the band, called them "filthy motherfuckers," and fired them on the spot.

The Whisky was one of the centers of the notorious "Sunset Strip Riots" in the fall of 1966 (documented for posterity in Stephen Stills's stirring anthem, "For What It's Worth"). The Whisky, which also was immortalized in the Love song "Maybe the People Would Be the Times or Between Clark and Hilldale," caught fire in 1971 after a "wild Humble Pie concert." After shutting down for nearly six months, the Whisky reopened, but it was a shadow of what it had been in the glory days. Scenes from Oliver Stone's *The Doors* were shot here. Robby Krieger and John Densmore appeared at the thirty-fifth anniversary of the Whisky on January 16, 1999, and performed "Love Me Two Times."

Fillmore Auditorium

The Doors made their debut at the Fillmore Auditorium in San Francisco on January 6–8, 1967, just days after releasing their self-titled debut album. By then, the Fillmore had evolved into a focal point for psychedelic rock and booked such bands as the Grateful Dead and Jefferson Airplane. Virtually unknown in "The City by the Bay," the Doors were third-billed behind Sopwith Camel and the Young Rascals, and received $350 for the gig. When introduced as "this band from Los Angeles," the audience booed. However, the Doors quickly won them over by opening the set with a mesmerizing version of "When the Music's Over."

Owned by legendary rock promoter, Bill Graham (real name: Wolfgang Grajonca), the Fillmore was a "rather nondescript brown brick music hall" on the edge of a rough neighborhood at Fillmore Street and Geary Boulevard, according to John Densmore. Ray Manzarek called it "a San Francisco psychedelic ballroom" and remarked that it "felt bohemian to be playing San Francisco, the city of poets and acid rock bands." Elektra Records president Jac Holzman had pleaded with Graham to book the Doors, later remarking, "San Francisco was the heart of spacey, rebellious rock and roll and the Doors had to be seen there." In a May 3, 1969, interview with *Rolling Stone* magazine, Graham called the Fillmore "a building that has made the San Francisco sound heard round the world."

While in San Francisco for the Fillmore gigs, the Doors attended the Human Be-In, called the "opening act to the Summer of Love," at Golden Gate Park on January 14, 1967, which featured Timothy Leary, Allen Ginsberg, Lawrence Ferlinghetti, Gary Snyder ("Japhy Ryder" in Kerouac's *The Dharma Bums*),

The Doors conquered New York City with powerful early performances at Ondine Discotheque, Steve Paul's the Scene, and Bill Graham's Fillmore East.   *Courtesy of Logan Janzen/mildequator.com*

Michael McClure (who would later become Morrison's friend and mentor), and other heroes of the counterculture, as well as performances by Jefferson Airplane, the Grateful Dead, Country Joe and the Fish, and Quicksilver Messenger Service. That night at the Fillmore, the Doors received third billing once again behind the Grateful Dead and the Junior Wells Chicago Blues Band.

The Doors eventually would perform five weekends at the Fillmore. During one of the gigs Morrison failed to show up and later admitted that he had instead sat through three showings of *Casablanca* at a movie theater in Sacramento. During another incident, Morrison was onstage swinging the microphone wildly when he hit Graham in the head. Graham yelled at him, "Are you out of your fucking mind?" Morrison later gifted Graham with a pith helmet painted in psychedelic colors as a humorous apology for his actions.

Other bands that took the stage at the Fillmore over the years included the Grateful Dead, Jefferson Airplane, Big Brother and the Holding Company, and Country Joe and the Fish. Graham would go on to serve as the coproducer of Oliver Stone's *The Doors*, although he was given little creative input and admitted disliking the final product. Tragically, Graham was killed in a helicopter crash on October 25, 1991, while returning home from a Huey Lewis and the News concert.

Hullabaloo Club

Located at 6230 Sunset Boulevard in downtown Hollywood, the Hullabaloo Club occupied the former Earl Carroll Theatre, an "entertainment palace" that first opened in 1938 and featured a marquee over the entrance that proclaimed: "Through these portals pass the most beautiful girls in the world." A glamorous supper club, the Earl Carroll Theatre boasted a "Wall of Fame" where Hollywood celebrities could leave personal inscriptions. Lucille Ball was one of the showgirls who performed here. The theater was sold in 1948 following the deaths of Carroll and his wife, Beryl Wallace, in a plane crash. The venue changed hands several times (at one point it was known as the "Moulin Rouge") before becoming the Hullabaloo Club.

A popular rock 'n' roll club billed as "The Rock 'n' Roll Showplace of the World!," the Hullabaloo Club was named to capitalize on the popularity of the *Hullabaloo* TV variety show. The Doors took the stage here on May 30, 1966, and opened the show with "Light My Fire." The Hullabaloo Club later became the Aquarius Theater, where the Doors performed several memorable concerts on July 21–22, 1969. These comeback performances, which took place four months after the disastrous Miami concert, were recorded for the *Absolutely Live* album.

Cheetah

Once known as the Aragon Ballroom (featuring Lawrence Welk and the "Champagne Music Makers"), the Cheetah was a rock 'n' roll club located adjacent to Pacific Ocean Park at 1 Navy Street on the Santa Monica Pier. According to Densmore, first the Doors "played clubs, then second bill at small two-thousand-seat auditoriums like the Cheetah . . . We were making the transition from dives to concerts."

The Cheetah featured early performances by the Doors, Buffalo Springfield, the Seeds, the Mothers of Invention, Love, Pink Floyd, and Alice Cooper. In *Light My Fire*, Manzarek described the Cheetah as "an insane psychedelic ballroom" that was "all wooden and warm and archaic . . . inside" like "something from the movie *They Shoot Horses, Don't They?*, a Depression-era tale of marathon dancing."

During a gig with Jefferson Airplane on April 9, 1967, at the Cheetah (the first time they received top billing over their San Francisco rivals),

The Doors finished off 1967 with three nights of performances at the historic Family Dog Theater in Denver, Colorado, along with the Allmen Joy and Gingerbread Blu. The famous "Pay Attention" or "Spaceman" promotional poster used for the event was created by Rick Griffin, one of the leading designers of psychedelic posters in the 1960s.

Courtesy of Robert Rodriguez

Morrison unveiled his "tightrope walk," balancing precariously on the edge of the stage eight feet off the ground while doing a shaman Indian dance. According to Manzarek, Morrison lost his balance and fell into the audience and "stage diving was born."

One of the Alice Cooper Band's early incarnations, the Nazz (not to be confused with the Todd Rundgren group), opened for the Doors at the Cheetah. The Cheetah closed in 1968, and the building was completely destroyed by fire in 1979.

Ondine Discotheque

The Doors signed for a one-month engagement (November 1–30, 1966) at the trendy Ondine Discotheque, then considered one of the hippest New York City nightclubs and a favorite place for out-of-town bands to come and play residencies. It was the Doors' first New York City gig and helped them establish their footing on the East Coast. Popular with the Andy Warhol crowd, Ondine was located at 308 East 59th Street on the Upper East Side. The club, which was named after an Olympic-winning sailboat, opened in 1965. The Doors visited Ondine for the first time on Halloween night, and Manzarek described it as a modern-day Babylon, a place where Morrison felt right at home. During the afternoons, the band mixed their debut album with producer Paul Rothchild.

The Doors' second trip to New York City involved a January 19–29, 1967, stint at Ondine that was enthusiastically reviewed by Richard Goldstein of the *Village Voice*, who described them as a "vital new group." The Doors' third and final gig at Ondine took place from mid-March through early April 1967. Also at Ondine, Robby Krieger met his future wife, Lynn Veres, who had briefly dated Morrison. Linda Eastman (later McCartney) photographed the Doors at Ondine and became friends with Morrison. In her 1992 book *Sixties: Portrait of an Era*, McCartney remarked, "It wasn't Jim Morrison's looks that struck me first about him. It was the poetry of his songs and the way he would get completely lost in the music. He had this habit of cupping his hand behind his ear so that he could hear his vocals in the way that traditional folk singers did. I thought the whole band was great; Ray Manzarek, Robby Krieger and John Densmore were all very creative musicians." Other performers that took the stage at Ondine ranged from the famous like Jimi Hendrix and Buffalo Springfield to the now-forgotten such as the Denims and the Druids of Stonehenge.

The Matrix

A renovated former pizza shop that once featured a huge mural of the Four Horsemen of the Apocalypse, the Matrix opened at 3138 Fillmore Street in San Francisco on August 13, 1965. The small, intimate club, which was originally owned by the Jefferson Airplane's Marty Balin, provided seating for just over

100 people. The front cover of the Airplane's 1967 album *Surrealistic Pillow* was shot inside the Matrix.

Released in 2008, the Doors' live album *Live at the Matrix 1967* features one of the band's earliest recordings from their memorable March 7 and 10, 1967, performances at the Matrix. In addition, *The Doors Box Set* (1997) includes two songs recorded live at the club: "The Crystal Ship" and "I Can't See Your Face in My Mind." Hunter S. Thompson, who used to hang out at the Matrix in the late 1960s, mentioned the club in *Fear and Loathing in Las Vegas*. The club closed in 1972 and has undergone many incarnations and name changes over the years, the latest being MATRIXFILLMORE.

Steve Paul's the Scene

A famous rock club located at 301 West 4th Street in New York City, the Scene opened in 1965 and was owned by Steve Paul, who had a knack for spotting up-and-coming talent. The Doors were booked at the Scene for the first time in June 1967 (the band was the biggest draw in the history of the club up to that time). It was a "very hip club," according to Manzarek.

Jimi Hendrix attended the Doors' performance at the Scene on June 14, 1967, on his way to the Monterey Pop Festival. Just a month away from hitting the top of the charts with "Light My Fire," the Doors were not even invited to perform at Monterey. The group also played with Howlin' Wolf at the Scene, a dream for Manzarek, who was a hardcore disciple of the Chicago blues scene. Even actor Paul Newman caught a Doors performance at the Scene and later talked with Morrison about the title song for a movie he was planning to produce.

Other acts to take the stage at the Scene included the Rascals, Janis Joplin, the Velvet Underground, Ten Years After, Moby Grape, the Seeds, Fleetwood Mac, and even Tiny Tim, who warmed up the house singing his campy showtunes.

10

Kingdoms of Our Own

Methods the Doors Utilized to Achieve Their Unique Sound

The Doors are basically a blues-oriented group with heavy dosages of rock 'n' roll, a moderate sprinkling of jazz, a minute quantity of classical influences and some popular elements. But basically, a white blues band.

—*Jim Morrison*

Legendary rock producer Rick Rubin remarked in *Canyon of Dreams*, "The key artist of the L.A. sound of the '60s for me was The Doors." Renowned Los Angeles DJ Jim Ladd added, "You've got to give it up in The Doors' case to producer Paul Rothchild and engineer and producer Bruce Botnick. They sound like they were recorded yesterday . . . There is a magic of this music that resonates deep within people because the songs are about the human experience." The Doors created a highly innovative sound that featured Jim Morrison's haunting baritone voice, the blues-influenced Ray Manzarek on keyboards, the classically trained Robby Krieger on guitar, and John Densmore with his jazz-based drumming style. In fact, the Doors stood out among other bands of the time with a sound driven by a keyboard rather than all guitars (with the possible exception of the Seeds and Question Mark & the Mysterians, which utilized a Vox organ on their No. 1 hit "96 Tears"). The band only hired session musicians to play bass guitar when it came time to record their studio albums.

A classically trained pianist with an affinity for the Chicago blues, Manzarek used a 32-note Fender keyboard bass, played with his left hand, which became the bass for the Doors. The compact model sat on top of his Vox organ, which he played with his right hand. Before joining the Doors, Densmore was an aspiring jazz drummer heavily influenced by Elvin Jones. Krieger's guitar style brought not only classical influences but flamenco and Indian music as well. Krieger started out using a 1964 Gibson Melody Maker and later switched to a Gibson SG Special. He utilized a Gibson Les Paul for bottleneck playing. Densmore started out with Gretsch drums and switched to Ludwig for the Doors' third album, *Waiting for the Sun*. As for Morrison, he brought a notebook of great song lyrics to the band but had no discernible musical ability. However, over the period of just under a year, he developed his unique singing voice at Sunset Strip clubs such as the London Fog and the Whisky A Go Go (the evolution of his voice can be traced by listening to the band's shaky demo in September 1965 compared to their solid debut album in January 1967).

The Doors—Released on January 4, 1967

Widely acknowledged as one of the greatest debuts in rock history, *The Doors* was produced by Paul Rothchild and recorded in just six days at Sunset Sound Recorders with a four-track tape machine at a cost of approximately $10,000. Owned by Tutti Camarata, Walt Disney's director of recording, Sunset Sound was located at 6650 Sunset Boulevard in Hollywood, California. Sunset Sound served as the recording studio for the Doors' first two albums, as well as many other classic rock albums, including the Rolling Stones' *Exile on Main Street* and the Beach Boys' *Pet Sounds*. According to audio engineer Bruce Botnick (*MOJO* magazine, June 2007), "Sunset Sound Recorders was the most advanced studio in Los Angeles at the time."

According to Manzarek, the band's first album was "an existential album" made by "four incredibly hungry young men," who "desperately" wanted to release a good record that the public would like. The entire album was recorded so quickly because the Doors knew the tracks inside and out from playing them nightly at Sunset Strip nightclubs such as the London Fog and the Whisky A Go Go for nearly a year before hitting the recording studio. According to Botnick (*MOJO* magazine, June 2007), "What you hear on the first album is what they did live. It wasn't just playing the song—it transcended that." In fact, the Doors had an abundance of material, enough to fill two albums (they didn't even have room to include "Moonlight Drive," the song that started it all on the beach in Venice). The Doors used session musician Larry Knechtel on bass for several songs on the album, although his work would go uncredited (Knechtel would later win a Grammy Award for his piano arrangement of Simon & Garfunkel's "Bridge over Troubled Water," a No. 1 hit in 1970). Morrison dropped acid while making the first album, but the rest of the band refrained, according to Manzarek.

The Doors' debut album featured a number of eclectic songs such as a cover of Willie Dixon's "Back Door Man" (which was originally a hit for Howlin' Wolf) and even a Kurt Weill/Bertolt Brecht composition, "Alabama Song (Whisky Bar)," which utilized a Marxaphone played by Manzarek. Both the Doors' signature song and first single, "Break on Through (to the Other Side)," and the Oedipal-influenced epic "The End" were released censored on the album. The line "She get high" in "Break on Through" became simply "She get," while the repeated use of "fuck" in "The End" was edited out. The album also featured the full-length "Light My Fire," the shorter version of which would go to No. 1 on the charts in July 1967. Rounding out the album were the tracks "Soul Kitchen,"

"The Crystal Ship," "Twentieth Century Fox," "I Looked at You," "End of the Night," and "Take It as It Comes," Morrison's tribute to Maharishi Mahesh Yogi.

A huge billboard in the middle of the Sunset Strip announced the release of the Doors' debut album: "THE DOORS: Break on Through with an Electrifying Album." In fact, the Doors started the trend of promoting rock albums via Sunset Strip billboards. In the liner notes to the album (in the *Perception* box set), Ben Fong-Torres calls *The Doors* "a near-perfect debut album." *The Doors* peaked at No. 3 on the charts and is ranked No. 42 on *Rolling Stone* magazine's list of the "500 Greatest Albums of All Time."

Strange Days—Released on September 25, 1967

The Doors was recorded on four-track, but after its release Sunset Sound Recorders was converted to eight-track, which opened the door for more experimentation. According to Manzarek, "Paul Rothchild took us into the control room at Sunset and showed [guitarist] Robby Krieger and I this beast of a machine. He explained to us that we now had *twice* the tracks to play with. Robby looked at me, and I looked at him, and we both rubbed our hands together and said, 'Let's get to work.'" In addition, Botnick had somehow picked up an early copy of the Beatles' latest album, *Sgt. Pepper's Lonely Hearts Club Band*, which inspired the Doors and Paul Rothchild to come up with some new methods of studio recording such as reversed tracks, tape manipulation, and use of the moog synthesizer.

For *Strange Days*, the Doors still had a wealth of material that they had honed in the clubs such as "When the Music's Over," "Moonlight Drive," "My Eyes Have Seen You," and "I Can't See Your Face in My Mind." The avant-garde "Horse Latitudes," which Morrison had scrawled in one of his notebooks in high school, contained drowning imagery that perfectly carried over into "Moonlight Drive," one of the earliest Doors songs. "When the Music's Over" was recorded without Morrison (he failed to show up that day), but when he came back the next day he nailed the lyrics. For the eerie "Strange Days," the first track on the album, the Doors hired Paul Beaver, a pioneer user of synthesizers, to distort the vocals.

Strange Days peaked at No. 3 on the Billboard charts but failed to produce any hit singles. According to Rothchild, "Strange Days was the best album . . . It said everything we were trying to say musically and it contains some of Jim's best poetry . . . We were confident it was going to be bigger than anything The Beatles had done. But there was no single. The record died on us. It never really conquered like it should have." Morrison claimed he was most proud of *Strange Days* since "it tells a story, it is a whole effort." He predicted that someday the album would "get the recognition it deserves."

In a review of *Strange Days* for the *L.A. Free Press*, Gene Youngblood wrote, "The Beatles and the Stones are for blowing your mind; The Doors are for afterward, when your mind is already gone." Youngblood called the Doors "the warlocks of pop culture," Morrison "an exterminating angel," and their music

The
Second
Coming
is
at
hand

Elektra Records announces the release of **STRANGE DAYS** EKS-74014 EKL-4014, a new album by **the doors**

In dramatic fashion ("The Second Coming Is at Hand"), the Doors released their second album, *Strange Days*, in September 1967. Although today considered to be the band's most complete album, *Strange Days* failed to produce any hit singles.   *Courtesy of Robert Rodriguez*

"more surreal than psychedelic, it is more anguish than acid." According to writer Barney Hoskyns in his book *Waiting for the Sun,* "Much of *Strange Days* addresses the flip side of California's lysergic utopianism, tells us there's a darker truth to chemical escapism." Hoskyns called the album "a masterpiece of post-psychedelic pop, beat poets, and deceptively solicitous love songs." According to the *Rolling Stone Album Guide,* "With the exception of the hard blues, 'Love Me Two Times,' and the rock tango, 'Moonlight Drive,' *Strange Days* didn't have the power of *The Doors;* it sounded instead like twilit, ominous carnival music." *Rolling Stone* magazine later ranked *Strange Days* No. 407 on its list of the "500 Greatest Albums of All Time."

Waiting for the Sun—Released on June 12, 1968

By the time they came to record their third album, the Doors had basically run out of material. Krieger called it the "third-album syndrome," claiming that most groups have enough songs to record one or two albums and then they go on tour, which does not leave them time to write new songs. So they are forced to write new material in the studio that has not been performed live. The Doors returned to Sunset Sound Recorders in late 1967 (but soon relocated to another studio called TTG) to record their third album. By this time, the recording studio was full of "hangers-on," and alcohol and marijuana were in abundance, according to Botnick.

Waiting for the Sun was originally supposed to feature a whole side dedicated to Morrison's epic, the "Celebration of the Lizard." When "Celebration" failed in the recording studio, the Doors scrambled to find new material to fill the side (only one section of the poem, "Not to Touch the Earth," eventually appeared on the album). Consequently, the album featured a strange blend of material, with Krieger contributing three of the eleven tracks: "Wintertime Love," "Spanish Caravan" (legendary acoustic bass player Leroy Vinegar played on the song), and "Yes, the River Knows." The album also contained the Doors' first protest song, "The Unknown Soldier." Critic Paul Williams of *Crawdaddy!* magazine just happened to be in the studio when the Doors recorded "The Unknown

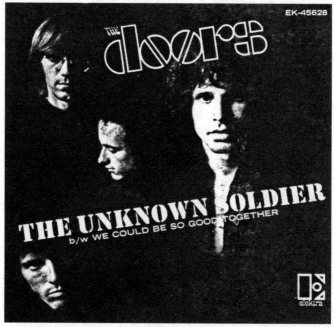

The first single released from *Waiting for the Sun*, "The Unknown Soldier," was the Doors' first true political song and peaked at No. 39 on the charts even though it encountered censorship on commercial radio.   *Courtesy of Kerry Humpherys/doors.com*

Soldier" and he assisted with the sound effects, which consisted of marching and cocking prop rifles. Meanwhile, "We Could Be So Good Together" had been considered and rejected for the first album. *Waiting for the Sun* also contained one of the band's most ambiguous political songs, "Five to One."

Ironically, *Waiting for the Sun* was a huge commercial success and became the Doors' first and only No. 1 album. It was also a huge hit in the UK where it reached No. 16 on the charts, mostly on the strength of the single "Hello, I Love You," which was dismissed by some critics and fans as a "bubblegum sellout" but became the Doors second No. 1 hit after "Light My Fire."

Reviewing the album for the *Philadelphia Inquirer*, critic Pete Johnson remarked, "*Waiting for the Sun* contains the fewest snakes, the least ugliness, the lowest number of freaks and monsters, and the smallest amount of self-indulgent mysticism of the trio of Doors' LPs. They have traded terror for beauty and the success of the swap is a tribute to their talent and originality."

On the same day that the Doors' third album, *Waiting for the Sun*, was released, July 12, 1968, the band put on a memorable show at the Seattle Center Arena—"one of the finest rock concerts offered in this city," according to Seattle's *Daily Times*.

Courtesy of Kerry Humpherys/doors.com

The Soft Parade—Released on July 5, 1969

A total departure from the sound of the first three Doors albums, *The Soft Parade* was recorded at Elektra Sound West on La Cienega Boulevard. Once again the band was totally out of original material and forced to write songs in the studio. Adding to the problems was the fact that Morrison's drinking had gotten even worse, and he was now "living the Dylan Thomas life as an Irish poet," according to Botnick.

The album was very controversial for its liberal use of brass and string instruments—a total departure from the sound of the first three albums. In addition, Krieger wrote half of the songs, including "Touch Me," "Runnin' Blue" (a bizarre bluegrass-style tribute to Otis Redding), and "Tell All the People," which Morrison hated so much that he demanded that individual writing credits be placed on the album for the first time. According to Densmore in *Riders on the Storm*, "We had a great time making that album . . . we spent more than $80,000 on it—we were making our 'Sgt. Pepper.' Just to show how ridiculous things got, we imported Jesse McReynolds and Jimmy Buchanan, a fiddler and a picker, from North Carolina, to play one solo on one song."

With "Touch Me," Morrison got the opportunity to sing in a crooning style reminiscent of his musical heroes, Frank Sinatra. The upbeat song, which featured the talents of saxophonist Curtis Amy, reached No. 3 on the charts, and the Doors performed it on *The Smothers Brothers Comedy Hour* in December 1968. The album itself reached No. 6 on the charts.

Morrison Hotel—Released on February 1, 1970

With *Morrison Hotel* (often viewed as the Doors' "comeback album" after the critical failure of *The Soft Parade*), the band moved away from the jazz-influenced sound of the previous album toward a more bluesy approach, which allowed Morrison to ditch his Lizard King persona and focus once again on the music. Morrison stated in a later interview that the band felt they had gone too far with the "orchestration" and desired to "get back to the original blues format." According to Botnick in the album's liner notes, "The band's goal for *Morrison Hotel* was to try and return to simplicity as best as they could, meaning no horns or strings."

The first side of the album was titled *Hard Rock Cafe* and the second side, *Morrison Hotel*. "Waiting for the Sun," a holdover from the Doors' third album, really stood out among the blues-oriented selection of songs since it was more reminiscent of the Doors' first two albums. John Sebastian, of the Lovin' Spoonful, played harmonica on "Roadhouse Blues." He was credited on the album with a pseudonym, "G. Puglese," so as not to jeopardize the deal he had with Reprise Records. Sebastian would later reach No. 1 on the charts with "Welcome Back," the theme to the TV sitcom *Welcome Back, Kotter*, on May 8, 1976. With the Lovin' Spoonful, Sebastian had a No. 1 hit, "Summer in the

City," on August 13, 1966. Lonnie Mack played bass on "Roadhouse Blues" and "Maggie M'Gill." For "Peace Frog," Rothchild found a poem in one of Morrison's notebooks called "Abortion Stories." Several songs on the album were inspired by Morrison's often-turbulent relationship with Pamela Courson—"Blue Sunday," "You Make Me Real," and "Queen of the Highway."

Morrison Hotel peaked at No. 4 on the charts. According to the Rolling Stone Album Guide, "A return to form, Morrison Hotel was the most cohesive record; aside from the throwaway grunter, 'Maggie McGill,' every song was masterful—and the band swings tougher and easier than it ever had before." In the album's liner notes, rock critic David Fricke called Morrison Hotel "one of rock's great resurrection records, a striking fight for life by a band under attack but uncompromised."

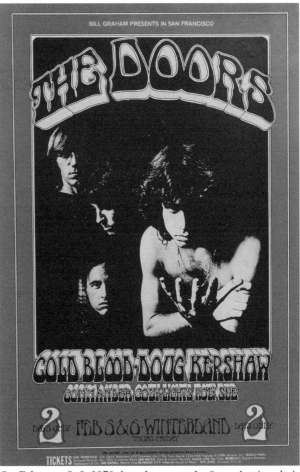

On February 5–6, 1970, less than a week after releasing their fifth album, Morrison Hotel, the Doors performed in two concerts at the Winterland Arena in San Francisco, their final performances in the "City by the Bay." *Courtesy of Robert Rodriguez*

L.A. Woman—Released on April 15, 1971

Recording for L.A. Woman began at Sunset Sound Recorders, but producer Paul Rothchild quit the project early on, and the Doors decided to produce the album on their own with the assistance of Botnick. The Doors' final studio album with Morrison was also their most blues-oriented record. It was recorded in the Doors Office, which was haphazardly transformed into a laid-back recording studio. Since the band desired to get back to basics, they recorded on the old eight-track board they had used on Strange Days (even though sixteen-track was already in widespread use). According to Elektra Records president Jac Holzman in Follow *the Music,* "I never felt that returning to eight-track from sixteen-track was a step backward. You pick the tool you need to do the job, and eight-track was more than sufficient for an organic location recording, which is what this was. Fewer tracks meant fewer mikes and less problems with microphone phasing, always a consideration in ad hoc studios. The result was a return to the original Doors sound before all the distractions of fame and fortune got in the way."

The Doors created a control room in the upstairs office of their manager, Bill Siddons. The recording studio became the downstairs rehearsal room with attached bathroom. Morrison recorded all of his vocals standing in the bathroom doorway with the gold Electrovoice microphone he used onstage. Densmore used the same drum kit he had used on the first album. Manzarek used a Wurlitzer, Fender Rhodes and Hammond B3. As a producer, Botnick turned out to be much more casual than Rothchild and only requested a couple of takes per song.

Morrison reworked "Texas Radio," a poem he had written in 1968, into the song "The WASP (Texas Radio and the Big Beat)." Morrison's poetry from Venice Beach produced "Cars Hiss by My Window." In addition, "Riders on the Storm" morphed out of "Ghost Riders in the Sky," which the band was playing in the studio one day just for fun. The album also featured a powerful cover of John Lee Hooker's "Crawling King Snake." Most of the tracks were recorded live except for a few overdubbed keyboard parts by Manzarek. The Doors used session musicians Jerry Scheff (Elvis's bassist) and Marc Benno (rhythm guitar) on the album, which was recorded in just six days. It was mixed at a new studio in West Hollywood called Poppi (disrupted once by an earthquake).

L.A. Woman reached No. 9 on the charts and is ranked 362 on *Rolling Stone* magazine's list of the "500 Greatest Albums of All Time." According to the *Rolling Stone Album Guide,* "Morrison's voice is the ghost of its former glory—doom, heartbreak and frustration sound in his every note. Difficult and sad, the record has some of the power of Neil Young's *Tonight's the Night*: it's a straining for catharsis."

Two days after *Strange Days* hit the record stores, the Doors sampled their newly released material from the album at the KRNT Theater in Des Moines, Iowa, on September 27, 1967.

Courtesy of Robert Rodriguez

The Music and Voices Are All Around Us

Doors Songs That Were "Inspired" by Other Sources

Jim was borrowing and quoting and paying homage to his masters, as I was borrowing quotes from all my favorite jazz and blues musicians.
—*Ray Manzarek*

J ust as Jim Morrison "borrowed" lines from literary figures such as William Blake and Louis-Ferdinand Celine to create some of his song lyrics, the rest of the band were inspired to utilize melodies from some of their musical influences, whether jazz, classical, or flamenco guitar. The Doors were not alone among rock bands in pilfering material from other sources. For example, in a June 2007 interview with *MOJO* magazine, Robby Krieger claimed, "I was positive that [the Beatles had] stolen the idea for that speeded-up bit on 'A Day in the Life' from 'The End,' because I know they'd heard the first Doors album by then."

"Break on Through (to the Other Side)"

Robby Krieger claimed that his guitar melody line in "Break on Through" was inspired by Paul Butterfield's version of "Shake Your Money Maker." A blues vocalist and harmonica player, Butterfield founded the Paul Butterfield Blues Band in 1963. The band, which was known for its electric Chicago blues style, backed Bob Dylan during his infamous "electric" performance at the Newport Folk Festival in 1965. Their self-titled debut album was released by Elektra Records in September 1965 (the same month the Doors recorded their demo at World Pacific Jazz Studios). "Shake Your Money Maker" was first recorded by Elmore James (the "King of the Slide Guitar") in 1961.

Another inspiration for "Break on Through" was American saxophonist Stan "The Sound" Getz and Brazilian guitarist Joao Gilberto's 1964 jazz bossa nova album *Getz/Gilberto*. One of the bestselling jazz albums of all time, *Getz/Gilberto*

EK—45611

BREAK ON THROUGH
B/W END OF THE NIGHT

elektra

In the "Dead Cats, Dead Rats" version of "Break on Through," Jim Morrison incorporated the lyrics "Dead cats, dead rats, did you see what they were at, alright/Dead cat in a top hat." *Courtesy of Kerry Humpherys/doors.com*

started a bossa nova craze in the United States that quickly spread throughout the world. The album won the 1965 Grammy Award for Best Album of the Year. Gilberto was known as the "Father of Bossa Nova." In *Light My Fire*, Manzarek called *Getz/Gilberto* "one of our favorite 'relaxing' albums—John Densmore and I were really into the whole Brazilian samba groove. And this record was the coolest. We'd get high, open the windows . . . and float away to Brazil."

"Light My Fire"

According to Ray Manzarek, the solos in "Light My Fire," the Doors' first No. 1 hit, were based on John Coltrane's "Ole" from the album *Ole Coltrane*, which was released in 1961 by Atlantic Records. An often overlooked jazz album, *Ole Coltrane* was Coltrane's last release for Atlantic before he moved to

Impulse! Records. Coltrane assembled a highly talented roster for the album that included McCoy Tyner, Reggie Workman, Art Davis, Eric Dolphy, Freddie Hubbard, and Elvin Jones (John Densmore's favorite jazz drummer).

The interplay and improvisation of the long version of "Light My Fire" was also influenced by Coltrane's "My Favorite Things," which was hugely influential among other musicians. Interviewed in the June 2007 issue of *MOJO* magazine, Patti Smith claimed that the song "taught me everything to know about improvisation . . . what he did on that record was a template not only for art but for human existence. Because as workers, as artists, we want to break boundaries and push ourselves harder in order to see new levels of things." In later concerts, Krieger started incorporating the melody from the Beatles' "Eleanor Rigby" into his guitar solo for "Light My Fire."

"Take It as It Comes"

In *Light My Fire*, Manzarek stated that the organ solo in "Take It as It Comes" was derived from German composer Johann Sebastian Bach (1685–1750). Morrison wrote the lyrics, while Krieger came up with the melody. Although he preferred LSD at the time, Morrison had attended a Transcendental Meditation lecture, and "Take It as It Comes" served as a tribute to Maharishi Mahesh Yogi. The song appeared on the Doors' self-titled debut album.

"Love Me Two Times"

Krieger's "Love Me Two Times" was inspired by Elektra recording artist "Spider" John Koerner's "Southbound Train." Koerner was part of a blues trio called Koerner, Ray & Glover along with Dave Ray and Tony Glover. In a 1991 *Guitar World* magazine interview, Krieger stated, "The lick is very similar to one that Koerner does on 'Southbound Train.' I told him that and he didn't see it, didn't think they sounded alike, but that was what inspired me. In fact, those guys inspired a lot of my licks." In January 1968, "Love Me Two Times" reached No. 25 on the charts. In addition to "Love Me Two Times," Krieger wrote "You're Lost Little Girl" for *Strange Days*.

"When the Music's Over"

According to Manzarek in *Light My Fire*, the opening organ passage of "When the Music's Over" was inspired by Herbie Hancock's "Watermelon Man." A jazz standard, "Watermelon Man" was first released on Hancock's critically acclaimed debut album, *Takin' Off*, in 1962. In the album's liner notes, Hancock stated, "In reflecting on my childhood, I recalled the cry of the watermelon man making his rounds through the back streets and alleys of Chicago's South Side. The wheels of his wagon beat out the rhythm on the cobblestones." In addition, "Watermelon Man" featured improvisations by Freddie Hubbard and Dexter

Gordon. "When the Music's Over" served as the epic to end *Strange Days*, similar to "The End" on the Doors' debut album.

"Hello, I Love You"

Although the Kinks never took legal action, "Hello, I Love You" sounded suspiciously close to their hit single "All Day and All of the Night," which reached No. 7 on the U.S. charts in 1964. In fact, *Rolling Stone* magazine even called the Doors' second No. 1 hit single a "jagged Kinks rip-off." However, in the liner notes to *The Doors Box Set*, Krieger stated, "We have been accused of ripping off the Kinks song 'All Day and All of the Night.' When Ray Davies was asked about this, he had no problem. The truth is, the drumbeat on this song was ripped off the Cream song, 'Sunshine of Your Love.' It was my fault. I suggested to John in the studio: 'Hey man, do that 'Sunshine of Your Love' beat.' The rest is history."

In a 1997 interview, Davies discussed bands that he felt ripped off the Kinks' sound: "That one is the most irritating of all of them . . . The other night I did a show where I played 'All Day and All of the Night' and stuck in a piece of 'Hello, I Love You.' There was some response, there were a few smiles. But I've never understood why nobody's ever said anything about it. You can't say anything about the Doors. You're not *allowed* to." One of the Doors' earliest songs, "Hello, I Love You" was written by Morrison on Venice Beach in the summer of 1965 and was one of six songs recorded on the band's original demo in September 1965.

"We Could Be So Good Together"

Manzarek claimed in *Light My Fire* that a Thelonius Monk lyric from "Straight, No Chaser" appeared in "We Could Be So Good Together," a song from *Waiting for the Sun*. A jazz standard first recorded by Monk on his *Blue Note Sessions* album in 1951, "Straight, No Chaser" became the title of a 1988 documentary on the jazz great, *Thelonius Monk: Straight, No Chaser*, directed by Clint Eastwood. "We Could Be So Good Together," an early Doors song that had been rejected for the band's debut album, served as the B-side to "The Unknown Soldier."

"Touch Me"

The Motown-like riff for the Krieger-penned "Touch Me," the biggest hit from *The Soft Parade*, was influenced by the Four Seasons' "C'mon Marianne," which appeared on the B-side of their single "Let's Ride Again" in 1967. In addition, the Doors borrowed a lick from an Ajax detergent commercial that was widely aired at the time. In fact, Morrison can be heard shouting "stronger than dirt" at the end of the song. "Touch Me" peaked at No. 5 on the charts in February 1969.

"The Soft Parade"

For "The Soft Parade," the Doors actually used the melody from an industrial film they had scored early in their careers. In May 1966, Ford Motor Company had hired the band to score the soundtrack for an industrial training film for mechanics. A light instrumental piece, the same melody from the film served as the opening sequence for the transitional passage in "The Soft Parade."

"Riders on the Storm"

Krieger has stated that the band was "fooling around with 'Ghost Riders in the Sky' one day and somehow it turned into 'Riders on the Storm.'" Written by Stan Jones in 1948, "Ghost Riders in the Sky" has been recorded by dozens of performers over the years such as Bing Crosby, Burl Ives, Marty Robbins, Johnny Cash, and, perhaps most famously, the Outlaws. The last song on *L.A. Woman*, "Riders on the Storm" peaked at No. 14 on the charts in September 1971.

12

Do It, Robby, Do It

Doors Songs Written by Robby Krieger

Most groups today aren't true groups. In a true group, all the members create the arrangements amongst themselves. Here, we use everyone's ideas.
—Robby Krieger

Jim Morrison's brilliant songwriting ability has overshadowed the important contributions of Robby Krieger, who wrote some of the Doors' most memorable songs such as the No. 1 hit "Light My Fire," "Love Me Two Times (No. 25)," "Touch Me" (No. 3), and "Love Her Madly" (No. 11), as well as lesser-known gems including "You're Lost Little Girl," "Wintertime Love" "Yes, the River Knows," "Runnin' Blue," "Wishful, Sinful," and "Spanish Caravan." Interestingly, after writing three songs on *Waiting for the Sun* and half of the songs on *The Soft Parade*, Krieger did not contribute any songs for *Morrison Hotel* and only one song, "Touch Me," for *L.A. Woman*.

"Light My Fire"

One day at rehearsal, Morrison challenged the rest of the band members to come up with some new songs. Krieger was the only one to take up the challenge, resulting in the classic "Light My Fire," which spent three weeks at the top of the charts in the summer of 1967. According to Krieger, "I figured I'd keep it on a universal scale and write about earth, air, fire or water. I picked fire, mainly because I always liked that song by the Stones, 'Play with Fire.'"

However, Krieger's song actually involved a true collaborative effort among all the band members. Manzarek came up with the lively intro and Morrison contributed the infamous lines "wallow in the mire" and "funeral pyre" to the otherwise upbeat song, while John Densmore added the distinctive beat. Rock critic Paul Williams of *Crawdaddy!* magazine likened the instrumental buildup in "Light My Fire" to the long version of the Who's "Won't Get Fooled Again." According to Manzarek, "The take we chose to put on the record had a marvelous solo by Robby. It's always been overlooked, but I think it's one of the best extended solos I've ever heard in a rock and roll song."

Released as a single in May 1967 (with "The Crystal Ship" as the B-side), "Light My Fire" reached No. 1 on the charts on July 29, 1967. In concert, Krieger played his guitar solo different each time.

"You're Lost Little Girl"

"You're Lost Little Girl" appeared as the second track on the Doors' second album, *Strange Days*. According to legend, Morrison's "cosmic mate," Pamela Courson, gave him a blow job while he overdubbed the vocals for "You're Lost Little Girl." Whatever the truth behind that rumor, Densmore remarked in *Riders on the Storm* that the final take of the song "had a tranquil mood like the aftermath of a large explosion." In addition, Manzarek lightheartedly suggested that Morrison's idol, Frank Sinatra, might be interested in covering the song. In an article that appeared in *Crawdaddy!* magazine, critic Sandy Pearlman wrote that the "bass entrance on 'You're Lost Little Girl' . . . smacks of the pulp mystery (crime-detective) movie music of the era 1940–1960." In the liner notes to the *Strange Days* album from the *Perception* box set, writer Barney Hoskyns referred to the song as "psychedelic Sinatra."

"Love Me Two Times"

Released as the second single (with "Moonlight Drive" as the B-side) from the Doors' second album, *Strange Days* (after "People Are Strange"), "Love Me Two Times" reached No. 25 on the charts in January 1968. The song concerned a sailor or soldier spending one last day with his girlfriend before shipping out to war.

In *Light My Fire*, Manzarek, who played a clavinet (not a harpsichord as sometimes alleged) on the final version of "Love Me Two Times," referred to the song as "Robby's great blues/rock classic about love and loss, or multiple orgasms." In fact, some radio stations at the time banned the song because of its sexual innuendo.

In 1972, the three surviving Doors often played "Love Me Two Times" in concert along with "Light My Fire" mixed in with new material from their post-Morrison studio albums, *Other Voices* and *Full Circle*. A live version of "Love Me Two Times" appeared on the Doors' 1983 live album, *Alive, She Cried*. Aerosmith covered the song for the soundtrack of the 1990 film *Air America* (a black comedy about a CIA-financed airline during the Vietnam War that starred Mel Gibson and Robert Downey Jr.), as well as on the Doors tribute album *Stoned Immaculate: The Music of The Doors*, which was released in 2000.

"Wintertime Love"

The perfect companion to Morrison's song "Summer's Almost Gone," which immediately preceded it on the Doors' third album, *Waiting for the Sun*, Krieger's

"Wintertime Love" was another song about lost love: "Wintertime winds blue and freezin' comin' from northern storms in the sea/Love has been lost is that the reason trying so desperately to be free." Light, mellow, and ultimately forgettable, the song was rarely, if ever, performed in concert.

"Spanish Caravan"

In his official Elektra biography, Krieger commented, "When I was seventeen, I started playing guitar. I used my friend's guitar. I didn't get my own until I was eighteen. It was a Mexican flamenco guitar. I took flamenco lessons for a few months. I switched around from folk to flamenco to blues to rock 'n' roll."

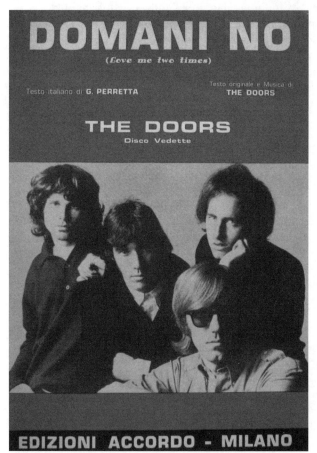

Doors music has been translated into dozens of different languages, including this Italian version of Robby Krieger's "Love Me Two Times," which reached No. 25 on the charts.
Courtesy of Ida Miller/idafan.com

Krieger got the opportunity to showcase his flamenco guitar skills during the introduction to "Spanish Caravan," which appeared on *Waiting for the Sun*. Krieger reportedly incorporated "Asturias" by Spanish pianist and composer Isaac Albeniz into the intro for "Spanish Caravan." In a review of the Doors' third album for the *L.A. Free Press*, critic Bob Shayne commented that *Waiting for the Sun* "contains absolutely the worst lyrics I have ever heard in my life in 'Spanish Caravan.'"

The Doors played the song as early as January 1967, during one of their gigs at the Fillmore Auditorium in San Francisco. According to John Densmore in *Riders on the Storm*, "That night we didn't blow anybody off the stage, but the faces in the first few rows stared at us like we were from another planet . . . In Robby's solo in 'Spanish Caravan,' Jim got down on his knees to get a closer look at Robby's fingers. In rehearsal I always asked Robby to play flamenco so I, too, could watch his picking. His right hand looked like a crab with many legs crawling over the strings." The Doors also performed the song (incorporating a prelude that featured some sections of "Celebration of the Lizard") at the famous Hollywood Bowl concert on July 5, 1968.

"Yes, the River Knows"

"Yes, the River Knows," which also appeared on *Waiting for the Sun*, provided the perfect crooning ballad for Morrison and featured some very eclectic lyrics such as "I promised I would drown myself/in mystic heated wine." Krieger moved away from the fire imagery in "Light My Fire" to the water imagery of "Yes, the River Knows," similar to Morrison's "The Crystal Ship," "Moonlight Drive," and "Horse Latitudes." Just as in "Moonlight Drive," the song's final images evoked drowning: "Breathe under water till the end." Krieger has stated that "Yes, the River Knows" is one of his favorites among all the songs he wrote.

"Touch Me"

One of the Doors' biggest hits, "Touch Me" appeared on the band's much-maligned fourth album, *The Soft Parade*, and was released as a single in December 1968, reaching No. 3 on the U.S charts on February 15, 1969, behind Sly & the Family Stone's "Everyday People" and Tommy James & the Shondells' "Crimson and Clover."

Krieger originally titled the song "Hit Me," with the opening line "C'mon, hit me, I'm not afraid," but Morrison informed him he would never sing those lyrics. Another working title was "I'm Gonna Love You" from the lyric, "Now I'm gonna love you till the heavens stop the rain." The song boasted a powerful solo by saxophonist Curtis Amy. In a May 1970 interview with *Downbeat* magazine, Morrison remarked, "One thing about [*The Soft Parade*] that I am very proud of, is that 'Touch Me' was the first rock hit to have a jazz solo in it." The Doors performed "Touch Me" (along with its B-side, "Wild Child") on *The Smothers Brothers Comedy Hour*, which aired on December 15, 1968.

Morrison can be heard saying the Ajax slogan, "stronger than dirt," at the end of the song since the last four chords of the song were lifted directly from an Ajax commercial that ran frequently on TV at the time. He was also reportedly mocking the other band members, who had "sold out" by accepting a lucrative offer to use "Light My Fire" in a Buick commercial (a furious Morrison squashed the deal). The Guess Who covered the song, as did the Cult's Ian Astbury (who would later become lead singer of the Doors of the 21st Century), who was backed by Krieger, Manzarek, and Densmore for the 2000 tribute album *Stoned Immaculate: The Music of the Doors*.

"Runnin' Blue"

Not only did Krieger write the lyrics for this rather strange, bluegrass-flavored tribute to legendary singer Otis Redding, but he sang the lyrics as well. Appearing on *The Soft Parade*, it was the only non-Morrison lead vocals to appear on any of the Doors' first six studio albums. Morrison actually opened the song, chanting the lyrics, "Poor Otis dead and gone/Left me here to sing his song." The song also featured the talents of two legendary musicians: mandolin player Jesse McReynolds and fiddler Jimmy Buchanan.

Tragically, on December 10, 1967, the private plane carrying Redding and five members of his backup group, the Bar-Keys, nosedived into an icy lake just outside of Madison, Wisconsin, killing all aboard. Redding had become a superstar after his electrifying performance at the Monterey Pop Festival in June 1967. He recorded a slew of hits such as "Mr. Pitiful," "Pain in My Heart," "That's How Strong My Love Is," "These Arms of Mine," "I've Been Loving You Too Long" and "Respect," which became a No. 1 hit for Aretha Franklin on June 3, 1967. Redding also covered the Rolling Stones' "(I Can't Get No) Satisfaction." His "(Sittin' on) the Dock of the Bay" became the first posthumous No. 1 single on March 16, 1968.

Redding, who was just twenty-six years old at the time of his death, had been scheduled to perform with the Doors at the Winterland Arena in San Francisco on December 28, 1967, and was replaced by one of the Doors' musical heroes, Chuck Berry. During the concert, in the middle of "When the Music's Over," Morrison sang the opening lyrics to "Runnin' Blue" in honor of Redding. "Runnin' Blue" was released as a single in August 1969 (with the Krieger-Morrison collaboration "Do It" as the B-side) and peaked at No. 64 on the charts. The song also appeared on the Doors' second compilation album, *Weird Scenes Inside the Gold Mine*, which was released in 1972.

"Wishful, Sinful"

"Wishful, Sinful" was released as a single in February 1969 with the B-side, "Who Scared You?" (which did not appear on *The Soft Parade* album). The single peaked at No. 44 on the charts. The Doors performed "Wishful, Sinful" on the PBS *Critique Recording Sessions*, which aired on June 25, 1969. The song featured some sexually suggestive lyrics such as "I know where I would like to be/Right back where I came." According to Krieger, Morrison liked the song, which was another crooning, Frank Sinatra-type ballad. Krieger claimed he really tried to "get in the subconscious mind" with "Wishful, Sinful," while Manzarek remarked that the song was simply about "love and sex."

"Love Her Madly"

"Love Her Madly," which appeared on *L.A. Woman*, the final Doors studio album with Morrison, was released as a single in April 1971 and peaked at No. 11 on the charts. In *Light My Fire*, Manzarek referred to "Love Her Madly" as "a chugging, tuneful tribute to a fight Robby Krieger had with a girlfriend." Jerry Scheff, a member of Elvis Presley's TCB Band, played bass on the song. The B-side of the single, "(You Need Meat) Don't Go No Further," a cover of a Willie Dixon song, did not appear on the album.

Doors producer Paul Rothchild admitted in a 1981 interview with *BAM* magazine that it was "Love Her Madly" (not "Riders on the Storm" as many have assumed over the years) that drove him out of the studio during the recording sessions for *L.A. Woman*, claiming "That it sold a million copies means nothing to me." The song appeared in the 1994 film *Forrest Gump*, when Jenny (Robin Wright) hastily exited a cheap motel with a black eye. In 2000, Krieger, Densmore, and Manzarek recorded a new version of "Love Her Madly" with one of their musical idols, blues legend Bo Diddley, for the tribute album, *Stoned Immaculate: The Music of the Doors*.

13

Girl, We Couldn't Get Much Higher

Jim said, "Hey guys, we don't have enough original songs, why don't you try writing." I went home and wrote "Light My Fire."

—*Robby Krieger*

The Doors scored a total of eight Top 40 hits during their brief recording career: "Light My Fire" (No. 1), "Hello, I Love You" (No. 1), "People Are Strange" (No. 12), "Love Me Two Times" (No. 25), "The Unknown Soldier" (No. 39), "Touch Me" (No. 5), "Love Her Madly" (No. 11), and "Riders on the Storm" (No. 14). Interestingly, half of the songs—"Light My Fire," "Love Me Two Times," "Touch Me," and "Love Her Madly"—were written by Robby Krieger, while the rest were written by Jim Morrison. The two No. 1 hits were separated by just over a year.

"Light My Fire"—July 29, 1967

What would the "Summer of Love" have been without its ever-present anthem "Light My Fire," which turned out to be both an early blessing and later curse for the Doors? Just two years after the mythical meeting on Venice Beach between Morrison and Ray Manzarek in July 1965 that resulted in the creation of the band, on July 29, 1967, the Krieger-penned "Light My Fire" skyrocketed to No. 1 on the Billboard Charts and remained there for three weeks before being knocked off by the Beatles' "All You Need Is Love." Rounding out the top five behind "Light My Fire" were "I Was Made to Love Her" by Stevie Wonder, "Windy" by the Association, "Can't Take My Eyes Off of You" by Frankie Valli, and "A Whiter Shade of Pale" by Procol Harum.

Without the phenomenal success of "Light My Fire," the Doors "probably would never have stayed together," according to Krieger. According to Manzarek, "That psychedelic band of acid head, Jungian, shamanistic, Dionysian, Indian mediators had made it to the top of the *Billboard* Hot 100. We had even knocked the Beatles out of first place." For better or worse, nothing would ever be the same for the Doors. It all started when Morrison suggested that the other band members take a shot at writing a song. Only Krieger accepted the challenge. "Light My Fire" was the first song Krieger ever wrote (he also wrote "Love Me Two Times" the same day). According to Krieger, "It's like I'd saved up all [these ideas] in my mind and got them out all at once." It was also the first rock song to have an instrumental section that utilized both a keyboard and a guitar. Finally, even though Krieger came up with the song, it was a total group effort. For example, Manzarek worked up the dynamic intro, Densmore added the beat, and Morrison contributed a darker edge with the stanza that included "wallow in the mire" and "funeral pyre." Producer Paul Rothchild later told Morrison that the "funeral pyre" stanza was the one part of the song he disliked, unaware of Morrison's contribution.

Honed in Sunset Strip clubs such as the London Fog and Whisky A Go Go, "Light My Fire" skyrocketed to No. 1 on the charts in the summer of 1967 and became both a curse and a blessing for the Doors.   *Courtesy of Ida Miller/idafan.com*

Once the Doors' debut album was released in January 1967 (the first single released, "Break on Through," stalled at No. 126 on the charts), local Los Angeles DJ Dave Diamond told the band he had been getting a lot of requests for "Light My Fire" and suggested they edit the song to three minutes for commercial radio play. Rothchild simply cut out most of the instrumental section to create the single version. The abbreviated "Light My Fire" was released in April 1967 with "The Crystal Ship" as the B-side. The song peaked at No. 1 between July 28 and August 12, 1967. Ironically, it is the longer version with the instrumental section intact that plays most frequently on commercial radio today.

According to rock critic Paul Williams in the September 17, 1981, issue of *Rolling Stone* magazine, "'Light My Fire' is simple—but quite sophisticated in its simplicity. The closest thing I can think of to its instrumental buildup is the long version of the Who's 'Won't Get Fooled Again.' Certainly, it was the inspiration for Cream's 'Spoonful,' out of which grew a whole generation of British blues-rock."

Although written by Robby Krieger, "Light My Fire" was a true collaborative effort by the Doors—featuring Ray Manzarek's dynamic intro, John Densmore's mesmerizing beat, and additional, darker lyrics from Jim Morrison (the infamous "funeral pyre" stanza).
Courtesy of Ida Miller/idafan.com

The Doors infamously sang "Light My Fire" on *The Ed Sullivan Show* on September 17, 1967, conveniently forgetting to censor the word "higher" as instructed by the show's producer. The song reappeared on the charts a year later when Jose Feliciano released a Latin-flavored cover that peaked at No. 5. Controversy ensued after the Doors' European Tour in 1968 when Morrison and Courson headed to London and the rest of the band returned to Los Angeles and agreed to a $75,000 deal with Buick to use "Light My Fire" in an advertising campaign for the Buick Opel ("Come on Buick, Light My Fire"). When Morrison returned to town, he was outraged by the Buick deal, and it was quickly terminated.

"Light My Fire" turned out to be both a blessing and a burden to the band. During the late 1960s, teenage fans screamed for the song throughout concerts, much to the chagrin of Morrison. In order to give the song a darker edge, Morrison would sometimes add his "Graveyard Poem" within "Light My Fire." The poem contained such macabre lines as "A girl got drunk and balled the dead/And I gave empty sermons to my head." At the Doors' last concert as a quartet—December 12, 1970, at the Warehouse in New Orleans—an exhausted Morrison ran out of energy halfway through "Light My Fire" and started smashing his microphone into the stage floor before being escorted backstage. It turned out to be the last song they played as a quartet. In addition, the three surviving Doors played "Light My Fire" as the last song in their last concert before breaking up at the Hollywood Bowl on September 10, 1972.

A live version of "Light My Fire" appeared on the 1983 live album *Alive, She Cried*. "Light My Fire" is No. 35 on *Rolling Stone* magazine's list of the "500 Greatest Songs of All Time." In addition, the song was inducted into the Grammy Hall of Fame in 1998, the same year that Manzarek released his autobiography titled *Light My Fire*. According to Manzarek, "People even today come up to me and say 'Don't you get tired of playing Light My Fire?' I say 'Are you kidding? Do you get tired of having sex?' [laughs] Come on, man! Do you get tired of fucking? No you don't, because there's always an improvisation, there's always a new position, there's always a little variation. We're always improvising. It's like Miles Davis playing 'All Blues.' Miles plays 'All Blues,' you play it different every night. That's the fun of Doors music, you play it different every night."

In addition to Feliciano, a diverse range of performers have covered "Light My Fire" over the years such as Etta James, Jackie Wilson, Shirley Bassey, Will Young, UB40, Nancy Sinatra, B. J. Thomas, the Beastie Boys, Train, Amii Stewart, and even Amorphis, a Finnish death metal band.

"Hello, I Love You"—August 3, 1968

It is interesting to note that the Doors never chose to record "Hello, I Love You" until their third album and only because they desperately needed to find some songs to fill the void left by the failure of the "Celebration of the Lizard," which was originally intended to take up one side of the album, *Waiting for the Sun*. In fact, it was Elektra Records president Jac Holzman's son Adam who remembered the song. In *Follow the Music*, Holzman stated, "When they were doing *Waiting for the Sun*, Adam reminded me about 'Hello, I Love You.' He said, 'Dad, I think that's a hit single.'" The origins of "Hello, I Love You" can be traced to Venice Beach in the summer of 1965. Morrison watched a beautiful black girl stroll across the beach and wrote the lyrics in his notebook: "Sidewalk crouches at her feet/Like a dog that begs for something sweet." The song appeared on the Doors' demo (pre-Robby Krieger), which was recorded on September 2, 1965.

The Doors' second (and final) No. 1 hit, "Hello, I Love You" (with "Love Street" as its B-side) was released in June 1968 and stayed on top of the charts for two weeks (August 3 and 10, 1968) before being knocked off by the Rascals' "People Got to Be Free." Rounding out the top five behind "Hello, I Love You" were "Classical Gas" by Mason Williams, "Stoned Soul Picnic" by the Fifth Dimension, "Grazing in the Grass" by Hugh Masekela, and "Hurdy Gurdy Man" by Donovan.

Rolling Stone magazine called "Hello, I Love You," a "jagged Kinks' rip-off in which Morrison comes on like a rapist," while Richard Riegel of *CREEM* magazine suggested that the song "sounded like Paul Revere & the Raiders slipped some LSD." Other critics referred to the song as "bubblegum pop," certainly uncharacteristic of the darker songs on the Doors' first two albums. "Hello, I Love You" proved to be the Doors' breakthrough hit in England, reaching No. 15 on the UK charts.

Artists who have covered "Hello, I Love You" over the years include Missing Persons, the Cure, Eurythmics, Simple Minds, Neil Young, Buddy Rich, Adam Ant, Siouxsie Sioux, and, perhaps most unlikely, Anal Cunt, an American grindcore band as a hidden track on their 1993 album, *Morbid Florist.*

The JAMES C. PAGNI COMPANY Presents:
HAPPENING NO. 3
THE doors
plus: the SHAG
fresno fairgrounds
friday, june 7th
8:30 pm
tickets now available:
gospel records
& village records
all seats
$3.50

Shortly before the Doors released "Hello, I Love You," which would become their second No. 1 hit, the band took the stage at the Fresno District Fairgrounds on June 7, 1968. Concert management threatened to "hold up the purse should the Doors' behavior be any less than 'in the public interest,'" according to a pre-concert article in the *Fresno Bee*.   *Courtesy of Robert Rodriguez*

14

Realms of Bliss, Realms of Light

Doors Songs That Feature Direct Literary References

I'm kind of hooked to the game of art and literature; my heroes are artists and writers.

—*Jim Morrison*

The Doors were totally unique among '60s rock bands for the myriad of literary references that can be found in their songs such as the reference to Louis-Ferdinand Celine's *Journey to the End of the Night* in the title "End of the Night," the reference to French symbolist poet Arthur Rimbaud in "Wild Child" and, of course, the infamous Oedipal section of "The End." Indeed, a rarity among rock bands, all four of the Doors attended college and Ray Manzarek and Jim Morrison earned degrees (Manzarek in economics and cinematography and Morrison in cinematography).

Morrison's only prized possessions were the boxes of tattered copies of books with titles such as Arthur Rimbaud's *A Season in Hell,* James Joyce's *Ulysses,* Albert Camus' *The Stranger,* and Jack Kerouac's *On the Road.* In the video companion to *No One Here Gets Out Alive,* Doors producer Paul Rothchild claimed, "I never saw [Morrison] without a book. It was the brightest band I'd ever worked with." In fact, Morrison always thought of himself more as a poet than a rock star and considered his lyrics as poetry put to music. He focused on universal themes of sex, violence and death. In a famous profile of the Doors titled "Waiting for Morrison," Joan Didion remarked, "The Doors are the Norman Mailers of the Top 40, missionaries of apocalyptic sex." In his foreword to *The Doors by the Doors,* Henry Rollins called Morrison "a dangerous mind" and an "intellectual and artistic anarchist" who "read books. Huxley, Rimbaud, Artaud, and perhaps Milton."

"Break on Through (to the Other Side)"

One of the most popular songs in the Doors' arsenal, "Break on Through (to the Other Side)" was the first single released by the band off their 1967 self-titled debut album (with the B-side being "End of the Night"). However, the song stalled at No. 126 on the U.S. charts and then faded away quickly in April 1967 during a time when the Turtles' lighthearted single "Happy Together" occupied the No. 1 spot. And yet "Break on Through" has proven to be the archetypal Doors song.

As he would later do in "L.A. Woman," Morrison borrowed imagery from John Rechy's 1963 novel *City of Night.* Doors biographer Doug Sundling in *The Ultimate Doors Companion* pointed out that the novel's nameless narrator uses the term "the other side" to delineate the "sexual boundary of the Hollywood world of hustling vagrants and wanderers." Indeed, one of Rechy's lines sounds very familiar: "He made it, instead, from place to place, week to week, night to night" sounds like the passage "day to day, hour to hour" in "Break on Through." According to Manzarek, "The first song on the first Doors album was 'Break on Through to the Other Side,' and a whole generation did just that." Morrison was quoted in a September 1967 issue of *Hit Parader* magazine claiming that he wrote "Break on Through" one morning in Venice crossing the canals: "I was walking over a bridge. I guess it's one girl, a girl I knew at the time."

"End of the Night"

"End of the Night" was one of the Doors' earliest songs. The lyrics "take the highway to the end of the night" revealed the influence of Louis-Ferdinand Celine's 1932 novel, *Journey to the End of the Night.* In addition, Morrison borrowed a line from eighteenth-century English poet and mystic William Blake. According to Morrison's friend Los Angeles poet Michael C. Ford, "When [Morrison] did the bridge to 'End of the Night,' he said 'Realms of bliss, Realms of light'—I said 'Jim, that's William Blake's "Songs of Innocence."'" He said, 'I know, but nobody's busted me yet.' The Doors really represented a rock band that really tapped into literature, and it worked." One of the six songs recorded on the Doors' demo (without Robby Krieger) on September 2, 1965, "End of the Night" appeared on the B-side of the band's first single, "Break on Through," which was released in January 1967 and only reached No. 126 on the charts.

"The End"

The Doors' first epic, "The End," which appears as the last song of their debut album, was originally conceived as a simple goodbye song to Jim Morrison's girlfriend Mary Werbelow, who had followed him from Clearwater, Florida, to Los Angeles. According to Manzarek, Werbelow was "a fox. We're talking nectar here. Hard, tight body. Large breasts, firm and pointy. Long, straight auburn hair. A body and a half and a dancer of sorts." By the time it appeared on the Doors' self-titled debut album, "The End" had swelled to a length of 11 1/2 minutes of "Joycean pop, with a stream-of-consciousness lyric in which images are strung together by association," according to critic Richard Goldstein in his article "The Doors Open Wide," which appeared in *New York* magazine.

In an interview with Paul Williams of *Crawdaddy!* magazine, Paul Rothchild referred to "The End" as "a changing piece. Jim used it as . . . almost an open canvas for his poetic bits and pieces and fragments and images and little couplets and things that he just wanted to say, and it changed all the time." Rothchild also remarked that "It was beautiful, it was one of the most beautiful moments I've ever had in a recording studio, that half hour when 'The End' was recorded. I was emotionally wrung."

In an interview in the May 1991 issue of *Guitar World* magazine, Robby Krieger described the evolution of the song: "It's funny because that started out as just a cute little love song: 'This is the end, my friend, my beautiful friend.' And I got the idea to do an Indian tuning because I was into Ravi Shankar in a big way. From there it started getting long and more weird. And every time we'd play it, Jim would add more weird stuff." Krieger also noted in *The Doors by the Doors* that "The End" was Morrison's "favorite song on acid."

The Doors honed "The End" during gigs at the London Fog and the Whisky A Go Go, culminating in the infamous set on August 21, 1966, when Morrison, out of his mind after dropping a legendary dose of acid, added the Oedipal sequence, which promptly got the band fired as house band. Oedipus was the mythical Greek king of Thebes made famous by Sophocles' Athenian tragedy *Oedipus the King*, which appeared circa 429 BC. According to Morrison, "Our last night at the Whisky, I invented that climactic part about 'Father, I want to kill you . . .' That's what the song had been leading up to."

"The End"—which has been variously interpreted as the end of a relationship, the end of innocence, the end of childhood or even the end of the world—appears as the final song on the Doors' debut album. The night that the Doors recorded the song at Sunset Sound Recorders, Morrison, high on acid, returned and hosed the whole studio down with a fire extinguisher.

Critic Kurt Von Meier, in his article "Love, Mysticism and the Hippies" for *Vogue* magazine, stated that in "The End" Morrison wrote "as if Edgar Allan Poe had blown back as a hippie." John Stickney of *The Williams College News* ("Four Doors to the Future: Gothic Rock Is Their Thing") called "The End" a "black masterpiece of narrative poetry about a physical and spiritual odyssey which ends in patricide and incest." At least one critic didn't get it at all. Pete Johnson of the *Los Angeles Times* commented: "The best example of [Morrison's] faults is 'The End,' an eleven-minute thirty-five-second exploration of how bored he can sound as he recites singularly simple, overelaborated psychedelic non sequiturs and fallacies." "The End" placed No. 336 on *Rolling Stone* magazine's list of the "500 Greatest Songs of All Time."

"Not to Touch the Earth"

Morrison's epic poem, "The Celebration of the Lizard" was originally intended to take up an entire side of the Doors' third album, *Waiting for the Sun*. However, only the segment "Not to Touch the Earth" made the cut. The lines "Not to touch the earth" and "Not to see the sun" were taken from the table of contents of Sir James George Frazer's *Aftermath: A Supplement to the Golden Bough*: "Chapter LXV—Not to Touch the Earth" and "Chapter LXVI—Not to See the Sun." Frazer, a Scottish social anthropologist, published *The Golden Bough: A Study in Magic and Religion* in 1890.

"Not to Touch the Earth" is full of dark, foreboding lyrics such as "Dead President's corpse in the driver's car." Most famously, the song ends with the lyrics "I am the Lizard King, I can do anything," which would come to haunt Morrison in later years. "The Celebration of the Lizard" can be heard in its entirety on the Doors' 1970 live album, *Absolutely Live*. "Not to Touch the Earth" has been covered by Deceased and Queens of the Stone Age.

"Wild Child"

"Wild Child" from *The Soft Parade* featured a bluesy solo by Krieger. The final line of the song, "You remember when we were in Africa?," refers to one of Morrison's favorite writers, the French Symbolist poet Arthur Rimbaud (*A Season in Hell*), who abandoned poetry at the age of nineteen, became a trader and gun runner in Africa, and died at the age of thirty-seven. "Wild Child" was released as the B-side of the single "Touch Me," which reached No. 3 on the charts in February 1969. The Doors performed "Wild Child" at the notorious Singer Bowl concert on August 2, 1968, which devolved into a full-scale riot.

"The Spy"

The lyrics of "The Spy"—"I'm a spy in the house of love"—were borrowed from the 1954 novel *A Spy in the House of Love* by French author Anais Nin (1903–77). Part of Nin's *Cities of the Interior* sequence, *A Spy in the House of Love* was erotic fiction that portrayed a character study of an adulterous woman named Sabina. Famous for her erotic literature and diaries, Nin shared a bohemian lifestyle with author Henry Miller (*Tropic of Cancer*) in the 1930s as documented in *Henry and June: From the Unexpurgated Diary of Anais Nin*. Her relationship with Miller was later filmed as *Henry & June* (1990), which starred Maria de Madeiros, Fred Ward, and Uma Thurman, and was the first movie in the United States to be given an NC-17 rating. "The Spy" appeared on the Doors' fifth studio album, *Morrison Hotel*.

"Been Down So Long"

"Been Down So Long" from *L.A. Woman* served as a tribute to Richard Farina's 1966 novel *Been Down So Long It Looks Like Up to Me*, in which the author wrote "I've been on a voyage, old sport, a kind of quest, I've seen fire and pestilence, symptoms of a great disease. I'm exempt." A close friend of Bob Dylan, Farina was a writer and folk singer, who married Mimi Baez, the teenage sister of Joan

Baez, in 1963. The couple made their debut as "Richard & Mimi Farina" at the Big Sur Folk Festival in 1964 and soon signed a contract with Vanguard Records.

A comic novel that has evolved into a cult classic, *Been Down So Long It Looks Like Up to Me*, which boasts an introduction by novelist Thomas Pynchon (*Gravity's Rainbow*), features the picaresque adventures of Gnossos Pappadopoulis. Tragically, Farina (1937–66) died in a motorcycle accident in Carmel, California, at the age of twenty-nine, just two days after the novel's publication.

"L.A. Woman"

Morrison borrowed the phrase "city of night" from John Rechy's 1962 novel *City of Night*, a largely autobiographical depiction of gay street hustling written in a stream-of-consciousness narrative style: "When the bars close on Main Street, their world spills into the streets. Malehustlers, queens, scores—all those who haven't made it yet one way or another—or have made it and are trying again—disperse into the night, squeezing every inch of nightlife into the streets."

Despite receiving critical acclaim, Rechy continued to ply his trade as a hustler for several years after the novel was published. In his book *The Sexual Outlaw*, Rechy remarked, "Even when I had good jobs, I was on the streets recurrently, pulled back as if by a powerful lover. Even when *City of Night* was riding the bestseller lists. I've seen copies of my books in the houses of people who have picked me up anonymously." Rechy has received the PEN Center USA West Lifetime Achievement Award and the William Whitehead Award for Lifetime Achievement. Interestingly, Rechy wrote a blurb for Judy Huddleston's memoir *This Is the End . . . My Only Friend: Living & Dying with Jim Morrison*: "Not only is Judy Huddleston's book wonderfully written and moving, but it provides an intimate view of Jim Morrison that other writers have only hinted at or missed entirely."

Manzarek later directed a music video of "L.A. Woman" that included a clip of Morrison smoking a cigarette while riding his bike, footage of the Doors at the beach, and views of the stars of Marlene Dietrich and Josef von Sternberg along the Hollywood Walk of Fame. In an interview with *Classic Rock* magazine (Summer 2007), Krieger stated that "L.A. Woman" was his favorite Doors song: "Jim'd had an idea about Los Angeles being a woman, and it just grew. And the way he repeats the refrain 'Mr. Mojo Risin' . . . it gets faster and faster. It's got a lot of good guitar stuff, some good organ stuff—it's got everything a Doors song should have."

"Hyacinth House"

One of the strangest Doors songs ever recorded, "Hyacinth House," which appeared on *L.A. Woman*, indirectly evoked the Greek myth of Hyacinth, who was the lover of Apollo. During a competition, Hyacinth was struck and killed by a discus during a competition. A grief-stricken Apollo created a flower, the hyacinth, which grew from his spilled blood. Morrison most likely first encountered the Hyacinth myth during his readings of Edith Hamilton's influential book on mythology.

In a May 1991 interview with *Guitar World* magazine, Krieger remarked, "It was a very *odd* vocal—a very, very odd vocal. I didn't know what to make of it then, and I still don't. We wrote that one night when Jim was over at my house, and we were watching these raccoons in my back yard. That's where he got the lions." According to Krieger, the line "I see the bathroom is clear" referred to Morrison's friend Babe Hill leaving the bathroom so Morrison could use it. In the liner notes for *The Doors Box Set*, Densmore stated that "Hyacinth House" was "possibly the saddest song Jim ever wrote."

The title of "Riders on the Storm" was reportedly adapted from Hart Crane's epic poem "The Bridge," although Robby Krieger later suggested that the song simply morphed out of an incident when the band started playing "Ghost Riders on the Sky" for fun during a studio session.   *Courtesy of Ida Miller/idafan.com*

"Riders on the Storm"

Morrison reportedly adapted the title of "Riders on the Storm" from the title of a poem by Hart Crane, an American poet best known for his epic poem "The Bridge," who was, like Morrison, strongly influenced by French Symbolist poet Arthur Rimbaud. Crane committed suicide in 1932 by jumping overboard from the steamship *Orizaba*. Doors biographer Chuck Crisafulli in *When the Music's Over* suggests that Crane was "hounded by a sense of personal failure." According to Manzarek, "Riders on the Storm" is a "song of desperation" and a "dark, gloomy song."

The last song Morrison recorded, "Riders on the Storm" (with "The Changeling" as the B-side) peaked at No. 14 on the charts in September 1971. Robert Harmon, the director of *The Hitcher* (1986), has claimed that the whole idea for the thriller was inspired by "Riders on the Storm." In 2010, "Riders on the Storm" was selected for induction into the Grammy Hall of Fame.

15

A River of Sadness

The Most Overtly Political Doors Songs

I don't think so far politics has been a major theme in my songs. It is there in a few songs, but it is a very minor theme. Politics is people and their interaction with other people, so you cannot really separate it from anything.

—Jim Morrison

Jim Morrison once remarked, "Who wants to hear revolution 24 hours a day?" Although Morrison claimed that Doors songs weren't political, several of the band's songs powerfully reflected on the turmoil of the 1960s. Some of the group's more notable political songs included "The Unknown Soldier," "Five to One," "When the Music's Over," "Peace Frog," and "Tell All the People." Morrison rarely would directly address the current political climate but instead write about universal themes (for instance, "The Unknown Soldier" could apply to any war, not just Vietnam). However, there were exceptions, such as onstage at a concert at the Arizona Veterans Memorial Coliseum in Phoenix when Morrison shouted to the crowd, "Four more years of mediocrity and horseshit. If [President Nixon] does wrong, we will get him."

"When the Music's Over"

An epic song that appeared at the end of the Doors' second album, *Strange Days*, "When the Music's Over" ran for nearly eleven minutes, making it the third-longest recorded Doors song behind "The End" (11:42) and the "Celebration of the Lizard" (17:01). The song features a powerful ecological rant using rape imagery: "What have they done to the earth?/ What have they done to our fair sister?/Ravaged and plundered." Morrison took the line "scream of the butterfly" from the title of a porn movie he had seen on a marquee while driving through Times Square in New York City. The lyric "feast of friends" later became the title of a Doors documentary, while "alive she cried" was taken for the title of the Doors' second live album and "dance on fire" was used for a Doors video.

"Five to One"

"Five to One" appeared on the Doors' third album, *Waiting for the Sun*. According to Robby Krieger, "Five to One" was "one of the predecessors to Heavy Metal."

Although the song strongly suggested an urge for an overthrow of the existing order, Morrison left the title open to interpretation (but claimed that the lyrics were not political). Was "Five to One" the ratio of old to young, whites to blacks or non-pot smokers to pot smokers? In the liner notes to *The Doors Box Set*, Robby Krieger remarked, "Jim figured that by 1969, there would be five times as many people under the age of 21 as would be over, therefore, why not rebel? We could take over."

"Five to One" was the song played during Morrison's infamous rant at the Dinner Key Auditorium in Miami on March 1, 1969. After slurring the first two stanzas, he called the audience "a bunch of fuckin' idiots" and then embarked on an extended (and often nonsensical) monologue inspired by ideas he garnered from the experimental Living Theater. Morrison later claimed he got the idea for the song while waiting in the audience before an early concert: "It was one of those big ballroom places and the kids were milling around and I just got an idea for a song." One of the lines from "Five to One"—"No one here gets out alive"—was used by Jerry Hopkins and Danny Sugerman as the title for their hugely successful 1980 biography of Jim Morrison.

"The Unknown Soldier"

"The Unknown Soldier" was the first single (with the B-side "We Could Be So Good Together") released from *Waiting for the Sun*. The song peaked at No. 39 on the charts even though it was strongly censored by commercial radio. According to Densmore in *The Doors by the Doors*, Rothchild had the Doors do "130 takes" of the song: "It was ludicrous . . . the heart was lost." Morrison may very well have been inspired to write the song after the Doors had visited the Tomb of the Unknown Soldier at Arlington National Cemetery during the day of a concert at the Hilton Hotel International Ballroom on November 25, 1967.

During live performances, the Doors devised an elaborate onstage mock execution. Manzarek would raise his arm, while Krieger pointed his guitar toward Morrison like a rifle. When Manzarek dropped his arm, Densmore used his drums to emulate a gunshot and Morrison would collapse onto the stage. The band even created a three-minute film for "The Unknown Soldier" that was shot on Venice Beach and featured Morrison being summarily executed. The film was enthusiastically received when the Doors played it at the Fillmore East. In a negative review of a Doors concert for the *Bridgeport Telegram* ("Doors Shout and Shriek to 5,000 in JFK Stadium"), critic Charles S. Gardner called "The Unknown Soldier" a "desperately anti-war ballad climaxing with Morrison's being thrown to the floor in a burst of exploding electronic feedback."

"Tell All the People"

Morrison hated the Krieger-penned "Tell All the People" so much that he demanded that individual writing credits be listed for the first time on the Doors' fourth (and most critically maligned) album, *The Soft Parade*. The third single

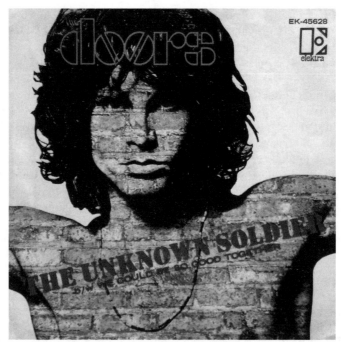

Even though "The Unknown Soldier" was strongly censored from commercial radio, the Doors publicized the song by creating one of the first music videos in rock history, a three-minute film that featured Jim Morrison getting summarily executed on Venice Beach.   *Courtesy of Kerry Humpherys/doors.com*

released off the album, "Tell All the People" (with "Easy Ride" as the B-side) reached No. 57 on the charts. "Tell All the People" was often known as "Follow Me Down" because of the use of the phrase throughout the song. Morrison's opinion was that it had "terrible, corny lyrics," but it was a "nice song." A reviewer for *CREEM* magazine called it "an innocuous enough hippie call-to-arms with none of the jumbled wit of John Lennon's 'Come Together.'"

"Peace Frog"

"Peace Frog" appeared on the Doors' fifth album, *Morrison Hotel*. Frantically looking for some new material to fill the album, producer Paul Rothchild discovered one of Morrison's poems called "Abortion Stories," which served as the basis for the song. In the liner notes for *The Doors Box Set*, Densmore referred to "Peace Frog" as the "most ridiculous title ever," while Krieger called the song "an early attempt at dance music."

"Peace Frog" features the line, "Blood in the streets in the town of New Haven," a reference to Morrison's December 9, 1967, onstage arrest at the New Haven Arena. Morrison also makes reference to the infamous 1968 Democratic

National Convention with the line "Blood in the streets of the town of Chicago." In addition, "Peace Frog" contains the spoken-word verse that begins with: "Indians scattered on dawn's highway bleeding." A childhood flashback, the lines referred to a terrible accident involving Native Americans that Morrison witnessed as a child on a desert highway near Albuquerque, New Mexico. Since "Peace Frog" blended so seamlessly into the next track, "Blue Sunday," radio stations often played the two songs consecutively. "Peace Frog" appeared on the soundtrack for the 1998 Adam Sandler comedy *The Waterboy* as well as the 2005 video game *Tony Hawk's American Wasteland.*

16

She Was a Princess

Doors Songs That Were Inspired by Pamela Courson

[Pam] was the dame of this film noir story. The gorgeous, tragic, little wisp of a girl who was destined to become Jim's inamorata . . . and his doomed partner.
—Ray Manzarek

Jim Morrison wrote many songs for his longtime girlfriend Pamela Courson, including "Love Street," "Queen of the Highway," "Blue Sunday," and "Indian Summer." According to Manzarek, Courson was Morrison's "cosmic mate" and he described their relationship in the liner notes of *The Doors Box Set* as "a burning flame, too hot to touch, too incendiary to last, but what a brilliant light they created together." Courson met Morrison during the band's early London Fog days on the Sunset Strip in the winter of 1966 and was with him until the end when he died under mysterious circumstances in the bathtub of their Paris apartment on July 3, 1971. Less than three years later, Courson died of a heroin overdose in her Los Angeles apartment at the age of twenty-seven on April 25, 1974.

"Love Street"

"Love Street," which appears on the Doors' third album, *Waiting for the Sun*, also served as the B-side to "Hello, I Love You," which rose to No. 1 on the charts in August 1968. The song is about Laurel Canyon Boulevard, where Morrison and Courson lived at 1812 Rothdell Trail. The couple would often sit on the balcony and watch all the hippies and freaks stroll by. The centrally located Canyon Country Store at 2108 Laurel Canyon Boulevard was "the store where the creatures meet."

Ironically, "Love Street" was also where Morrison and Courson engaged in some of the most legendary fights of their turbulent relationship. Fittingly, "Love Street" ends on a note of uncertainty: "I guess I like it fine, so far." In the liner notes of *Waiting for the Sun* in the *Perception* box set, critic Paul Williams refers to "Love Street" as "edgy, even visionary music." The song was rarely played in

Jim Morrison's "cosmic mate," Pamela Courson, served as the inspiration for several classic Doors songs, including "Love Street," which described the couple's often tumultuous relationship in Laurel Canyon.   *Courtesy of Kerry Humpherys/doors.com*

concert but did make the set list in Sweden during the 1968 European Tour. In the poem "Don't Start That . . . ," which appears in *The American Night*, Morrison made two references to "Love Street."

"We Could Be So Good Together"

Reportedly considered for inclusion on the Doors' debut album, "We Could Be So Good Together" may have been about one of Morrison's girlfriends prior to Courson. The song contains darker imagery than the other songs dedicated to her such as "The time you wait subtracts from joy/Beheads these angels you destroy." Author Patricia Butler used a line from the song as the title of her 1998 biography *Angels Dance and Angels Die: The Tragic Romance of Pamela and Jim Morrison*. "We Could Be So Good Together" served as the B-side to "The Unknown Soldier," which peaked at No. 39 on the charts.

"Roadhouse Blues"

Morrison (who preferred staying in cheap motels like the Tropicana and the Alta Cienega) purchased a small bungalow for Courson in secluded Topanga Canyon. It was up the hill from a small roadhouse called the Topanga Grill that offered cold beer, a jukebox, and live bands such as Spirit, Little Feat, and Canned Heat, who recorded a live album there in 1971 called *Live at Topanga Grill.* Neil Young recorded a sizable portion of his 1970 album *After the Gold Rush* (which featured such hits as "Southern Man," "Tell Me Why," and "Only Love Can Break Your Heart") in his basement studio in Topanga Canyon.

The opening lines for "Roadhouse Blues"—"Keep your eyes on the road, your hands upon the wheel"—were Morrison's instructions to Courson as she sometimes took the wheel for the precarious drive along Topanga Canyon Boulevard. The "King of Shock Rock" himself, Alice Cooper, an early drinking buddy of Morrison's, later claimed that he uttered the line "Woke up this morning and got myself a beer" in a conversation with Morrison that eventually ended up as a line in "Roadhouse Blues." As with "Love Street," "Roadhouse Blues" ends on a tentative note: "The future's uncertain and the end is always near."

"Roadhouse Blues" featured the talents of legendary blues guitarist Lonnie Mack, as well as John Sebastian, formerly of the Lovin' Spoonful, on harmonica. A hard-hitting, raw, and gritty booze-drinking song popular on jukeboxes everywhere, "Roadhouse Blues" served as the B-side of "You Make Me Real," a single from *Morrison Hotel* that reached No. 50 on the charts. At one point, the Doors even considered naming the album *Roadhouse Blues.* The song became a favorite opener at Doors concerts. A live version appeared on *An American Prayer.* In the liner notes to *Morrison Hotel,* Doors recording engineer Bruce Botnick hailed "Roadhouse Blues" as "the all-time American bar band song."

"You Make Me Real"

"You Make Me Real" was released as the only single from *Morrison Hotel* in March 1970, with "Roadhouse Blues" as the B-side. It reached No. 50 on the charts. "You Make Me Real" features sexual imagery such as "So let me slide in your tender sunken sea." In the liner notes to *Morrison Hotel,* rock critic David Fricke called the uptempo, bluesy song "a three-minute preview of the garage-blues napalm the Doors would take into arenas throughout 1970."

"Blue Sunday"

Morrison got to show off his crooning style for "Blue Sunday," a Frank Sinatra-style ballad reportedly dedicated to Courson. A mood piece with minimal lyrics, "Blue Sunday" served almost as a coda to "Peace Frog" on *Morrison Hotel,* and the two songs were often played together on commercial radio. Densmore referred to "Blue Sunday" as "Frank Sinatra meets Carlos Castaneda."

"Queen of the Highway"

In "Queen of the Highway," which also appeared on *Morrison Hotel,* Courson is characterized as a "princess," while Morrison is a "monster, black dressed in leather." As with most of the songs about Courson, "Queen of the Highway" also ends on a note of uncertainty: "Hope it can continue a little while longer." Describing the song in the liner notes for *The Doors Box Set*, Manzarek remarked, "Imagine yourself at a smoky jazz joint in the Village circa 1962 with Jim as a world-weary, existential balladeer singing a tale of love. That's the mood we were going for." According to John Densmore in *Riders on the Storm*, "['Queen of the Highway'] had some nice autobiographical lyrics from Jim, but the track never settled into a good groove. It was the first time I ever felt we let Jim down in supporting his words."

"Indian Summer"

One of the Doors' first songs, "Indian Summer" was actually considered for the first album. Facing a shortage of material for *Morrison Hotel*, the Doors threw in the song as a last-minute addition. The ambiguous ending suggests Morrison loves Courson "the best"; however, she is just one of his many lovers: "Better than all the rest."

17

Must Be Something Else We Say

Why *The Soft Parade* Was So Different from Other Doors Albums

We're on a monstrous ego trip and people resent it.

—*Jim Morrison*

Due to Jim Morrison's growing indifference and ever-worsening alcoholism, Robby Krieger wrote about half of the songs on the Doors' fourth album, *The Soft Parade*, such as "Tell All the People," "Touch Me," "Runnin' Blue," and "Wishful, Sinful." The album was a total departure from the band's first three albums and met with criticism from fans and critics alike for its liberal use of brass and string instruments. Also, for the first time, the songs on the album were credited to individual band members.

"Jimbo"

According to Doors producer Paul Rothchild in *The Doors by the Doors*, "Jim was really not interested after about the third album. It became very difficult to get him involved with the records. When we made *The Soft Parade*, it was like pulling teeth to get Jim into it." In fact, Morrison showed up drunk to the recording studio most of the time (if he bothered to show up at all) and was usually surrounded by an entourage of flunkies, groupies, and hangers-on. It was around this time that Ray Manzarek came up with the name "Jimbo" to describe Morrison's raging alcoholic alter ego.

Recording Sessions

The album took nine grueling months to complete. Recording began in November 1968 and was not completed until June 1969. In contrast, the first album had taken just six days to record. Produced by Paul Rothchild, *The Soft Parade* was recorded at the new Elektra recording studio, known as Elektra

Sound West on La Cienega Boulevard in West Hollywood. Rothchild brought in arranger Paul Harris to handle the string and horn overdubs, while session musicians Doug Lubahn and Harvey Brooks were hired to play bass guitar. The band utilized strings from the Los Angeles Philharmonic and horns from local jazz musicians to create the unique sound on *The Soft Parade*. Manzarek claimed that the horns and strings were his idea since he didn't feel like making the same album over and over again.

The album cost more than $80,000 to create (in contrast to the first album, which only cost $10,000). One bright spot during the recording sessions was when George Harrison dropped by the studio in November 1968. According to Doors biographer Greg Shaw, Harrison remarked that the session resembled "the complexity required for the *Sergeant Pepper* recordings."

Individual Writing Credits

Since half of the songs were written by Krieger and half by Morrison (they collaborated on one song, "Do It"), *The Soft Parade* lacked a unified feel. In addition, Morrison hated the line "Can't you see me growing, get your guns," in Krieger's song "Tell All the People." According to Krieger, "He was afraid of people coming to our shows with guns." Morrison demanded that individual writing credits be listed on the album for the first time in the band's history. Ironically, his contributions to the album were particularly weak (especially throwaway songs like "Easy Ride" and "Shaman's Blues"), while the Krieger-penned "Touch Me" (original titles: "Hit Me" and "I'm Gonna Love You") became one of the Doors' biggest hits, reaching No. 3 on the charts.

Last night, while the over-30s watched Bonanza, 27.1 million of the turned-on tuned in Smothers Brothers and heard The Doors break their next million-selling single TOUCH ME (b/w Wild Child) EK 45646 Stock it now. You will be richer for the experience.

An unlikely hit, the Robby Krieger-penned "Touch Me" from *The Soft Parade* album reached No. 3 on the charts and featured a stirring saxophone solo from legendary musician Curtis Amy.
Courtesy of Robert Rodriguez

The Morrison-penned "Wild Child" contained a tribute to his favorite poet, Arthur Rimbaud, who had abandoned poetry at the age of nineteen for a reckless life as a trader and gun runner in Africa: "You remember when we were in Africa?" Another bizarre aspect of the album was that five of the nine tracks were released as singles over an eight-month period before the album was released in July 1969.

Critical Reaction

Several of the songs from *The Soft Parade*—including "Tell All the People," "Wishful, Sinful," and "The Soft Parade"—were performed on the PBS *Critique* show, which was hosted by *Village Voice* music critic Richard Goldstein and first aired on June 25, 1969. An Elektra ad promoting the new album read, "The Doors. Their new album is here. The Soft Parade. It is Jim Morrison. And John Densmore and Ray Manzarek and Robby Krieger. The Soft Parade. It is Touch Me. It is Wishful Sinful. It is Tell All The People. It is much more. It is today and tomorrow. It is emotion. It is perception and poetry. It is the Doors and their search for things known and unknown. For things real and unreal. The Doors. The Soft Parade."

In a review of *The Soft Parade* that appeared in *Rolling Stone* magazine, critic Alec Dubro called the album "worse than infuriating, it's sad," claiming that "one of the most potentially moving forces in rock & roll has allowed itself to degenerate." In a review in *Jazz & Pop* magazine, Patricia Kennealy praised the album, claiming that "most of it is very superior music and some of it is absolutely glorious." However, the *Rolling Stone Album Guide* called it the Doors' "shakiest album" and "cluttered with horns and strings." *The Soft Parade* also appeared just four months after the notorious Miami concert amid an avalanche of cancelled tour dates, so the timing could not be any worse. Despite everything, *The Soft Parade* reached No. 6 on the charts and earned the Doors their fourth consecutive Gold Record Award.

18

The Mask You Wore

The Real Story Behind the Doors' Album Covers

They ran in, got behind the window, and I took one roll of film before anyone noticed . . . Then Jim said, "Let's get a drink."
— Henry Diltz

The Doors created two very memorable album covers: the European circus shot for *Strange Days* and the pose inside of the downtown Los Angeles hotel for *Morrison Hotel*. The cover of the debut album, *The Doors*, was memorable for its image of Jim Morrison that overshadows the other three band members. The *Waiting for the Sun* cover finally treated all of the band members as equals even though they all seem to have bored and/or impatient looks on their faces. The arty, rather pretentious cover for *The Soft Parade* was perhaps the least memorable of the band's album covers. Finally, the cover for *L.A. Woman* that simply states "Doors" across the top perfectly matches the back-to-basics, bluesy feel of the album.

The Doors (1967)

The front cover of the Doors' first album features a huge shot of Morrison on the left-hand side and much smaller images of the other three Doors on the right-hand side. Morrison was outraged by the image, which served to diminish the contributions of the other band members on the album. The front cover photo was taken by Guy Webster, while the back cover photo was credited to Joel Brodsky. A legendary rock photographer, Webster also shot album covers for the Rolling Stones, the Beach Boys, the Mamas and the Papas, Sonny & Cher, Simon & Garfunkel, the Who, and Chicago, among others. He currently runs a photography studio in Venice, California.

William S. Harvey, Elektra's Art Director, designed the album (he also created both the Doors logo and the Elektra butterfly). According to Harvey in *Follow the Music*, "When we were shooting the album cover, we had the idea of overlapping the faces. Because at that time I didn't know who the star was . . . the fact that Jim was the lead singer had nothing to do with it,

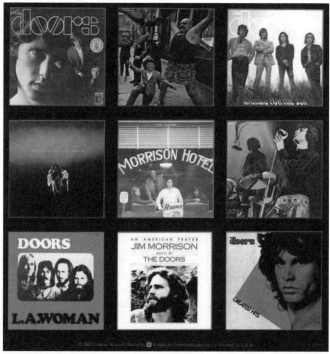

Each of the Doors' first six studio album covers were strongly characteristic of the songs contained within their sleeves, especially the carnivalesque *Strange Days*, the artsy *Soft Parade*, the back-to-basics *Morrison Hotel,* and the bluesy *L.A. Woman.* Later greatest hits compilations often featured the Jim Morrison "Lizard King" persona on their album covers.   *Courtesy of Ida Miller/idafan.com*

except that he was absolutely beautiful. I mean, he was a gorgeous-looking kid. You begin to realize that in front of the camera he was the one." The back cover photo (which actually featured Manzarek prominently) was later utilized on a large illuminated billboard overlooking the Sunset Strip that screamed: "THE DOORS: Break on Through with an Electrifying Album."

Strange Days (1967)

According to Morrison in a 1968 interview with John Carpenter of the *L.A. Free Press,*

> I hated the cover on the first album. So I said, "I don't want to be on this cover. Where is that? Put a chick on it or something. Let's have a dandelion or a design." The title, *Strange Days,* came and everybody said, yeah, 'cause that was where we were, what was happening. It was right. Originally I wanted us in a room surrounded by about thirty dogs, but

that was impossible 'cause we couldn't get the dogs and everybody was saying, "What do you want dogs for?" And I said that it was symbolic that it spelled God backwards. (Laughs) Finally we ended up leaving it up to the art director and the photographer. We wanted some real freaks though, and he came out with a typical sideshow thing. It looked European. It was better than having our fucking faces on it though.

The album's Felliniesque artwork was designed by William S. Harvey and photographed by Joel Brodsky. The cover photo was taken in Sniffen Court, a small residential mew between Lexington and Third Avenue in New York City in August 1967. The shot was inspired by Federico Fellini's 1954 circus film, *La Strada*. A small poster of the band members appears very discreetly on the right-hand side of the album cover (it was actually the back cover photo from the band's first album). The cover featured two acrobats who were actual circus performers if somewhat inept. According to Brodsky, "They were terrible . . . The guy underneath could only hold up his partner for a few seconds—he kept on dropping him." The trumpet player was actually a passing cab driver who agreed to appear in the shot for $5. The juggler was Brodsky's assistant, Frank Kollegy, who "couldn't juggle worth a damn," according to Brodsky. The strongman was a doorman at the Friars Club. The dwarves were Lester Janus, who appeared on the front cover, and his younger brother, Stanley, who appeared on the back cover. The woman on the back cover was Brodsky's wife, Zazel Loven.

Waiting for the Sun (1968)

The album cover for *Waiting for the Sun* was shot by Paul Ferrara in a canyon above Malibu and featured a group shot that treated the band as equals. Ferrara was Morrison's friend from the UCLA Film School who would later work on the experimental film *HWY* as well as the Doors' documentary, *Feast of Friends*. Ferrara also claimed to have cowritten "Waiting for the Sun" with Morrison (a song that would later appear on the *Morrison Hotel* album). According to Ferrara in his 2007 memoir *Flash of Eden* (the title of which came from the first line in "Waiting for the Sun": "At first flash of eden we raced down to the sea"), "I wanted to do something that showed them in a glamorous type portrait for their third cover. They had one album with four heads and the second with a juggler. I wanted the sunrise behind them, which was kind of hard on the west coast. The easiest thing to accomplish was a sunset that doubled for a sunrise." Ferrara crouched atop a Rambler station wagon and used a rented Hasselblad camera for the shot.

The Soft Parade (1969)

By far the weakest album cover (and some critics and fans believe the worst album) of the Doors' first six studio albums, *The Soft Parade* features the four

Doors standing around a tripod in an artistic shot that appeared like something out of Michelangelo Antonioni's 1966 film *Blow Up*. Ironically, by the time the album was released in July 1969, Morrison, who had gained weight and grown a scraggly beard, looked nothing like the shot on the album cover. The cover for *The Soft Parade* was once again photographed by Joel Brodsky, who worked on *The Doors* and *Strange Days*. Brodsky, who died of a heart attack in 2007, photographed approximately 400 album covers during his prolific career such as B. B. King, Carly Simon, Barry Manilow, Iggy Pop, Kiss, and Gladys Knight and the Pips.

In addition, Brodsky was responsible for the famous bare-chested shot of Morrison (that would later appear on the cover of *No One Here Gets Out Alive*). In a July 3, 1981, interview with *BAM* magazine, Brodsky described the photo shoot, which took place in a New York City studio in 1966. According to Brodsky, Morrison was "totally plastered . . . so drunk he was stumbling into the lights . . . You know, Morrison never looked that way again, and those pictures have become a big part of the Doors' legend . . . I think I got him at his peak."

Morrison Hotel (1970)

Manzarek and his wife, Dorothy, were driving around Los Angeles when they spotted the seedy Morrison Hotel ("rooms $2.50 and up") at 1246 South Hope Street in downtown Los Angeles that inspired arguably their greatest album cover for *Morrison Hotel*. The hotel's owner forbade a photo shoot on his property, so photographer Henry Diltz waited until he left. The Doors then ducked in and did a quick, five-minute session. At one point, a food delivery man made an unexpected cameo strolling past the hotel's window in front of the band. Lights from a Christmas tree can be seen in the lobby. According to Henry Rollins in his foreword to *The Doors by the Doors*, "On the cover of the album, Henry Diltz's portrait of the band in the window of the Morrison Hotel, Morrison's expression seems distracted and somewhat hollow. Like a man who was peering into the abyss."

Diltz began his love for photography while performing with the folk revival band Modern Folk Quartet (MFQ) in the early 1960s. He was the official photographer of both the Monterey International Pop Festival in 1967 and Woodstock in 1969. Diltz has more than 200 album and CD covers to his credit such as James Taylor's *Sweet Baby James*, the debut albums of Crosby, Stills & Nash and Jackson Browne, five albums for America, the Mamas and the Papas' *People Like Us*, and the Eagles' first album and *Desperado*. He is the cofounder of the Morrison Hotel Galleries, based in New York and California, the premier venue for rock photography.

After the photo shoot at the Morrison Hotel, the group drove around and discovered the Hard Rock Cafe at 300 East 5th Street. A photo of the Hard Rock Cafe, the kind of bar where Los Angeles writer and barfly Charles Bukowski would feel right at home, appeared on the back cover. The founders of the unrelated Hard Rock Cafe chain of restaurants reportedly got the idea for their name after viewing the back cover of *Morrison Hotel.*

L.A. Woman (1971)

The Doors' sixth studio album (and final album with Morrison) was mixed at a new studio in West Hollywood called Poppi, where the band also did their photo shoot for the album cover. A somewhat bloated and heavily bearded Morrison appeared like he was slouching in the far corner of the shot (a far cry from his dominant position on the cover of the debut album). The cover shot was credited to photographer Wendell Hamick. According to Elektra Records president Jac Holzman in *Follow the Music,* "I wasn't sure there'd be another album ever, so I had Bill Harvey create a collector's cover. The Doors' faces were printed on clear film. The backing color of the inner sleeve could be changed and would affect the mood of the package. This is the first album on which Jim is bearded. His photo is on the right, no bigger, no smaller than the others, just another guy in the band."

Jim Morrison's friend Paul Ferrara designed this cover for the Doors' 1968 *Tour Book* and also photographed the band for the *Waiting for the Sun* album cover.   *Courtesy of Robert Rodriguez*

19

A Beast Caged

The Failure of the "Celebration of the Lizard"

That piece "Celebration of the Lizard" was kind of an invitation to the dark forces.

—Jim Morrison

The "Celebration of the Lizard" was an epic performance piece conceived by Jim Morrison and originally intended to take up one full side of the 1968 album *Waiting for the Sun*. Unfortunately, the Doors could not find a way to meld its disparate sections into a unified song. Eventually, only one musical passage, "Not to Touch the Earth," ended up on the album (although a live performance of the entire "Celebration of the Lizard" can be heard on the Doors' 1970 live album *Absolutely Live*).

Recording Sessions

By the time it came to record the third album, Morrison had become less and less interested in recording albums. He frequently showed up drunk at the studio if he bothered to show up at all. One night in the studio Morrison got so inebriated that he collapsed on the floor and urinated. Densmore threw down his drumsticks and stormed out, only to return the next day. According to producer Paul Rothchild, "Jim was really not interested. He wanted to do other things like write. Being lead singer of The Doors was really not his idea of a good time now. It became very difficult to get him involved with the record."

Worse yet, the Doors had exhausted all of their best material in the first two albums and now found themselves having to create songs in the studio for the first time. Robby Krieger referred to the dilemma as "third album syndrome" and remarked that "Usually a group will have enough songs to record one, maybe two albums, then they'll go off on tour and not have time to write any more material. So by the third album, you find yourself trying to write stuff in the studio . . . and it shows, usually."

Writer Joan Didion, who referred to the Doors as "missionaries of apocalyptic sex," perfectly caught the band's mood during the recording sessions for

During the Doors' Hollywood Bowl concert on July 5, 1968, the band performed several selections from Jim Morrison's epic poem, the "Celebration of the Lizard" such as "A Little Game," "The Hill Dwellers," and "Wake Up!" Sitting in the front row with his then-girlfriend, Marianne Faithfull, Mick Jagger later remarked that the show was "boring."

Courtesy of Kerry Humpherys/doors.com

Waiting for the Sun in "Waiting for Morrison," which appeared in the *Saturday Evening Post.* Morrison showed up a couple of hours late (as he usually did) for the session and no one even acknowledged his arrival: "An hour or so passed, and still no one had spoken to Morrison . . . There was a sense that no one was going to leave the room, ever."

An Epic Poem

For the Doors' third album, Morrison had originally wanted to recite some of his poetry between songs (similar to how *An American Prayer* eventually turned out).

During a concert at the L.A. Forum on December 14, 1968, the Doors followed "Light My Fire" with a complete version of the "Celebration of the Lizard" to a somewhat bewildered and ultimately bored audience.   *Courtesy of Ida Miller/idafan.com*

The album title changed from *American Night* (the name of a lengthy Morrison poem) to *Celebration of the Lizard* (Morrison wanted the cover to be an imitation lizard skin) to *Waiting for the Sun*. Ironically, the title track did not even make the album and later showed up on the Doors' fifth album, *Morrison Hotel*.

In a 1970 interview for *Poppin* magazine, Morrison claimed that the "Celebration of the Lizard" concerned a "band of youths who leave the city and venture into the desert" where they "tell stories and sing around a fire." He later told Bob Chorush in a January 1971 interview with the *L.A. Free Press* that the "Celebration of the Lizard" was "kind of an invitation to the dark forces." The "Celebration of the Lizard" was divided into seven sections: "Lions in the Street," "Wake Up!," "A Little Game (Go Insane)," "The Hill Dwellers," "Not to Touch the Earth," "Names of the Kingdom," and "The Palace of Exile."

The Lizard King

As Manzarek remarked in *Light My Fire*: "We worked on 'The Celebration of the Lizard' but it kept resisting us . . . But we did manage a very intense completion of 'Not to Touch the Earth' section, including Jim's infamous line . . . 'I am the Lizard King I can do anything.'" The Doors filled the gap left by the "Celebration of the Lizard" with songs such as "Hello, I Love You," "Wintertime Love," and "My Wild Love."

The only consolation to the "Celebration of the Lizard" besides the inclusion of "Not to Touch the Earth" was the entire poem being printed inside the album sleeve. *Waiting for the Sun* was released in July 1968, and ironically it was the throwaway pop tune "Hello, I Love You" that skyrocketed to No. 1 on the charts. In addition, the term "Lizard King" would come to haunt Morrison as he later tried to shake the rock star image.

"Undergraduate Imagery"

In a review for the *Philadelphia Inquirer*, critic Pete Johnson remarked, "*Waiting for the Sun* contains the fewest snakes, the least ugliness, the lowest numbers of freaks and monsters, and the smallest amount of self-indulgent mysticism of the trio of Doors LPs. They have traded terror for beauty, and the success of the swap is a tribute to their talent and originality." Bob Shayne of the *L.A. Free Press* was somewhat less kind: "This album is unbelievably bad . . . *Waiting for the Sun* contains three new versions of 'Break on Through,' which go by the euphemisms 'Not to Touch the Earth,' 'Unknown Soldier' and 'We Could Be So Good Together.' It contains 'Hello, I Love You,' which was better when The Kinks did it as another song . . . It contains the worst lyrics I have ever heard in my life in 'Spanish Caravan.' The set has none of the vitality, originality, enigmatic quality, believable passion or musicality of the first two Doors LPs."

In reviewing *Absolutely Live*, legendary rock critic Lester Bangs remarked, "Mention should also be made of 'Celebration of the Lizard,' complete on record for the first time. But that's about all that should be made of it. It's real low comedy, typical Morrisonian undergraduate imagery, but without the support this time of a good melody and arrangement. 'Not to Touch the Earth' was definitely the only part worth preserving. I get a pretty good laff out of it, but I don't want to play it again."

"Celebration of the Lizard" also appeared in *The Doors Box Set* on the *Live in New York* CD. In the album's liner notes, Krieger remarked, "Jim got an awful lot of shit for proclaiming himself the 'Lizard King.' But he really loved lizards and snakes. He was serious about this. Many of his acid trips were very lizard-laden."

A rare performance of the entire version of the "Celebration of the Lizard" took place at the Felt Forum on January 18, 1970. Urging the audience to be quiet, Jim Morrison called the piece "a little tour de force that we've only done a couple of times in front of strangers."

Courtesy of Ida Miller/idafan.com

20

If You Don't Give a Listen

The Most Essential (and Least Essential) Doors Albums

I think albums have replaced books . . . and movies . . . You measure your progress mentally by your records.

—Jim Morrison

I n addition to all of the first six studio albums—*The Doors, Strange Days, Waiting for the Sun, The Soft Parade, Morrison Hotel,* and *L.A. Woman*—there are several essential releases for Doors collectors such as *The Complete Studio Recordings,* a seven-CD set released by Elektra in 1999, as well as rare Doors recordings, bootlegs, live albums, and tribute albums such as *Stoned Immaculate: The Music of the Doors,* which was released in 2000. The Jim Morrison spoken-word album (with music by the Doors) *An American Prayer* is also essential listening for any hardcore Doors fan.

Conversely, over the years there have been a dozen or so Doors compilation albums that provided little else than a good introduction for the casual fan such as *13* (1970), *Weird Scenes Inside the Gold Mine* (1972), *The Best of the Doors* (1973), and *The Doors Greatest Hits* (1980), among many others. In addition, the two post-Morrison studio albums, *Other Voices* (1971) and *Full Circle* (1972), have never been released on CD in the United States (for good reason!). Finally, over the last ten years, the Bright Midnight Archives has made available a variety of previously unreleased material from the Doors archive, the latest being *Live in Vancouver 1970* (2010).

13 (1970)

13, the first Doors compilation album and the only one that came out before Jim Morrison's death, was released in November 1970 without much input from the band. According to Ray Manzarek, "We never wanted those compilations released at all." Along with such recognized hits as "Light My Fire" and "Hello, I Love You," *13* contained some unique selections not normally included on

Doors compilation albums such as "Wild Child" and "Land Ho!" The *13* album cover featured a huge image of Morrison and much smaller photos of the other band members at the bottom. The album peaked at No. 25 on the charts. It has never been issued on CD and neither has the band's second compilation album, *Weird Scenes Inside the Gold Mine*, which was first released in 1972.

Live at the Hollywood Bowl (1987)

Recorded on July 5, 1968, *Live at the Hollywood Bowl* features "Wake Up," "Light My Fire," "The Unknown Soldier," and "Spanish Caravan," as well as two songs from the "Celebration of the Lizard"—"A Little Game" and "The Hill Dwellers." Unbeknownst to the rest of the band, Morrison had dropped acid before the show and turned in a rather lackluster performance, according to John Densmore, who called the show "a drag." In contrast, Manzarek considered the Hollywood Bowl concert a milestone for the band: "We had made it . . . We had come all the way . . . It was one of the high points of our careers." Reviewing the concert for the *L.A. Free Press*, critic Harvey Perr wrote, "It was a good show and nothing more. The mystique has turned mundane . . . the evening failed not only as Theater but it failed, as well, as a rock concert." Unfortunately, *Live at the Hollywood Bowl* does not include the Doors' finale that night, "The End," which Morrison interrupted to recite his "Ode to a Grasshopper."

In Concert (1991)

A live double album, *In Concert* includes all the tracks from the Doors' live albums, *Absolutely Live* and *Alive, She Cried*, as well as three bonus tracks: "Roadhouse Blues" from *An American Prayer*, "The Unknown Soldier" from *Live at the Hollywood Bowl*, and a previously unreleased version of "The End" from the Hollywood Bowl concert. *Absolutely Live* was recorded at several venues, including the

Rushed into release in November 1970, the Doors' first compilation album, *13*, featured a mythical cover image of Morrison towering over his bandmates, much to their chagrin.

Courtesy of Ida Miller/idafan.com

Aquarius Theater in Hollywood (July 21–22, 1969), the Felt Forum in New York City (January 17–18, 1969), Boston Arena (April 10, 1970), the Spectrum in Philadelphia (May 1, 1970), Civic Center in Pittsburgh (May 2, 1970), and Cobo Arena in Detroit (May 8, 1970). *Alive, She Cried* featured live recordings from concerts in Los Angeles, New York, Detroit, and Copenhagen between 1968 and 1970.

The Doors: Original Soundtrack Recording (1991)

Produced by Paul Rothchild, the soundtrack to Oliver Stone's film contains the typical slew of Doors hits such as "Light My Fire" and "Riders on the Storm," as well as the Velvet Underground and Nico's "Heroin" and some of Morrison's spoken-word poetry, including "The Movie," "Ghost Song," and "Stoned Immaculate." The album cover features Val Kilmer portraying Morrison with his hair the color of burning flames.

The Doors Box Set (1997)

The Doors' first box set features four CDs: *Without a Safety Net, Live in New York* (recorded at Madison Square Garden in 1970), *The Future Ain't What It Used to Be*, and *Band Favorites*. *The Doors Box Set* includes rare and unreleased demo recordings such as "Go Insane" and "Summer's Almost Gone" from the band's September 1965 session at World Pacific Studios. Some of the songs included in the box set had been previously available as bootlegs. Other highlights of *The Doors Box Set* include the seventeen-minute "Rock Is Dead" from a 1969 studio jam, the notorious Morrison "Five to One" rant from the Dinner Key Auditorium in Miami in 1969, "Orange County Suite" (Morrison's tribute to Courson), and "Tightrope Ride" from the first post-Morrison studio album, *Other Voices*.

On the *Band Favorites* CD, Krieger picked "Light My Fire," "Peace Frog," "Wishful, Sinful," "Take It as It Comes," and "L.A. Woman"; Densmore chose "Love Me Two Times," "When the Music's Over," "The Unknown Soldier," "Wild Child," and "Riders on the Storm"; and Manzarek selected "I Can't See Your Face in My Mind," "Land Ho!", "Yes, the River Knows," "Shaman's Blues," and "You're Lost Little Girl." *The Doors Box Set* was dedicated to producer Paul Rothchild, who passed away in 1995.

The Doors: The Complete Studio Recordings (1999)

A seven-CD box set, *The Complete Studio Recordings* contains six of the original eight Doors albums digitally remastered and a CD titled *Essential Rarities* (later released on its own in 2000) that features studio cuts, live cuts, and demos taken from *The Doors Box Set*. The title of the box set is misleading since it does not include the two post-Morrison studio albums—*Other Voices* and *Full Circle*—or the posthumous Jim Morrison spoken-word album *An American Prayer*, which was released in 1978.

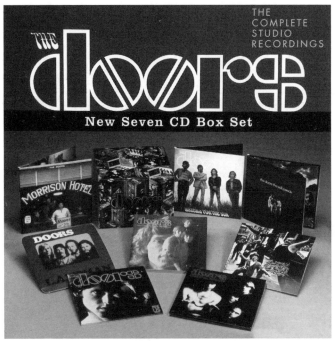

Released in 1999, *The Doors: The Complete Studio Recordings* is a rather misleading title since it does not include the two post-Morrison studio albums, *Other Voices* and *Full Circle*.

Courtesy of Kerry Humpherys/doors.com

Live in Detroit (2000)

One of the first releases from the Bright Midnight Archives, which was formed by the Doors Music Company to make available live, previously unreleased material from the Doors archives, *Live in Detroit* was recorded on May 8, 1970, at the Cobo Arena. In the CD's liner notes, Danny Sugerman called the Detroit concert "easily . . . the longest Doors set ever performed." Other releases from the Bright Midnight Archives include *The Bright Midnight Sampler* (2000), *Bright Midnight: Live in America* (2001), *Live in Hollywood* (2002), *Boot Yer Butt: The Doors Bootlegs* (2003), *Live in Philadelphia '70* (2005), *Live in Boston* (2007), *Live at the Matrix 1967* (2008), *Pittsburgh Civic Arena* (2008), *Live in New York* (2009), and *Live in Vancouver 1970* (2010), among others.

Stoned Immaculate: The Music of the Doors (2000)

Released in the fall of 2000, *Stoned Immaculate* is an eclectic Doors tribute album produced by Ralph Sall that features a variety of new, classic, and iconic musical artists. Unusual for a tribute album, the surviving members of the Doors played on several of the tracks. In the album's liner notes, Sall remarked, "The Doors showed that a group of disparate characters with different musical tastes and influences could, for a brief yet brilliant moment, create music that, quite simply, sounded like nothing that came before." In addition, recordings of Jim Morrison were used posthumously in the creation of four tracks: "Under Waterfall," "Cosmic Movie," "Is Everybody In?," and "Children of Night." Sall stated, "It was both exciting and challenging to create 'new' Doors material through the use of beats and samples. Juxtaposition creates new meaning in the work."

Stoned Immaculate featured Doors covers by musicians influenced by the band such as Stone Temple Pilots ("Break on Through"), Train ("Light My Fire"), Smash Mouth ("Peace Frog"), "Days of the New ("L.A. Woman," "The End"), Creed ("Riders on the Storm"), Aerosmith ("Love Me Two Times"), the Cult ("Wild Child"), Oleander ("Hello, I Love You"), Ian Astbury ("Touch Me"), and Perry Ferrell/Exene ("Children of Night"), as well as artists who influenced the Doors such as John Lee Hooker ("Roadhouse Blues"), Bo Diddley ("Love Her Madly"), and even legendary Beat author William S. Burroughs ("Is Everybody In?"). The album cover features a painting by the late Rick Griffin, one of the leading designers of psychedelic posters during the 1960s. The album title was taken from a lyric from "The WASP (Texas Radio and the Big Beat)"—"Out here we is stoned—immaculate."

Perception (2006)

A 12-disc box set "Celebrating The Doors' 40th Anniversary 1967–2007," *Perception* contains the 1999 remastered editions of the first six Doors studio albums, 24 rare and previously unreleased bonus clips and 12 live video clips, while the DVD-AUDIO discs feature 2006 "40th-anniversary" remixes. Each CD also includes extra tracks that consist of previously unreleased session outtakes.

When You're Strange: Music from the Motion Picture (2010)

The soundtrack to the Doors documentary directed by Tom DiCillo and narrated by Johnny Depp, *When You're Strange* features fourteen songs from the Doors' first six studio albums mixed with Morrison's poetry read by Johnny Depp. The album also contains live performances at venues that include the notorious performance of "Light My Fire" from *The Ed Sullivan Show*; "When the Music's Over" from Television-Byen in Gladsaxe, Copenhagen; "Roadhouse Blues" from the Felt Forum in New York City; and "Break on Through (to the Other Side)" from the Isle of Wight Festival.

Poems featured on the soundtrack include "Cinema," "The Spirit of Music," "The Doors of Perception" (William Blake), "A Visitation of Energy," "Wasting the Dawn," "Inside the Dream," "We Have Been Metamorphosized," "Touch Scares," "Naked We Come," "O Great Creator of Being," "The Girl of the Ghetto," "Crossroads," "Ensenada," "As I Look Back," and "Goodbye America."

21

The Lights Are Getting Brighter

Bands That Shared the Bill with the Doors During the Early Years

The general idea was to blow the headliners off the stage.

—*John Densmore*

As house band at the Whisky A Go Go in the spring and summer of 1966, the Doors were fortunate enough to open for such legendary bands as Them (featuring Van Morrison), Buffalo Springfield, and the Turtles. As they traveled outside Los Angeles to promote their first album starting in January 1967, the little-known band had to perform second and third billing behind bands that soon faded into obscurity such as Sopwith Camel and the Peanut Butter Conspiracy. However, everything changed during the summer of 1967 when "Light My Fire" skyrocketed to No. 1 on the U.S. charts, and the same bands that headlined over the Doors just months before now found themselves in the awkward position of opening for them.

Alice Cooper

"Welcome to my nightmare, I think you're gonna like it . . ." Before he became the "Godfather of Shock Rock," Alice Cooper (real name: Vincent Damon Furnier) was just a struggling rock musician trying to hit the big time with his band in Los Angeles. The son of a preacher, Furnier was born in Detroit, Michigan, on February 4, 1948. The family moved to Phoenix, Arizona, when Furnier, a severe asthmatic, was three years old. In 1965, Furnier and some of his high school buddies on the track team formed a band called the Earwigs, mainly performing covers of Beatles and Rolling Stones songs. The band changed their name to the Spiders the following year, scored a local hit with "Don't Blow Your Mind," and eventually headed to Los Angeles in 1968, morphing first into the Nazz and later Alice Cooper. The band featured Furnier (vocals/harmonica), Glen Buxton (lead guitar), Michael Bruce (rhythm guitar/keyboards), Dennis Dunaway (bass), and Neal Smith (drums). Furnier soon adopted the band's name as his own.

The Doors were one of the first bands to befriend Alice Cooper and invited them to the recording studio. According to Cooper, Morrison would arrive at the studio and start taking any drugs that were available, pills or acid, and washing it all down with shots of whisky. Needless to say, Morrison and Furnier soon became drinking buddies and often hung out on the Santa Monica Pier chugging beer after beer. The Alice Cooper Band opened for the Doors at the Cheetah, which was located at the end of the pier, as "Light My Fire" skyrocketed up the charts during the summer of 1967. According to Cooper, "The thing about Jim was it was sometimes dangerous being around him because there was no such thing as a dare. He would jump out of cars and roll down hills." At a big party for the Doors at 6000 Sunset Boulevard, Morrison's "got a bottle of whiskey in each hand, on top of the building balancing like a high wire act. One gust of wind and he is over. I'm sitting there going 'How come no one is pulling him off the ledge? It's Jim Morrison!' and they're like 'If he falls, he falls.'"

During the late 1960s, the Alice Cooper Band earned a reputation as "the worst band in Los Angeles." They eventually signed with Frank Zappa's Straight Records label and released two albums: *Pretties for You* (which the *Rolling Stone Album Guide* called "strictly inept psychedelia") and *Easy Action* in 1970. On September 13, 1969, the Alice Cooper Band turned in an infamous performance at the Toronto Rock 'n' Roll Revival festival. The Doors headlined the event, which also featured the Plastic Ono Band, as well as Chuck Berry, Bo Diddley, Jerry Lee Lewis, Little Richard, and Gene Vincent. During the Alice Cooper Band's set, someone threw a live chicken onstage. Unaware that the bird could not fly, Cooper hurled the bird off the stage, and it was torn to pieces by the audience.

Unable to gain any momentum in Los Angeles, the Alice Cooper Band decided to head to Detroit, where they received a somewhat better reception and befriended local bands such as the Stooges and MC5. In 1971, the band released *Love It to Death*, which featured the hit single "Eighteen"—an instant teen anthem first recorded by Question Mark and the Mysterians as "8-Teen" that reached No. 21 on the charts. By this time, the band started indulging in rock theatrics and incorporating elaborate stage props into their live shows that included black makeup, fake blood, guillotines and electric chairs, live boa constrictors, and six-foot-long, inflatable phalluses. No strangers to excess, the Alice Cooper Band bought a 42-room mansion in Greenwich, Connecticut, and boasted of spending $300,000 a year on booze. Cooper later remarked, "We were the *National Enquirer* of rock 'n' roll." *Love It to Death* was followed by *Killer* (1971) and *School's Out* (1972), which reached No. 2 on the U.S charts, and *Billion Dollar Babies* (1973), which reached No. 1. In Cooper's 1976 autobiography, *Me, Alice: The Autobiography of Alice Cooper*, he wrote that the song "Desperado" on his *Killer* album was a tribute to Morrison.

Cooper's first solo effort, *Welcome to My Nightmare* (1975), featured narration by Vincent Price and the ballad "Only Women Bleed." Cooper provided the song "He's Back (The Man Behind the Mask)" for the *Friday the 13th, Part VI* soundtrack. *Trash* (1989) boasted the hit single, "Poison," which hit No. 7 on the U.S. charts. Alice Cooper has influenced such performers as Kiss, Marilyn Manson, and Rob Zombie, among others. He was selected for induction into the Rock and Roll Hall of Fame as part of the class of 2011 along with Tom Waits, Dr. John, Neil Diamond, and Darlene Love.

Canned Heat

A Los Angeles-based blues rock band, Canned Heat was formed in 1965 by blue enthusiasts Alan "Blind Owl" Wilson and Bob "the Bear" Hite (both of whom collected thousands of blues records during the 1960s) and took its name from influential blues musician Tommy Johnson's 1928 song "Canned Heat Blues." Canned Heat was one of the Doors' favorite bands because of their strong affinity for the blues. The band's original lineup included Hite (singer), Wilson (guitar/harmonica), Henry Vestine (lead guitar), Larry "the Mole" Taylor (bass guitar), and Frank Cook (drums), who was later replaced by Fito de la Parra.

Canned Heat played on the same bill as the Doors in one of the earliest rock festivals, the Fantasy Faire & Magic Festival, on June 10, 1967. Also featuring the 13th Floor Elevators, Spanky and Our Gang, Sparrow (later known as Steppenwolf), Jefferson Airplane, Country Joe and the Fish, the Seeds, and others, the festival was overshadowed by the legendary Monterey Pop Festival a week later. In fact, Canned Heat gained recognition during a stellar performance at the Monterey Pop Festival and also turned in an electrifying performance at Woodstock in 1969 with a set that featured "A Change Is Gonna Come"/"Leaving This Town," "Woodstock Boogie," "Going up the Country," "Let's Work Together," "Too Many Drivers at the Wheel," and "Little Red Rooster." They also joined the Doors at a concert in Frankfurt, West Germany, during their 1968 European Tour.

Canned Heat signed with Liberty Records and reached the U.S. charts with the single, "On the Road Again," followed by "Going up the Country." During Morrison's Miami trial in August 1970, he sat in with Canned Heat for a 45-minute set at a nightclub called the Hump. In 1971, the group recorded an album with one of their idols, John Lee Hooker. Wilson joined the so-called "27 Club," which also would eventually include Morrison, Jimi Hendrix, and Janis Joplin, when he died of a drug overdose on September 3, 1970, at the age of twenty-seven. Canned Heat performed with the three surviving Doors for the last time at the Rock Liberation Festival at Balboa Stadium in San Diego on August 13, 1972.

Chambers Brothers

The four Chambers Brothers (yes, they were actual brothers) began as a gospel quartet from a sharecropper family in Lee County, Mississippi, but by the late 1960s had evolved into "funk/hippie-fusion psychedelized soul," according to the *Rolling Stone Album Guide*, which labeled the group as "sloppy, overheated, but gifted haphazardly with prophetic instinct."

Formed in 1954, the band consisted of bassist George, guitarist Willie, harpist Lester, and guitarist Joe. The Doors opened for Johnny Rivers and the Chambers Brothers several times during the summer of 1966 as part of their stint as house band at the Whisky A Go Go. In 1968, the Chambers Brothers scored their biggest hit with "Time Has Come Today" and also broke into the Top 40 with a cover of Otis Redding's "I Can't Turn You Loose." However, times had changed, and it was the Chambers Brothers (along with Steppenwolf) who opened for the Doors at the Hollywood Bowl concert on July 5, 1968.

Country Joe and the Fish

Formed in 1966 by lead singer Country Joe McDonald, one-time boyfriend of Janis Joplin, Country Joe and the Fish was one of the original and most popular San Francisco psychedelic bands. In October 1967, Country Joe and the Fish released the psychedelic album *Electric Music for the Mind and Body*, immediately followed by *I-Feel-Like-I'm-Fixin'-to-Die*, which featured the satirical, antiwar title song ("Be the first one on your block to have your boy come home in a box."). On March 3–4, 1967, the Doors headlined the Avalon Ballroom with Country Joe and the Fish (and Sparrow).

A true product of the times, Country Joe and the Fish focused primarily on free love, protest politics, and LSD. McDonald notoriously performed his version of "Fixin'-to-Die" at Woodstock in 1969. He later admitted, "I get kind of mystical about my solo performance at Woodstock . . . I was hanging around, and I was just filling time, singing a few country and western songs and folk songs. Then I did [the anti-Vietnam war song], 'Feel-Like-I'm-Fixing-to-Die-Rag'—the F-U-C-K cheer—the rest is history. From the first response to 'Give me an f' when they all stopped talking and looked at me and yelled, F, I knew there was no turning back."

According to the *Rolling Stone Album Guide*, "The political significance of this happy Haight-Ashbury crew is undeniable. Sixties agitators of the prankster variety, they aimed blows against the empire by developing a famous F-U-C-K cheer (gimme an 'F') to be bellowed at demonstrations and concerts, they starred at Woodstock— they summed up hippie rebellion . . . But the music the Fish made now demands the indulgence of nostalgia."

Grateful Dead

The late, great rock promoter Bill Graham once remarked that the Grateful Dead "aren't the best at what they do, they're the *only ones* who do what they do." According to the *Rolling Stone Album Guide*, "The Grateful Dead embodied hippie utopianism, the acid love-in and the endless, mystic jam. The Doors' California

In the pre-"Light My Fire" period in early 1967, the Doors would often get third billing behind bands like Country Joe and the Fish and Sparrow.

Courtesy of Kerry Humpherys/doors.com

was a construct of the darker psyche; it was L.A. crash pads and needle fever, Hollywood bungalows and film-noir threats."

The Grateful Dead traced its history from a jug band called Mother McCree's Uptown Jug Champions. Formerly known as the Warlocks (Courtney Love's father, Hank Harrison, was the band's original manager), the Grateful Dead served as house band during Ken Kesey and the Merry Pranksters' infamous

Acid Trips. Band members included Jerry Garcia, Bob Weir, Ron "Pig Pen" McKernan, Bill Kreutzmann, and Phil Lesh. The Grateful Dead's leader, Garcia, was known as "Captain Trips." LSD "changed everything" for the band, according to Garcia. Neal Cassady, the inspiration for Dean Moriarty, Jim Morrison's hero from Jack Kerouac's *On the Road*, drove the Merry Pranksters' bus. Cassady also took the stage before early Grateful Dead concerts to deliver "free-associational monologues." Garcia referred to Cassady as "the ultimate *something*—the ultimate person as art."

The Grateful Dead made their debut at the Avalon Ballroom in San Francisco on May 19, 1966. The group had a communal home at 710 Ashbury Street in that city. They performed along with Quicksilver Messenger Service and Jefferson Airplane at the "First Human Be-In," the prelude to the "Summer of Love" that attracted 20,000 attendees at Golden Gate Park in San Francisco on January 14, 1967. (The Doors were in attendance and dropped acid but did not perform at the event.) That night at the Avalon, the Doors received third billing behind the Grateful Dead and the Junior Wells Chicago Blues Band at the Fillmore Auditorium.

One of the Grateful Dead's earliest non-San Francisco gigs took place with the Doors at the Earl Warren Showgrounds in Santa Barbara on April 29, 1967. Morrison gratefully accepted some high-quality acid backstage courtesy of the

The Doors took the stage at the Earl Warren Showgrounds on May 27, 1967. In a previous concert a month earlier at the same venue with the Grateful Dead, Jim Morrison received some "purple-barrel acid" from the Dead's legendary sound engineer, Augustus Owsley Stanley.   *Courtesy of Kerry Humpherys/doors.com*

Dead and their legendary sound engineer, Augustus Owsley Stanley. Kesey later commented, "The Doors were playing and it was *such* a different feeling than our scene with the Acid Test. Lots of Hell's Angels. Really very, very dark. Slickly put on." According to Manzarek, the Dead had their own extensive support system and were completely insulated from other bands, rarely interacting with the Doors or any of their other contemporaries.

Tragically, the Dead's McKernan rejected LSD in favor of immense quantities of booze (he is rumored to have introduced former girlfriend Janis Joplin to the joys of Southern Comfort), and joined the "27 Club" when he died of liver disease in 1973. Over the years, the Grateful Dead evolved into the ultimate cult band with their dedicated fans, known as Deadheads.

Jefferson Airplane

Jefferson Airplane was formed by Marty Balin in 1965. Notable as the first rock band from San Francisco to get a major recording contract, Jefferson Airplane released the phenomenally successful album, *Surrealistic Pillow*, which spawned the hits "Somebody to Love" and "White Rabbit," in September 1967. Jefferson Airplane shared the bill with the Doors on numerous occasions, including an infamous concert at the Cheetah on April 9, 1967, in front of a crowd of approximately 3,000 fans. It was the first time the Doors were top-billed over Jefferson Airplane and also the concert where Morrison introduced his "tightrope walk," balancing precariously along the edge of the stage. Morrison then accomplished the first unintentional stage dive after losing his balance and falling eight feet into the crowd.

Jefferson Airplane also joined the Doors on their 1968 European Tour, which consisted of concerts at The Roundhouse in London, as well as shows in Stockholm, Frankfurt, and Amsterdam. As both bands wandered the streets of Amsterdam the afternoon before the concert, Morrison ingested every drug that was handed to him. Jefferson Airplane opened the concert that night and Morrison came out onstage during their set and started dancing wildly. Jefferson Airplane in turn reacted by playing "Plastic Fantastic Lover" faster and faster. Morrison eventually collapsed and was sent to the hospital. The Doors took the stage without him and performed admirably, with Manzarek taking over vocal duties. Morrison and Slick even enjoyed a one-night stand during the European Tour that she detailed in her autobiography, *Somebody to Love?* Slick and Paul Kantner of Jefferson Airplane introduced and narrated *The Doors Live in Europe 1968*.

Peanut Butter Conspiracy

A Los Angeles-based psychedelic rock band, the Peanut Butter Conspiracy formed in 1966 as a spin-off of a folk rock group called the Ashes. The band signed with Columbia Records in 1966 and released a single, "It's a Happening

Thing," which reached No. 93 on the U.S. charts. They soon released their debut album, *The Peanut Butter Conspiracy Is Spreading*, followed by *The Great Conspiracy*. The group featured Alan Brackett (bass/vocals), Lance Baker Fent (guitar), Jim Voight (drums), John Merrill (guitar/vocals), and Barbara "Sandi" Robison (vocals).

The Doors performed with the Peanut Butter Conspiracy several times, including a series of shows at Ciro's on April 21–23, 1967, that also included other long-forgotten Los Angeles bands, UFO and Kaleidoscope. The group also recorded music for such films as *Jud*; *Cherry Harry, and Raquel*; *Hell Ride*; and *Beyond the Valley of the Dolls* before breaking up around 1970.

Still relatively unknown in San Francisco in early 1967, the Doors were booked to open for the Peanut Butter Conspiracy, along with "the world's greatest light show."

Courtesy of Mark Smigel/mildequator.com

The Seeds

A truly bizarre Southern California proto-punk garage band, the Seeds claimed to have coined the term "flower power." One of the most popular acts during the peak years of the Sunset Strip scene, the Seeds were led by a true eccentric, Sky Saxon (real name: Richard Marsh), who was born a Mormon in Salt Lake City, and best known for the hit song "Pushin' Too Hard," as well as such classics as "Mr. Farmer" and "Can't Seem to Make You Mine."

According to the *Rolling Stone Album Guide*, "Compared to the Seeds, the Mothers of Invention seem labored, Arthur Lee comes across as a logician, and the Troggs sound tame. The band virtually defines the term 'guilty pleasure.'" Early on, the Seeds could often be heard at the Turkey Joint West before Rick and the Ravens started performing there, as well as at Bido Lito's and the Sea Witch. An early Bido Lito's ad for the band stated "Flower-Rock Sounds of The Seeds Five Nights a Week—It's Flower Music—It's Earthy—You'll Dig It!"

Since the band didn't use a bass player onstage, the keyboardist, Darryl Hooper, utilized a Fender Rhodes bass the same way Ray Manzarek did in the Doors. While they were still employed as house band at the Whisky A Go Go, the Doors opened for the Seeds at the Earl Warren Showgrounds in Santa Barbara on August 6, 1966. The Seeds released what was intended to be their psychedelic masterpiece, *Future*, in 1967. One of the highlights of the Seeds' brief career was a performance at a benefit concert with Buffalo Springfield, Johnny Rivers, and the Supremes for the United Negro College Fund at the Hollywood Bowl in April 1967. Unfortunately, the Seeds never caught on outside of Los Angeles and soon faded into obscurity. In the 1970s, Saxon joined a hippie spiritual cult called the Yahowha.

Sopwith Camel

Named after a British World War I biplane fighter and notable as the second San Francisco psychedelic rock band (after Jefferson Airplane) to be signed by a major record label, Sopwith Camel consisted of vocalist and saxophone player Peter Kraemer, guitarists Terry MacNeil and William Sievers, bassist Martin Beard, and drummer Norman Mayell. Formed in 1965, the band released their first album, *Sopwith Camel*, in 1967. It contained a hit single, "Hello, Hello," which reached No. 26 on the U.S. charts in January 1967, the same month that the Doors released their self-titled debut album. The Doors were third billed behind the Young Rascals and Sopwith Camel during their first gigs at the Fillmore Auditorium January 6–8, 1967.

Surprisingly, the band disbanded later that year but reformed in 1971 and recorded their second album in 1973 called *The Miraculous Hump Returns from the Moon* (which included such eclectic songs as "Coke, Suede and Waterbeds" and "Monkeys on the Moon") before breaking up for good in 1974.

Sparrow

Originally known as the Sparrows, this blues-influenced band was established in 1964 (and spawned from the same Venice Beach scene as the Doors) by brothers Dennis and Jerry Edmonton and Nick St. Nicholas. John Kay (born Joachim Fritz Krauledat in Germany) joined the band the following year. The group shortened its name to the Sparrow in May 1966, and somewhat later, to simply Sparrow. The Doors returned to San Francisco as headliners performing with Sparrow and Country Joe and the Fish at the Avalon Ballroom March 3–4, 1967.

The name change from Sparrow to Steppenwolf was suggested to Kay by record producer Gabriel Mekler, being inspired by Hermann Hesse's novel of the same name. As Steppenwolf the band released two classics—their proto-metal album, "Born to Be Wild" (which appeared on the soundtrack for the 1969 cult movie *Easy Rider*) and "Magic Carpet Ride." Most notably, "Born to Be Wild" introduced the phrase "heavy metal" to rock terminology. Steppenwolf's version of Hoyt Axton's "The Pusher" also appeared on the *Easy Rider* soundtrack.

The Doors often shared the stage during the early years with such classic 1960s bands as Steppenwolf (formerly known as Sparrow) and the Paul Butterfield Blues Band. *Courtesy of Kerry Humpherys/doors.com*

22

Under Television Skies

The Doors' Most Notable TV Performances

Good evening, now the Doors, here they are with their newest hit record!
                                                    —*Ed Sullivan*

In order to promote their self-titled debut album, which was released on January 4, 1967, the Doors turned in some rather forgettable performances on TV shows like *Shebang, American Bandstand,* and *Malibu U.* Everything changed when "Light My Fire" hit No. 1 on the charts on July 29, 1967, and the band was soon inundated with offers to appear on primetime shows such as *The Ed Sullivan Show, The Jonathan Winters Show,* and *The Smothers Brothers Comedy Hour.* Morrison hated lip-synching on these shows and the band started experimenting with short films to promote their new material such as the three-minute "Unknown Soldier" video, which was filmed in part on Venice Beach.

Shebang—January 1, 1967

On New Year's Day, just three days before the release of their first album, the Doors made an inauspicious television debut—lip-synching to "Break on Through (to the Other Side)"—on *Shebang,* a dance show that aired weekday afternoons on Los Angeles television station KTLA, Channel 5, Los Angeles. Hosted by disc jockey Casey Kasem and produced by *American Bandstand's* Dick Clark, *Shebang* was cancelled shortly thereafter.

Dressed in slacks and a jacket, the pre-leather Morrison looked like a college student and spent most of the performance hanging onto the microphone with his eyes closed. He looked extremely bored with the whole ordeal, while the rest of the Doors also went through the motions in a totally uninspired manner. The Doors' appearance on *Shebang* did little to help their first single, "Break on Through," which stalled at 126 on the Billboard Charts.

American Bandstand—July 22, 1967

The Doors made their national television debut on July 22, 1967, appearing on *American Bandstand* just one week before "Light My Fire" overtook "Windy" by the Association to assume the No. 1 spot on the charts. The midsummer edition of *American Bandstand* featured a countdown of the top ten hit songs for July 1967 with Jefferson Airplane's "White Rabbit" at No. 3, the Doors' "Light My Fire" at No. 2, and Procol Harum's "Whiter Shade of Pale" at No. 1. The Doors lip-synched both the hit single "Light My Fire" and "The Crystal Ship" at ABC Studios in Hollywood.

Host Dick Clark rather ineptly interviewed the band between songs. Clark: "A lot of people seem to think you come from San Francisco. Is that true?" Morrison: "Uh, no. We actually got together in L.A. But we do play in San Francisco a lot." Clark: "That's the explanation of why you have that association. Why is so much happening in San Francisco? You figured it out yet?" Morrison: "The West is the best." Clark: "All right! Fair enough . . . Have you selected a name for the new album yet?" Morrison: "I think it's *Strange Days*." Clark: All right, fair enough. We'll do the thing that set the whole music business on fire. Ladies and gentlemen, again—the Doors!"

Malibu U—August 25, 1967

"Light My Fire" reached No. 1 on the charts on July 29, 1967, and four weeks later the Doors performed the hit song on *Malibu U*, an American variety TV series that aired briefly for a total of just seven episodes in the summer of 1967. With a ridiculous premise that featured Ricky Nelson as the dean of a mythical college called Malibu U, the show aired on Friday nights at 8:30 p.m. *Variety* referred to *Malibu U* as "a 'cutesy' show—the gospel of young Americans according to Gidget."

The Doors taped their appearance in late July or early August in front of a 1940s-era fire engine at Leo Carrillo State Beach near Malibu, California. However, Morrison, who had become tired of lip-synching for these type of shows, never showed up for the filming. Krieger's nonidentical twin brother, Ron, stood in for the lead singer, who later agreed to film some close-ups, which were spliced into the performance.

The August 25 episode also featured Buffalo Springfield ("Bluebird"), Marvin Gaye ("Ain't That Peculiar"), Chad and Jeremy ("Distant Shores"), Lou Christie ("Something to Remind Me"), Robbie Porter ("Sure Good Loving You"), Sandy Posey, and Captain Beefheart and the Magic Band. During another infamous episode, *Malibu U* actually aired Leonard Nimoy's performance of the novelty song "The Ballad of Bilbo Baggins." The last episode of the show aired on September 1, 1967.

CBC Television Studios (Toronto)—September 14, 1967

Billed as "The Rock Scene: Like It Is," this Canadian Broadcasting Corporation (CBC) showcase on rock music, which was emceed by actor Noel Harrison, featured the Doors performing "Wake Up!" (from the "Celebration of the Lizard"), followed by a rare televised version of "The End" that omitted the entire Oedipal section. According to a review in *Variety*, "In their sequence, the Doors did one number 'The End' with the audience standing, dancing, lying on the floor and hugging the stage. Shots of the group were super-imposed on the audience and into it, giving the effect of confluence. There were many visual treats in this number and some superb musicianship was demonstrated particularly by the group's drummer."

Other performers included Jefferson Airplane ("White Rabbit"), Dionne Warwick ("Don't Make Me Over"), Eric Anderson, and Sergio Mendes with Brasil '66 ("Day Tripper"). Later that night, the Doors performed for a small audience at the Music Carnival in Cleveland. The CBC show aired on CBC-TV on October 16, 1967, while the Doors were performing at Steve Paul's the Scene in New York City. It was first aired in the United States on August 1, 1970, in a show called *Now Explosion*.

The Ed Sullivan Show—September 17, 1967

During their infamous appearance on *The Ed Sullivan Show*, the Doors were instructed by the show's producer, Bob Precht (Sullivan's son-in-law), to delete the word "higher" from the line "Girl we couldn't get much higher" from "Light My Fire," which had reached No. 1 on the charts in July of that year. Precht recommended that the band change the line to something like "Girl, you couldn't get much better."

The Doors were already used to such censorship as their own record company had made them remove the word "high" from "Break on Through," the first single from their self-titled debut album. Morrison assured Precht that they would come up with another line. Once Precht left, all four band members agreed that the leather-clad Morrison should sing the original lyrics anyway. According to Manzarek in *Light My Fire*, "The Doors' communal mind had gone conspiratorial. We were going to flip the bird at the Establishment. On national television!"

When they took the stage, the Doors were appalled by the tacky set, which was crowded with hanging doors of different sizes and colors. After the band performed a riveting version of "Light My Fire" that included the word "higher" before an audience of approximately ten million viewers, Sullivan refused to shake their hands and a furious Precht informed them they would never appear on the Sullivan show again. Morrison casually replied, "We just *did* the Sullivan show." Indeed, the Doors were never asked back. According to Manzarek, "We played the shit out of the song and Jim was magnificent. His performance was blood stirring. He was every girl's wet dream and every guy's idol of emulation. You either wanted him for your boyfriend or you wanted to be like him. He was great. *We* were great."

Somewhat forgotten in all the controversy is the fact that the Doors also performed a rather mediocre version of their new single "People Are Strange" on the show that night before "Light My Fire." Also appearing on the show with the Doors were Yul Brynner, Flip Wilson, Rodney Dangerfield, Steve Lawrence and Eydie Gorme, the Kessler Twins, and the Skating Bredos.

The Ed Sullivan Show, which made its debut in 1948, was no stranger to controversies over censorship. Sullivan personally booked the acts himself. During Elvis Presley's first performance on the show in 1956, the television host had ordered that Elvis be filmed from the waist up. In 1963, Bob Dylan refused to perform on the show when CBS censors banned him from singing "Talkin' John Birch Society Blues." During the Rolling Stones' 1965 performance, the band agreed to Sullivan's request to change the lyrics "Let's spend the night together" to "Let's spend some time together." However, just a year after the Doors appeared on the show, Sly & the Family Stone were allowed to sing the lyrics "Wanna take you higher" on *The Ed Sullivan Show*.

September 17, 1967, proved to be a truly historic night for rock 'n' roll since immediately following *The Ed Sullivan Show* the Who appeared on *The Smothers Brothers Comedy Hour* and set off a huge explosion during a performance of "My Generation" that singed Pete Townshend's hair and injured Keith Moon's arm. Fellow guests Bette Davis and Mickey Rooney sat in stunned silence, appalled by the anarchic display.

Murray the K in New York—September 22, 1967

An influential New York disc jockey, Murray Kaufman (1922–82) was an early supporter of the Beatles and often referred to himself as the "fifth Beatle." Known as "Murray the K," he produced a successful television special called *It's Happening, Baby*, which led to another show called *Murray the K in New York* that featured a music video-style format and an eclectic lineup of musicians that included the Doors, Otis Redding, Aretha Franklin, Spanky and Our Gang, and the Four Tops. The Doors video showed the performers in a windy New York City setting at Battery Park with Morrison lip-synching "People Are Strange" while the other Doors stood around awkwardly without instruments.

The Jonathan Winters Show—December 27, 1967

On December 27, 1967, the Doors appeared on the debut of *The Jonathan Winters Show*, performing "Light My Fire" and "Moonlight Drive." The band had actually taped the songs just before Christmas at CBS TV Studios in Los Angeles. They performed "Light My Fire" on a set that featured some psychedelic special effects. Sporting dark sunglasses, Morrison got caught in a chicken wire stage prop at the end of "Moonlight Drive." According to Densmore in *Riders on the Storm*, "It was an uptight, stiff vocal performance" and the Doors drummer felt that Morrison was "hurting the band" and "giving nothing as far as emotional singing goes."

Also appearing on the show that night were Red Skelton, Barbara Eden (*I Dream of Jeannie*), and Ivan Dixon (*Hogan's Heroes*). The Doors performed at Winterland Arena in San Francisco on the night the show aired and wheeled out a black-and-white TV onstage to catch their performance. When their segment aired, they stopped playing "Back Door Man" and sat onstage watching their performance in front of a somewhat bewildered audience. Densmore later remarked in *Riders on the Storm*, "We turned the TV off, went back to our instruments, and started playing 'Back Door Man' from the middle of the song where we'd left off. I'm sure most of the Winterland audience thought we were out of our minds."

The Doors Are Open (BBC)—October 4, 1968

Broadcast on BBC/Granada TV, *The Doors Are Open* featured the Doors performing at the London Roundhouse, a former railroad station converted into a 2,500-seat concert hall, interspersed with newsreel footage of various student demonstrations, including the 1968 Democratic Convention in Chicago and a demonstration known as the "Battle of Grosvenor Square" that took place at the American Embassy in London that year.

The Doors performed a slew of their greatest hits, including "When the Music's Over," "Five to One," "Spanish Caravan," "Hello, I Love You," "Back Door Man," "Crawlin' King Snake," "Wake Up!," "Light My Fire," and "The Unknown Soldier." The 65-minute, black-and-white video (originally titled *When the Mode of the Music Changes, the Walls of the City Will Shake*) also featured an interview with the Doors.

Morrison was impressed with *The Doors Are Open*, later remarking in an interview, "I thought the film was very exciting . . . The thing is, the guys that made the film had a thesis of what it was going to be before we even came over. We were going to be the political rock group, and it gave them the chance to whip out some of their anti-American sentiments, which they thought we were going to portray . . . but I still think they made an exciting film."

The Smothers Brothers Comedy Hour—December 15, 1968

The Doors appeared on "The Smother Brothers Comedy Hour" for the first and only time on December 15, 1968, and performed "Wild Child" and "Touch Me." The show had actually been taped two weeks earlier. During "Touch Me," the Doors were accompanied by the Smothers Brothers Orchestra and Curtis Amy, who lip-synched the saxophone solo, while Morrison skillfully crooned the lyrics in the style of one of his musical heroes, Frank Sinatra. Unfortunately, he blatantly missed his cue and came in late at the beginning of the second verse.

Robby Krieger sported a black eye of mysterious origin during the performance (ironically the Krieger-penned tune "Touch Me" was originally titled "Hit Me"). Krieger, who wore the black eye like a badge of honor, later confessed that he and Morrison had been accosted by some "rednecks" in a bar, and he got punched in the face while Morrison escaped unscathed.

The other song the Doors performed, "Wild Child," was the B-side to "Touch Me," which would reach No. 3 on the U.S. charts on February 15, 1969, behind Sly & the Family Stone's "Everyday People" and Tommy James & the Shondells' "Crimson and Clover."

Comedian George Carlin also appeared on the show that night. *The Smothers Brothers Comedy Hour* faced a variety of censorship issues during its brief tenure. In one famous instance, Joan Baez was censored for appearing on the show and paying tribute to her then-husband David Harris, who had been jailed for refusing military service. The show finally aired the segment but edited out the reason Harris had gone to prison. *The Smothers Brothers Comedy Hour* was abruptly cancelled on June 8, 1969. The whole story behind the show's cancellation was recounted in the 2002 documentary *Smothered*.

Critique Recording Sessions (PBS)—June 25, 1969

During the PBS *Critique Recording Sessions*, which were recorded in New York City April 28–29, 1969, the Doors performed a thirty-five-minute set that included "Five to One," "Tell All the People," "Alabama Song," "Back Door Man," "Wishful, Sinful," "Build Me a Woman," "Light My Fire," and "The Soft Parade," which Manzarek later referred to as "a song of the anguish of Jim's internal life. His turmoil. His need to rest. His need for succor."

The band also sat down for a ten-minute interview with influential *Village Voice* music critic Richard Goldstein, who was a big fan of the band and had praised them in early performances at New York City clubs such as Ondine and the Scene in 1966–67. It was in fact the band's first interview following the notorious concert at the Dinner Key Auditorium in Miami on March 1, 1969. In introducing the band, Goldstein stated, "A successful rock group has to combine technical virtuosity with a savage kind of grace."

Morrison, who sported a heavy beard, sunglasses, and a cigar, had obviously abandoned the "Lizard King" persona he had so carefully crafted just a couple of years before. The interview touched on the idea of a performer as shaman, with Morrison commenting, "I don't think the shaman from what I've read, is really too interested in defining his role in society. He's just more interested in pursuing his own fantasies. If he became too self-conscious of a function, you know, I think it might tend to ruin his own inner trip."

Morrison also expressed nostalgia for the days the band honed their material in the smaller clubs as opposed to the huge outdoor stadiums and other larger venues they were now playing. Performing night after night in clubs allowed the Doors to develop songs so well that eventually the music became a hypnotic undercurrent over which Morrison would improvise freely as a singer and front man.

At the end of the interview, Morrison even predicted the development of electronic music: "I guess in four or five years, the new generation's music will have a synthesis of those two elements, and some third thing that . . . might rely heavily on electronics . . . tapes . . . I can envision maybe one person with a lot of machines, tapes and electronic set-ups, singing or speaking and using machines."

The PBS special also featured a fifteen-minute discussion roundtable that consisted of Goldstein, WNEW-FM's William "Rosko" Mercer, Patricia Kennealy (who later "married" Morrison in a Celtic handfasting ceremony), and Alfred G. Aronowitz.

23

Blood on the Rise

The Top Ten Most Notorious Doors Concerts

There are no rules at a rock concert. Anything is possible.

—*Jim Morrison*

With Jim Morrison onstage, each Doors concert became progressively more unpredictable, thrilling, and potentially dangerous. Ironically, when Morrison started performing at Sunset Strip dives such as the London Fog in 1966, he usually sang with his back to the audience because he lacked confidence in his singing abilities. However, as he honed his skills at the Whisky A Go Go, Morrison started to slowly build upon his "Lizard King" persona. With the success of "Light My Fire," things changed overnight, and the Doors started playing huge arenas and outdoor stadiums where audiences expected Morrison to exhibit outrageous behavior. He never failed to disappoint, culminating with the disastrous Dinner Key Auditorium in Miami on March 1, 1969.

Whisky A Go Go, August 21, 1966

The infamous night that the Doors got fired from their gig as house band at the Whisky A Go Go started with Morrison missing the first set. Whisky management demanded that the other Doors go find him. Hiding under the bed in his room at the Tropicana Motel, Morrison had dropped a heroic amount of acid. The other Doors had to coax him back to the Whisky to perform the set.

During the middle of the set, Morrison surprisingly requested that the band play "The End," traditionally a song that closed each night's performance. The song became more and more hypnotic, and then Morrison launched into the Oedipal portion, which the band had never heard him do before: "Father, I want to kill you! . . . Mother . . . I want to fuck you!" The audience was totally mesmerized by the performance, but the owners of the Whiskey were outraged and fired the band.

Forest Hills Tennis Stadium, August 12, 1967

In one of the classic booking mistakes of all time, the Doors got hired to open for Simon & Garfunkel at Forest Hills Tennis Stadium in Queens, New York. Both Paul Simon and Art Garfunkel were hometown heroes who had graduated from Forest Hills' P.S. 164 (they had met during a sixth grade production of *Alice and Wonderland*, Simon playing the white rabbit and Garfunkel the Cheshire cat). The duo, who originally performed as "Tom and Jerry," scored a No. 1 hit with "Sounds of Silence" in January 1966.

The night got off to a rough start even before the show began when Simon dropped backstage to wish the Doors good luck and Morrison totally ignored him. According to Densmore in *Riders on the Storm*, Simon was very friendly, but Morrison gave him "the worst vibes, in short of saying, 'Get the fuck out of our dressing room.'" The Doors performed an abbreviated set that included "Break on Through," "Back Door Man," "Light My Fire," and "The End." The crowd was totally unresponsive. According to Manzarek in *Light My Fire*, it was "the worst reception" of the Doors' entire career: "The audience hated us! They had come to see smarm and were instead getting rock abyss from the opening act." Morrison later told Manzarek it was "the worst gig he had ever played and the worst audience he had ever experienced."

In *Follow the Music*, Elektra Records president Jac Holzman remembered "escaping" from the concert with "crowds jostling the car and pounding on the windows, with Jim sitting in the back seat, unbelieving yet loving every minute." The Doors were not the first band to get a hostile reception at Forest Hills. When Bob Dylan performed there three days before his infamous Newport Folk Festival appearance in 1965, he faced a belligerent crowd. In addition, the Jimi Hendrix Experience faced animosity from the crowd when they opened for the Monkees at Forest Hills.

University of Michigan, October 20, 1967

Jim Morrison took the stage drunk in a gymnasium at the University of Michigan Homecoming Dance, and chaos ensued. A band called the Long Island Sound was the opening act and performed a well-received set that included a couple of Beatles tunes from the recently released *Sgt. Pepper's* album. Then the Doors took the stage without Morrison and started jamming to "Soul Kitchen." When drunk and/or stoned Morrison was finally coaxed onstage, he could barely stand up. After a tepid response from the crowd, which was basically full of frat boys and sorority chicks, Morrison decided to mock them relentlessly, making weird sounds into the microphone, dropping F-bombs, and throwing things into the crowd. The crowd responded by booing, throwing paper cups at the stage, and finally leaving the concert in droves.

Frustrated by Morrison's antics, Densmore threw down his drumsticks and stormed off the stage, followed shortly by Krieger. Densmore later remarked that the concert was "the first leak, coming from some demon in Jim's psyche." Manzarek then grabbed a guitar and accompanied Morrison, who started to sing an early version of "Maggie M'Gill." They then made a hasty and unceremonious exit from the stage. Dance organizers were able to get the Long Island Sound to perform another set.

Morrison's antics inspired at least one audience member: James Osterberg (a.k.a. Iggy Pop), a University of Michigan dropout who was able to gain admittance with his old college ID. In *Please Kill Me*, Pop remarked that the band initially took the stage without Morrison and "sounded like pure shit." When an obviously inebriated Morrison came out and started singing, "he sang in a pussy voice—a falsetto. He sang like Betty Boop and refused to sing in a normal voice . . . I was very excited. I love the antagonism; I loved that he was pissing them off . . . The gig lasted only fifteen or twenty minutes because they had to pull Morrison offstage and get him out of there fast, because the people were gonna attack him. It made a big impression on me. That's when I thought, Look how awful they are, and they've got the number-one single in the country! If this guy can do it, I can do it. And I gotta do it now. I can't wait any longer."

New Haven Arena, Hartford, Connecticut, December 9, 1967

Just one day after his twenty-fourth birthday, Jim Morrison became the first rock star to get arrested onstage during a performance. Several days before the concert, the New Haven Police Department had faced criticism for using excessive force during an antiwar demonstration. Built in 1924, the New Haven Arena accommodated more than 4,000 people and was at that time the home to the New Haven Blades of the Eastern Hockey League.

Before the concert, Morrison was backstage making out with a coed from nearby Southern Connecticut State University (*not* Patricia Kennealy as portrayed in Oliver Stone's 1991 film) when he got maced by a police officer who failed to recognize him as the lead singer of the Doors. The concert began with a typical set that included "Five to One," "Unhappy Girl," "People Are Strange," and "Break on Through." However, as the rest of the band launched into "When the Music's Over," Morrison embarked on an extended rant about his treatment by the cop backstage: "I want to tell you about something that happened just two minutes ago right here in New Haven. This is New Haven, isn't it? New Haven, Connecticut, United States of America?"

Morrison proceeded to describe the incident backstage and concluded by shouting, "We want the whole fucking world and we want it . . . NOW!" The police then ordered the stage manager to turn on the house lights. Lieutenant James P. Kelly appeared with several other officers onstage. Morrison demanded the lights be turned off. When Kelly headed toward him, Morrison pointed the

Oliver Stone dramatized Jim Morrison's New Haven arrest in his 1991 film *The Doors*, complete with inaccuracies such as labeling the date of the concert "1968" and placing Patricia Kennealy backstage with Morrison.   *Author's Collection*

mic at him and remarked, "Say your thing, man." The officers then arrested him. They took him backstage where they reportedly roughed him up a bit and then drove him to the station, where he was charged with a lewd and obscene performance, breach of peace, and resisting arrest. Morrison was released on $1,500 bond. The charges against him were later dropped. In the resulting confusion immediately after the concert, three journalists working on a feature for *Life* magazine were also arrested: Michael Zwerin, jazz critic for the *Villlage Voice*; Tim Page, a *Life* photographer; and Yvonne Chabrier, a *Life* researcher. All were eventually acquitted. The story appeared in the April 12, 1968, issue of *Life*.

According to Densmore, "The group was too out of hand. Jim was crazy. And I wanted to escape from the growing fear that this was just the beginning. Ray later said that at the time, he, too, was worried that New Haven was the beginning of the erosion of everything we'd worked for." A portrayal of the New Haven incident in the *New York Times* ("New Haven Police Close 'The Doors'") somewhat comically described the reason police had given for making the arrest: "The police contended they had received complaints from audience members who did not like foul language that the performer allegedly used."

Morrison later paid offhand tribute to the New Haven incident in "Peace Frog" with the line "Blood in the streets in the town of New Haven." In addition, a fan captured some footage of the onstage arrest that was later used in the "Roadhouse Blues" video. Ironically, the former site of the New Haven Arena is now the headquarters of the New Haven Division of the FBI.

Chicago Coliseum, May 10, 1968

The Doors' first performance in Chicago, Manzarek's hometown, was disastrous as Morrison attempted to provoke the crowd of 4,000 fans into a riot. Morrison brazenly encouraged the audience to move past the flimsy police barricades toward the stage. After the house lights came on and the Doors retreated backstage, a teenage fan took a swan dive from the balcony into the crowd below and amazingly escaped unharmed (according to eyewitnesses, he exclaimed "Wow! what a turn on!"). The crowd then made it to the stage and destroyed some of the band's equipment before the police were able to assume control.

The set list at the Chicago concert included "Soul Kitchen" (which featured the intro to "Runnin' Blue" in tribute to Otis Redding), "Break on Through," "Alabama Song," "Back Door Man," "Five to One," "When the Music's Over," "The Crystal Ship," "Wake Up!," and "Light My Fire."

Singer Bowl, Flushing Meadows, Queens, New York, August 2, 1968

The Doors' notorious performance at the Singer Bowl (which had been built by the Singer Sewing Machine Company for the 1964 World's Fair) on a hot and humid summer night before a boisterous crowd turned into total mayhem. Billed as "The New York Rock Festival at the Singer Bowl in Queens," the concert drew approximately 17,000 people and also featured the Kangaroo and the Who. Things got off to a bad start with the breakdown of the "state-of-the-art" revolving stage at the venue. Tensions arose among fans after there was a one-hour delay between the time the Who's set ended and the Doors took the stage. Fights erupted throughout the stadium during the Doors' performance. At the conclusion of the performance, fans started charging the police barricades and tearing up the wooden seats and throwing them in all directions.

According to Jeff Silverman, a Doors fan who attended the concert and was quoted in *Follow the Music*, it all started with some "incredible eye contact" between Morrison and a Hispanic girl near the stage. During the break of a song, Morrison stared at the girl and shouted, "Mexican whore, come suck my prick." Silverman claimed that the girl's boyfriend then grabbed a wooden folding chair "and just heaped it on the stage and all of a sudden chairs started flying." With the place in total pandemonium, Morrison "is just dancing around, having the time of his life," according to Silverman. The Doors were eventually forced to abandon the stage.

Doors road manager Vince Treanor later commented, "People were hurt, equipment was stolen, a tremendous amount of damage was done." Watching the chaos from one side of the stage, the Who's Pete Townshend was reportedly both fascinated and appalled, leading him to write the song, "Sally Simpson," which later appeared in the rock opera, *Tommy*. The song's title character gets injured after trying to touch Tommy: "Tommy whirled around as a uniformed man/Threw her off the stage."

In a review of the Singer Bowl concert, *Variety* commented, "The kids were restless due to the concert's late start, a long intermission, and the addition of a third act, the Kangaroo. Perhaps topping off these events were The Doors' lyrics, many of which refer to death, power, violence, and comment on society's bizarre aspects, and the wild theatrics of the group's lead singer and new contemporaneous sex symbol, Jim Morrison."

Footage of the Singer Bowl debacle was captured for the *Feast of Friends* documentary and appears in the 2010 documentary *When You're Strange*. In one scene,

(Directions other side)

Just two weeks after the notorious New Haven concert, the Doors performed two shows at the Shrine Exposition Hall in Los Angeles on December 22–23, 1967. On the second night, the show was interrupted by police because of some "violent behavior" exhibited by audience members.   *Courtesy of Mark Smigel/mildequator.com*

Morrison was filmed backstage tending to a female fan who had suffered a head injury from a flying chair.

Cleveland Public Auditorium, August 3, 1968

Just one night after the Singer Bowl debacle, the Doors performed at Musicarnival in Cleveland, where another riot nearly broke out. Briefly interviewed backstage before the show, an extremely intoxicated Morrison was asked to define the band's act. "We're erotic politicians," he responded. Asked what his interests were, Morrison paraphrased a line from his official Elektra biography: "Anything that has to do with revolt, disorder, chaos, activity that's got no meaning."

Morrison reportedly took the stage with a bottle of whisky in one hand, while flipping off the audience of approximately 9,200 people with the other. Similar to the Miami concert in 1969, Morrison kept interrupting songs to talk with the audience (saying things like "We're gonna have a real good time, right?"), while the band tried desperately to steer him back into performance mode. At one point during "Light My Fire," Morrison jumped off the stage into the restless audience, which eventually started tearing up the auditorium's wooden seating. The concert was filmed for the Doors' documentary, *Feast of Friends*.

Concertgebou, Amsterdam, Holland, Netherlands, September 15, 1968

During the afternoon before the Amsterdam concert, which was part of the 1968 European Tour, the Doors and Jefferson Airplane wandered around the city sightseeing. Morrison ingested every bit of hashish that was offered to him by fans on the street. When Jefferson Airplane opened the concert, Morrison staggered onstage and started dancing wildly. The band launched into "Plastic Fantastic Lover" as Morrison spun maniacally around until he collapsed. He was then taken to the hospital, where he spent the night under observation. According to Grace Slick in her memoir *Somebody to Love?*, "We all ingested heavily, but Jim was the champ. An all-day, all-night consumption of everything available had turned him into a running pinwheel. Airplane opened that night and he came flying onto the stage during our set and collapsed. Dancing toward death, he was rushed to the hospital . . . Jim recuperated through the next day and was back onstage for the following evening's performance; that he lived as long as he did was amazing to me."

Doors road manager Vince Treanor took the stage, announced that Morrison would not be able to perform, and gave the audience the option of hearing the other three Doors perform or getting a refund. The audience chose to hear the Doors, and they performed a lively set with Manzarek assuming vocal duties. The set included "Break on Through," "Soul Kitchen," "Alabama Song," "Back Door Man," "Hello, I Love You," "Light My Fire," and "The Unknown Soldier."

Densmore remarked that Manzarek "handled the vocals fairly well." In the local newspaper the next day, the focus was on Densmore's performance, which had him beaming in front of the other band members. According to Manzarek, Densmore's ego had become "bloated," and he suffered from "delusions of grandeur."

Dinner Key Auditorium, Miami, Florida, March 1, 1969

The infamous Dinner Key Auditorium concert signaled the beginning of the end for the Doors. It led to an arrest warrant for Morrison, cancelled tour dates, and a forty-day trial. The Dinner Key Auditorium originally had been built as a hangar at the Pan American World Airways seaplane base at Dinner Key, which was located in the Coconut Grove neighborhood of Miami. The overstuffed venue contained approximately 13,000 fans on a hot and humid South Florida night. A totally inebriated Morrison arrived in Miami late after missing his flight and drinking heavily during the journey.

Bearded and wearing a leather hat with a skull and crossbones, Morrison was in no mood to sing "Light My Fire" that night. Fueled with ideas from the radical Living Theatre (Morrison had attended every one of their performances of *Paradise Now* the week before), the lead singer started berating the audience with an extended monologue during "Five to One," calling them "a bunch of fuckin' idiots." The sixty-five-minute "concert" devolved into chaos as the stage began to collapse, and at one point Morrison was thrown into the crowd. As Densmore and Krieger fled the stage, Manzarek continued to play the keyboards, and Morrison led a snake dance through the crowd.

Morrison was later charged with one felony and three misdemeanors: lewd and lascivious behavior, indecent exposure, open profanity, and drunkenness.

Seattle Center Coliseum, June 5, 1970

Just one-third of the seats at the 15,000-seat Seattle Center Coliseum had been sold for the concert. For no apparent reason, hostilities erupted between the crowd and the Doors from the beginning of the show. Most of the fans just shouted for "Light My Fire" throughout the duration of the concert, while Morrison appeared remote, distracted, and totally uninterested in performing. He even recited his poem, "Adolf Hitler Is Still Alive," sang mediocre versions of "Roadhouse Blues" and "When the Music's Over," and even made a crack about Seattle during the performance, remarking, "Seattle reminds you of a late 1930's version of 20 years in the future." During the Doors' finale, a forgettable version of "The End," the power in the Coliseum was abruptly cut off, and the house lights were turned on. On a positive note, blues legend Albert King also performed a well-received set that included the songs "Born Under a Bad Sign" and "Oh, Pretty Woman."

In a review of the concert for the *Seattle Times* ("The Doors Stumble Through a Concert"), critic Victor Stredicke remarked that Morrison "dawdled inexcusably between selections" and "got the coldest reception this town has ever accorded a superstar." In the *Seattle Post-Intelligencer*, reviewer Patrick MacDonald called Morrison "a parody of his former self . . . He seems to be quite bored with what he is doing. Morrison and the Doors . . . are well on their way to becoming an anachronism." In *The Doors on the Road*, Doors biographer Greg Shaw called the Seattle concert "undoubtedly one of the most difficult and regrettable shows of the 1970 tour."

24

See Me Change

Songs Modified by the Doors During Live Performances

Jim was magical—he never knew quite what he was going to do each night, and that's what was so exciting, the suspense, because obviously we didn't really know either.

—John Densmore

The Doors were known for their unpredictable stage performances, and Jim Morrison would often insert bits of poetry and stories within some of the songs for greater impact. It all started back in the early days at Sunset Strip clubs such as the London Fog and the Whisky A Go Go when the band extended songs like "Light My Fire" and "The End" just to fill the sets. According to Frank Lisciandro in his memoir *Jim Morrison: An Hour of Magic*, "Jim was the first rocker to reunite all of the elements of theater and restore them to original use. It was like street theater or a happening. It was guerilla theater, the Living Theater, and mime."

"Build Me a Woman"

Morrison's bluesy "Build Me a Woman" became controversial once he inserted the lines, "I'm a Sunday trucker, Christian motherfucker." The song also contains a sexual reference in "I've got the poontang blues." The Doors actually sang "Build Me a Woman" on the PBS *Critique* show, which aired on June 25, 1969. The unedited version can be heard on the *Live in New York* CD that is included with *The Doors Box Set* (1997). "Build Me a Woman" also appeared on the Doors' first live album, *Absolutely Live*, which was released in 1970.

"Break on Through #2"

During live performances of "Break on Through (to the Other Side)," Morrison liked to incorporate a version known as "Dead Cats, Dead Rats" into the song, which featured lyrics such as "Dead cats, dead rats, did you see what they were at, alright/Dead cat in a top hat." When the Doors performed during their induction into the Rock and Roll Hall of Fame in 1993, Eddie Vedder of Pearl Jam joined them onstage and sang the "Dead Cats, Dead Rats" version of "Break on Through."

"Gloria"

Them's classic hit "Gloria," which was written by Van Morrison and first recorded in 1967, soon became a garage rock staple. As the house band at the Whisky A Go Go, the Doors even got the opportunity to perform "Gloria" with Them onstage during the summer of 1966. The Doors loved performing "Gloria" in concert, and Morrison even added some new, dirtier lyrics to the song: "Wrap your legs around my neck, wrap your arms around my feet/Wrap your hair around my skin, wrap your lips around my cock." In fact, "Gloria" was included on the Doors' live album *Alive, She Cried*, which was released in 1983. Them's "Gloria" received the Grammy Hall of Fame Award in 1999.

During a December 26, 1967, concert at the Winterland Arena, Jim Morrison paid tribute to the late Otis Redding, who died in a plane crash several weeks earlier.

Courtesy of Ida Miller/idafan.com

"Light My Fire"

Morrison got bored with performing "Light My Fire," and one of the ways he would liven it up in concert was to add the macabre "Graveyard Poem" to the middle of the song: "A girl got drunk and balled the dead/And I gave empty sermons to my head/Cemetery, cool and quiet/Hate to leave your sacred lay/Dread the milky coming of the day."

"The End"

One of the earliest Doors songs, "The End," started out as a simple, three-minute goodbye song. However, it morphed into an eleven-minute epic by the time the Doors recorded it for their debut album. In concert, Morrison performed multiple versions of the song. For instance, at the Hollywood Bowl concert on July 5, 1968, Morrison incorporated a story within the song, "Have you seen the accident outside? . . . Six bachelors and their bride." He then recited an "Ode to a Grasshopper" after seeing what he thought was a grasshopper

During the "Roadhouse Blues" Tour, the Doors performed at the Felt Forum on January 17, 1970, and Jim Morrison incorpo-rated a morbid "Bring out your dead" dirge into the night's version of "The End."

Courtesy of Logan Janzen/mildequator.com

onstage (it turned out to be a moth): "I have a big green grasshopper out there/ Have you seen my grasshopper, mama?"

"When the Music's Over"

During the New Haven Arena concert on December 9, 1967, the Doors per-formed "When the Music's Over." Just before the song's climax, Morrison launched into a rant about having been maced backstage while he was making out with a coed from a nearby college before the show: "I want to tell you a story. It happened just a few minutes ago, right here in New Haven, Connecticut . . ." After relating the whole incident and firing up the audience, Morrison returned to "When the Music's Over," screaming "We want the whole fucking world and we want it . . . NOW!" After the song, the house lights came on, and the police arrested Morrison onstage, making him the first rock singer ever arrested onstage. At the precinct, Morrison was charged with a lewd and obscene perfor-mance, breach of peace, and resisting arrest (the charges were later dropped).

"Five to One"

At the notorious Miami concert at Dinner Key Auditorium on March 1, 1969, a heavily inebriated Morrison was in no mood to sing, but the band kept trying to bring him back in the fold and continue singing. He would have none of it and during "Five to One," Morrison slurred his way through two stanzas before berat-ing the audience: "You're all a bunch of fuckin' idiots! Lettin' people tell you what you're gonna do! Lettin' people push you around." This infamous version of "Five to One" can be heard on the *Without a Safety Net* CD in *The Doors Box Set*.

"Soul Kitchen"

During the middle of a rendition of "Soul Kitchen" at the Chicago Coliseum on May 10, 1968, Morrison inserted the first lines from "Runnin' Blue" in tribute to singer Otis Redding, who had died in a plane crash on December 10, 1967: "Poor Otis dead and gone/Left me here to sing his song." Redding had been scheduled to perform with the Doors at the Winterland Arena in San Francisco on December 26 and was replaced by Chuck Berry. Robby Krieger actually wrote "Runnin' Blue" for *The Soft Parade* album.

In one of their longest performances ever, at the Long Beach Sports Arena on February 7, 1970, the Doors performed extended versions of both "When the Music's Over" and "Light My Fire."   *Courtesy of Mark Smigel/mildequator.com*

25

C'mon People, Don't You Look So Down

The Biggest Events and Festivals Where the Doors Played

When we perform, we're participating in the creation of a world, and we celebrate that with the crowd.

—*Jim Morrison*

The Doors missed out on two of the biggest rock festivals in history: Monterey Pop in 1967 (they were not invited) and Woodstock in 1969 (they declined the invitation). The band simply did not do well at outdoor concerts, especially those held during the daytime. The vibe at these festivals was all wrong and simply could not accommodate Jim Morrison's dark lyrics combined with the mesmerizing sounds of Ray Manzarek's hypnotic keyboards, Robby Krieger's intricate guitar playing, and John Densmore's intense drumming style. In addition, if Morrison disliked the venue, he would often just slump over the microphone, drink himself into a stupor, and half-heartedly go through the motions. However, the Doors did manage to perform at several historic festivals such as the Toronto Rock and Revival Concert in 1968 that featured the first performance of John Lennon with his Plastic Ono Band and the Isle of Wight Festival (where an exhausted Morrison turned in a notably lackluster performance) in 1970 that drew approximately 600,000 people and remains one of the biggest rock festivals of all time.

The Fantasy Faire & Magic Festival—June 10, 1967

One of the first true rock festivals, the Fantasy Faire & Magic Festival has been completely overshadowed in history by the Monterey Pop Festival, which took place just a week later. Billed as "a thousand wonders and a two-day collage of beautiful music," the Fantasy Faire & Magic Festival took place at the Mt. Tamalpais Outdoor Theater in Marin County, California, before a sold-out crowd of approximately 15,000 people. Morrison was unusually animated during the Doors sets, reportedly swinging on flagpoles located on both sides of the stage and going into some of his shamanistic dance routines during instrumental portions of songs.

The eclectic lineup at this early rock festival included the Fifth Dimension, Dionne Warwick, Canned Heat, Jim Kweskin Jug Band, Moby Grape, 13th Floor Elevators, Spanky and Our Gang, Roger Collins, Blackburn and Snow, Sparrow, Every Mother's Son, Kaleidoscope, Chocolate Watch Band, Mojo Men, Merry Go Round, Jefferson Airplane, the Byrds, P. F. Sloan, the Seeds, the (New) Grass Roots, the Loading Zone, Tim Buckley, Hugh Masekela, Steve Miller Blues Band, Country Joe and the Fish, Smokey Robinson and the Miracles, Captain Beefheart and the Magic Band, Sons of Champlin, Lamp of Childhood, Mystery Trend, Penny Nichols, Merry Go Round, and New Salvation Army Band.

According to a review in the *San Francisco Chronicle* ("Bash on Mt. Tam" by Maitland Zane), the festival featured "wild sounds and wild colors, skydivers and side-shows, bizarre hippies from the Haight-Ashbury and T-shirted fraternity boys from Cal., young people necking on the sunburnt slopes and children sitting wide-eyed in a real teepee, Hell's Angels munching peanut butter sandwiches at a health food bar . . . There was something for everyone."

Northern California Folk-Rock Festival—May 19, 1968

The two-day Northern California Folk-Rock Festival took place at the Santa Clara Fairgrounds in San Jose, California. Other performers on the bill included the Grateful Dead, Steve Miller Band, Big Brother & the Holding Company, Jefferson Airplane, the Animals, Kaleidoscope, the Youngbloods, the Electric Flag, Taj Mahal, and others. The concert was filmed for the Doors' documentary, *Feast of Friends*.

As the afternoon wore on, the heat became intense as the sun scorched the crowd. Tempers flared and the Hell's Angel's reportedly beat up some people backstage. The crowd, which preferred San Francisco bands such as the Grateful Dead and Jefferson Airplane, treated the Doors with indifference. The band's forgettable performance at the festival—an outdoor concert during the day, which Morrison especially hated—would factor into their decision not to attend Woodstock the following year. In a later interview, Morrison remarked, "We've never done too well in those outdoor daytime concerts. I think that we need the night and a sort of theater-type atmosphere and mood in which to work. There's something about the daylight and the open spaces that just sort of dissipates the whole magic."

Seattle Pop Festival—July 27, 1969

This three-day festival took place at Gold Creek Park in Seattle with an estimated crowd of 40,000. The Doors' set list included "When the Music's Over," "Light My Fire," "Five to One," and "The End." During "When the Music's Over," a fan threw a paper cup at Morrison, who sported a full beard and was overweight, and

The Doors closed the two-day Northern California Folk-Rock Festival (May 18–19, 1968), following the Grateful Dead, the Animals, Big Brother and the Holding Company, Jefferson Airplane, and others. *Courtesy of Mark Smigel/mildequator.com*

SATURDAY		SUNDAY	
10:30 AM - 11:00 AM	MORNING REIGN	10:30 AM - 10:45 AM	OMAR
11:00 AM - 11:30 AM	INDIAN HEADBAND	10:45 AM - 11:00 AM	ELGIN MARBLE
11:30 AM - 12:00 Noon	TRANSATLANTIC RAILROAD	11:00 AM - 11:30 AM	MINT TATOO
12:00 Noon - 12:30 PM	CHROME SYRCUS	11:30 AM - 12:10 PM	TAJ MAHAL
12:30 PM - 1:00 PM	SONS OF CHAMPLIN	12:10 PM - 12:50 PM	PEOPLE
1:00 PM - 1:30 PM	PEOPLE	12:50 PM - 1:30 PM	LOADING ZONE
1:30 PM - 2:15 PM	YOUNGBLOODS	1:30 PM - 2:15 PM	ASHISH KHAN, SHAMIN AHMED, TARANOTH RAO
2:15 PM - 3:00 PM	STEVE MILLER BAND	2:15 PM - 3:00 PM	YOUNGBLOODS
3:00 PM - 3:45 PM	GRATEFUL DEAD	3:00 PM - 3:45 PM	ELECTRIC FLAG
3:45 PM - 4:30 PM	BIG BROTHER & HOLDING COMPANY	3:45 PM - 4:30 PM	COUNTRY JOE & THE FISH
4:30 PM - 5:30 PM	JEFFERSON AIRPLANE	4:30 PM - 5:30 PM	DOORS

A year before they headlined the Toronto Rock & Roll Revival, the Doors performed a long-forgotten show at Toronto's Coliseum Exhibition Park on April 20, 1968.
Courtesy of Derek Pattison/mildequator.com

Morrison flipped him off. The versions of "Light My Fire" and "Five to One" were uninspired.

This was the only time the Doors performed with Led Zeppelin. Other performers included Bo Diddley, Chuck Berry, the Flying Burrito Brothers, Vanilla Fudge, Ten Years After, Guess Who, Albert Collins, Santana, the Youngbloods, Tim Buckley, It's a Beautiful Day, the Byrds, the Flock, Charles Lloyd, Lee Michaels, Spirit, Blacksnake, Chicago Transit Authority, Lonnie Mack, and others. The Black Panthers provided security.

Reviewing the festival for *Poppin*, Edd Jeffords remarked, "Once one of the vital influences in rock, The Doors apparently have been captured entirely by the ego-tripping of Morrison. Instead of giving their audiences the music that turned us all on a couple of years back, The Doors now come on like some kind of carnival sideshow, with Morrison as the geek out front."

Toronto Rock & Roll Revival Concert—September 13, 1969

This one-day, 13 1/2 hour festival was originally promoted as a tribute to '50s rockers, but tickets sold poorly, and the promoters added other groups such as the Doors and the up-and-coming Alice Cooper Band. Even with the Doors as headliners, only 800 tickets had been sold just a week before the concert. In desperation, the promoters contacted John Lennon and asked him if he would like to emcee the show. Surprisingly he offered to perform at the concert with his newly formed Plastic Ono Band. With Lennon on the bill, ticket sales took off, and the venue completely sold out its 22,000 seats.

It was Lennon's first gig without the Beatles. The Plastic Ono Band consisted of Lennon, Yoko Ono, Eric Clapton on guitar, Klaus Voorman on bass, and Alan White on drums. The band played "Blue Suede Shoes," "Money," "Cold Turkey," and "Give Peace a Chance." Other performers included many of the Doors' earliest musical influences such as Chuck Berry, Gene Vincent, Bo Diddley (who later would sing a cover of "Love Her Madly" on the Doors tribute album *Stoned Immaculate*), Little Richard, Jerry Lee Lewis, and Lord Sutch. During

Alice Cooper's set, the shock rocker launched a live chicken into the audience (he later confessed that he thought it could fly), and the poor bird was torn to pieces by the crowd.

The Doors' set list included "When the Music's Over," "Break on Through," "Back Door Man," "The Crystal Ship," "Light My Fire," and "The End." During "Back Door Man," Morrison inserted a line from a new song, "Roadhouse Blues," that he was still working on: "Keep your eyes on the road, your hands upon the wheel." During the intro to "The End," Morrison paid tribute to the other performers, stating that it was "a great honor to perform on the same stage with so many illustrious musical geniuses." An album of the performance, *Live Peace in Toronto*, was released by Apple Records on December 15, 1969.

The Toronto Rock & Roll Revival Concert was the only time the Doors shared a bill with any of the Beatles. However, Morrison had met Lennon once before on September 23, 1968, when he stopped by Abbey Road Studios during one of their recording sessions. The Beatles were working on "Happiness Is a Warm Gun." According to an unfounded rumor, Morrison sang a chorus on one take. Lennon was murdered at the age of forty in 1980 on December 8 (coincidentally Morrison's birthday; he would have been thirty-seven years old).

Isle of Wight Festival—August 30, 1970

The Doors took a break from the Miami Trial (Judge Murray Goodman granted a five-day recess) and flew across the Atlantic to perform at the third annual Isle of Wight Festival, off the coast of England. Supposed to be the "British Woodstock" and billed as "the largest and most spectacular Festival ever," the three-day festival drew approximately 600,000 attendees (surpassing the crowd at Woodstock the year before and still the biggest UK rock festival of all time). The festival featured a star-studded lineup that included the Who, Jimi Hendrix, the Moody Blues, Sly & the Family Stone, Miles Davis, Joni Mitchell, Donovan, Richie Havens, Leonard Cohen, and others. Tiny Tim even took the stage! In *Light My Fire*, Manzarek called Isle of Wight "the last great hippie fest."

The Isle of Wight Festival had inauspicious beginnings in 1968 when Jefferson Airplane headlined to an estimated 10,000 people. Other acts that year included Arthur Brown, the Move, Tyrannosaurus Rex, Plastic Penny, and the Pretty Things. In his first performance since his 1966 motorcycle accident, Bob Dylan headlined the 1969 festival, and attendance rose to approximately 300,000. The 1969 Isle of Wight Festival began just eleven days after Woodstock ended. Accommodating upwards of 600,000 for the 1970 festival fans proved to be a nightmare for concert organizers. The island itself was home to a population of less than 100,000. Gate-crashing was a major problem.

Morrison and Roger Daltrey shared two bottles of Southern Comfort before the show in front of a huge bonfire and got "very plastered," according to the Who lead singer. A writer who saw Morrison before he took the stage commented, "He was like a ghost, man, walking around backstage with a can of beer in his hand." The Doors' set was sandwiched between Emerson Lake & Palmer and the Who. Still exhausted from the long flight, preoccupied with the Miami trial, and totally inebriated, Morrison put on a rather uninvolved performance in front of the record-breaking crowd. Barely moving from the microphone and chain-smoking cigarettes, a heavily bearded Morrison was "just going through the motions," according to Krieger. In *The Doors by the Doors*, Manzarek remarked, "He sang for all he was worth but moved nary a muscle. He remained rigid and fixed to the microphone for the entire concert. Dionysus had been shackled. They had killed his spirit." It didn't help that the Doors took the stage at 2 a.m. on October 30. The set list included "Back Door Man," "Break on Through (to the Other Side)," "When the Music's Over," "Ship of Fools," "Light My Fire," "The End," "Wake Up!," and "Roadhouse Blues." Isle of Wight proved to be the Doors' last filmed and recorded concert. Hendrix died just eighteen days after the festival. *A Message of Love: The Isle of Wight Rock Festival* was released theatrically in 1996 and features the Doors' performances of "When the Music's Over" and "The End," which was full of improvisation, including the "Wake Up" section of the "Celebration of the Lizard."

26

Trade in Your Hours for a Handful of Dimes

Why the Doors Didn't Perform at Woodstock

Once you saw the film and they said 750,000 hippies attended and you see the aerial shots I thought "Oh, shit . . ."

—Ray Manzarek

Sixties icon Wavy Gravy famously remarked, "If you can remember Woodstock, you probably weren't there." Considered a potential performing band at Woodstock, the Doors cancelled at the last minute and quickly regretted the decision. Conspicuously absent from the all-star lineup were both the Doors and Bob Dylan. The Doors had missed out on the other great rock festival of the 1960s—Monterey Pop Festival in June 1967 (but in that case they weren't even invited).

The Doors vs. Outdoor Concerts

The Doors did not perform well in outdoor concerts. According to Jim Morrison, the reason was that the band "needed the night and a sort of theater-type atmosphere and mood in which to work." Morrison claimed that there was something about daylight that "dissipates the whole magic." The band had negative experiences at several outdoor venues, including the Northern California Folk-Rock Festival (where the crowd treated them with total indifference) on May 19, 1968, and the more recent Seattle Pop Festival on July 27, 1969. Another reason they didn't want to do Woodstock, according to Doors manager Bill Siddons in *The Doors by the Doors*, was that "our policy had always been 'The Doors headline.' They don't play in multiple act bills. And be part of an event. They're an event in and of themselves. But I thought that Woodstock warranted a change in the policy, and so did Jac Holzman, who came over to the office and put his two cents in. And Bill Graham lobbied them too. But the band didn't want to do it."

Although the Doors shunned Woodstock, they did agree to perform at the Toronto Rock 'n' Roll Revival just a month later on September 13, 1969.

Courtesy of Kerry Humpherys/doors.com

"A Sea of Faces"

The only Door to appear at Woodstock was John Densmore (along with his then-girlfriend, Julia Negron) but only in the role of a spectator. Densmore vin *The Doors by the Doors* remarked, "I stole a glimpse of the audience. *This was it!* A sea of faces cresting at the top of a hill about a quarter of a mile away. The biggest gig ever, and The Doors weren't even playing! Oh well, I was there."

The Greatest Rock Festival Ever

Billed as "Three Days of Peace and Music," the greatest rock festival ever took place at Max Yasgur's 600-acre farm in Bethel, New York, and drew an estimated 500,000 people: a massive influx of tie-dyed shirts, peace signs, painted buses, acid trips, pot, skinny-dipping, and free love. Tickets cost $18 in advance. Richie Havens opened the festival with a riveting set that began at 5:07 p.m. on Friday afternoon, August 15, 1969. Featured acts at Woodstock also included: John B. Sebastian, Sweetwater, Tim Hardin, Melanie, Joan Baez, Country Joe McDonald, Incredible String Band, Bert Sommer, Ravi Shankar, and Arlo Guthrie on August 15; Quill, Canned Heat, Janis Joplin, Grateful Dead, the Who, Santana, Mountain, Sly & the Family Stone, and Creedence Clearwater Revival on August 16; Jefferson Airplane; Country Joe and the Fish; the Band; Johnny Winter; Joe Cocker; Ten Years After; Blood, Sweat, & Tears; and Crosby, Stills, Nash, and Young on August 17; and Paul Butterfield Blues Band, Sha-Na-Na, and Jimi Hendrix Experience on August 18.

Sample performer salaries were Jimi Hendrix Experience, $18,000; the Who, $12,500; Jefferson Airplane, $12,000; Creedence Clearwater Revival, $11,500; Grateful Dead, $7,500; and Santana, $1,500. Three deaths were reported during Woodstock: one heroin overdose, one ruptured appendix, and one person run over by a tractor. Directed by Michael Wadleigh, a documentary of the festival, *Woodstock*, was released in 1970. Director Martin Scorsese (*Taxi Driver*) served as one of the film's editors. Densmore can be glimpsed briefly in the background during Joe Cocker's set.

"A Bunch of Young Parasites"

While the bands at Woodstock were busy making rock history, Morrison made a personal appearance representing the Doors' documentary *Feast of Friends* on August 18 at a Creative Arts Conference ("The Film Maker Series") at the campus of United States International University in San Diego. Morrison remarked in a 1970 interview that "Woodstock seemed to me to be just a bunch of young parasites being spoon-fed for three or four days . . . They looked like the victims and dupes of a culture more than anything else. Of course that may sour grapes because I wasn't there, not even as a spectator. But some free celebration of a young culture, it's still better than nothing, and I'm sure that some of the people take away a kind of myth back to the city with them."

Woodstock 99

At Woodstock 99, Robby Krieger joined Creed onstage for renditions of "Roadhouse Blues" and "Riders on the Storm." Billed as "Three More Days of Peace and Music," Woodstock 99 took place at Griffiss Air Force Base in Rome, New York, July 23–25, 1999. The crowd numbered approximately 220,000 for the three-day festival, which also featured an eclectic lineup that included the Red Hot Chili Peppers, Rage Against the Machine, Willie Nelson, Metallica, Megadeath, Live, Limp Bizkit, Kid Rock, Jewel, Everclear, Ice Cube, Dave Matthews Band, Counting Crows, George Clinton and the P-Funk All Stars, Bush, and James Brown.

However, the legacy of Woodstock 99 may perhaps be looted vendor tents, smashed ATM machines, toppled porta potties, overturned cars, damaged speaker towers, raging bonfires, and state troopers in riot gear. In fact, Anthony Kiedis of the Red Hot Chili Peppers remarked from the stage, "Holy shit, it looks like *Apocalypse Now* out there!"

Interestingly, in his first novel, *The Poet in Exile*, which was published in 2001, Manzarek places the band at Woodstock, perhaps envisioning what might have been: "He closed his eyes and I could see him envisioning our transcendent night at Woodstock. Half a million people under his control, caught up in our music and taken to the free space on the other side. Half a million people breaking through, breaking free of their chains. An instant in time, perhaps never to be repeated, but realized and attained at least *once* in a collective lifetime. A vision of a new American possibility."

27

Everything Is Broken Up and Dances

Doors Concerts Recorded for the *Absolutely Live* Album

I think it's a true document of one of our good concerts: not insanely good, but a true portrait of what we usually do on a good night.

—Jim Morrison

T he Doors released *Absolutely Live*, their first live album, in July 1970. In a later interview, Jim Morrison remarked, "I think [*Absolutely Live* is] a fairly true document of what the band sounds like on a fairly good night. It's not the best we can do and it's certainly not the worst. It's a true document of an above average evening." In *Light My Fire*, Ray Manzarek remarked, "We wanted to get the Doors experience on tape. Live. One time. For the ages. And in doing so, perhaps we could capture the moment of escape. Live."

2,000 Edits

The album's liner notes featured this disclaimer: "Aside from the editing necessary to assemble the music into album form, the recording is an organic documentary and absolute live!" However, *Absolutely Live* was actually edited from many different concert recordings between July 1969 and May 1970 to create the illusion of one cohesive performance. According to producer Paul Rothchild, "I couldn't get a complete take of a lot of songs, so sometimes I'd cut from Detroit to Philadelphia in midsong. There must be 2,000 edits on that album."

Aquarius Theater

The original concept for the live album was to record the band's triumphant return to the Whisky A Go Go for a couple of shows in May 1969. Those concerts never took place, most likely because of the fallout surrounding the notorious

Miami concert two months earlier. The Doors then decided to record the live album at two shows that were part of the Elektra Records Showcase Concert Series at the Aquarius Theater July 21–22, 1969 (widely regarded today as the band's "comeback" performances after the Miami debacle). A heavily bearded Jim Morrison took the stage at the Aquarius Theater and announced, "For a long time we've wanted to record a live album. Tonight's the night . . . but we're going to keep it loose and almost casual. Ready? Let's go!" The Doors performed two very successful shows at the Aquarius Theater. However, when the band listened to the recording in the studio, they "found that it didn't really add up to a very good album," according to Morrison. So they decided to record seven or eight other concerts at venues such as the Felt Forum in New York (January 17–18, 1969), Boston Arena (April 10, 1970), the Spectrum in Philadelphia (May 1, 1970), Civic Center in Pittsburgh (May 2, 1970), and Cobo Arena in Detroit (May 8, 1970).

Eclectic Song Selection

A double album, *Absolutely Live* is notable for containing a complete performance of Morrison's failed epic, the "Celebration of the Lizard," which was originally intended to take up a whole side of the *Waiting for the Sun* album. "Celebration of the Lizard" featured seven sections: "Lions in the Street," "Wake Up," "A Little Game," "The Hill Dwellers," "Not to Touch the Earth," "Names of the Kingdom" and "The Palace of Exile." In an interview with Salli Stevenson in the Winter 1970 issue of *Circus* magazine, Morrison remarked,

> I like "The Celebration," though it's not a great version of that piece, but I'm glad we went ahead and put it out, because I doubt if we would have ever put it on a record otherwise because it's a couple of years old. We tried to do it at the time we were doing *Waiting for the Sun* and it just didn't seem to make it in the studio, so we used one piece out of it, "Not To Touch The Earth." If we hadn't put it on a live album, we would have just shelved it forever. I'm glad that we did it even in the imperfect form in which it exists. It's better than if we had never done it.

Both the "Celebration of the Lizard" and "Universal Mind" were recorded at the Doors' Aquarius Theatre concert in July 1969.

Another unusual aspect of *Absolutely Live* is the inclusion of the Willie Dixon classic "Close to You," featuring lead vocals by Ray Manzarek, who was familiar with singing blues covers from his days with Rick and the Ravens at the Turkey Joint West. Other songs on *Absolutely Live* include Bo Diddley's "Who Do You Love?," "Alabama Song," "Back Door Man," "Love Hides," "Five to One," "Build Me a Woman," "When the Music's Over," "Break on Through (to the Other Side) No. 2," and "Soul Kitchen."

Album Cover

The *Absolutely Live* album cover featured Morrison at the Hollywood Bowl concert on July 5, 1968, more than two years before the release of *Absolutely Live* (in 1993 the Hard Rock Cafe purchased the brown leather pants Morrison wore in the shot for $43,700). None of the other Doors were included on the cover. Ironically, when the album was released, Morrison had already shed his "Lizard King" persona and now sported a full beard and beer belly. He was reportedly enraged by the album cover, as well as by Elektra's decision to name the album *Absolutely Live* (he had supposedly wanted to name it *Lions in the Streets* from the first line in the "Celebration of the Lizard").

Critical Reception

Absolutely Live peaked at No. 8 on the Billboard charts in September 1970. According to Doors manager Bill Siddons, *"Absolutely Live* was absolutely nothing like the band was live . . . Most of the time, when they were onstage, they were crazed, and they could transport you. Invariably, the bootleg recordings from that time are better than *Absolutely Live."* Reviewing the album for the *New York Times,* critic Don Heckman panned the live effort, remarking that the Doors had "overextended themselves with this collection" and were "beginning to sound as dated as a Frankie Avalon surfing song." However, Patricia Kennealy of *Jazz & Pop* magazine (and also one of Morrison's love interests briefly) called it "one of the absolutely finest live rock 'n' roll albums ever made."

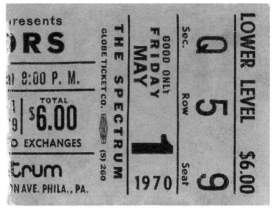

The Doors performed a highly energetic show at the Spectrum in Philadelphia on May 1, 1970, that was recorded for *Absolutely Live.* In addition, the recording of "Roadhouse Blues" from this show ended up on the 1978 album *An American Prayer.*

Courtesy of Ida Miller/idafan.com

In addition, legendary rock critic Lester Bangs enjoyed the album, especially the unique moments such as Morrison

> stopping "When the Music's Over" to scream at the audience to shut up; the way he says "Pritty neat, pritty neat, pritty good, pritty good" before "Build Me A Woman," which begins with the line, "I got the poontang blues;" the intro to "Close to You": "Ladies and gentlemen . . . I don't know if you realize it, but tonight you're in for a special treat" —crowd

cheers wildly—"No, No, not that not that . . . last time it happened grown men were weeping, policemen were turning in their badges . . ."; and, best of all, the (almost certainly improvised) sung intro to "Break on Through #2": "Dead cat in a top hat/dead rat/thinks he's an aristocrat/that's *crap* . . ."—true street poetry indeed. Plus the bonus of a brief reprise of the "Petition the Lord with prayer" bit, in which this time he sounds like no one so much as Lenny Bruce doing Oral Roberts in his "Religions, Inc." routine.

In a 1970 interview with *ZigZag* magazine, Morrison stated that *Absolutely Live* and *Morrison Hotel* were his two favorite albums. In 1991, *Absolutely Live* was repackaged with the Doors' 1983 live album *Alive, She Cried* and released as a two-disc set entitled *In Concert*.

28

In a Darkened Room

How Morrison's Alcoholism Affected the Doors' Performances and Studio Albums

People would tell Jim he should drink less and he'd take them out and get them drunk.

—*Robby Krieger*

Doors producer Paul Rothchild called Jim Morrison "a Jekyll and Hyde" who would suddenly "turn into a maniac" after drinking heavily. According to Elektra Records president Jac Holzman in an interview in *MOJO* magazine (June 2007), "There was danger around Morrison. You never knew what was going to happen. He was always graceful with me but when he had too much liquor he was a nasty drunk." In an interview that appeared on the *No One Here Gets Out Alive* video, Ray Manzarek remarked that Morrison "had to live on the edge 24 hours a day. He was always out there." In a 1969 interview with Jerry Hopkins for *Rolling Stone* magazine, Morrison stated, "Getting drunk . . . you're in complete control up to a point. It's your choice, every time you take a sip. You have a lot of small choices. It's like . . . I guess it's the difference between suicide and slow capitulation."

From Acidhead to Boozer

When Morrison first started writing lyrics during the summer of 1965, he had dropped down to about 135 pounds, had basically stopped eating and was dropping acid and smoking pot frequently. However, he changed very quickly, according to Manzarek, from a "psychedelic pothead and acidhead" to "a closing off of consciousness, and a favoring of pills, uppers and downers, and alcohol." Alice Cooper, who was one of Morrison's early drinking buddies, described him as one of the "most self-destructive" individuals he had ever met. According to Danny Sugerman in *Wonderland Avenue*, "It almost appeared Jim was intentionally trying to ruin everything he had worked so hard to establish—hellbent on bringing the whole house down with him."

Bloated, bearded, and increasingly drunk and belligerent onstage, Jim Morrison spent his last couple of years in the Doors attempting to shed his "Lizard King" persona.

Courtesy of Kerry Humpherys/doors.com

Drunken Recording Sessions

About the time of the *Waiting for the Sun* recording sessions, Morrison lost interest in recording albums. He would frequently show up at the recording studio drunk or simply not show up at all. Often he would be accompanied by groupies and drinking buddies like Tom Baker. Manzarek labeled the drunken Morrison persona "Jimbo." Morrison would occasionally disappear for several days at a time. As *Waiting for the Sun* neared completion, he often would pass out on the studio floor, "peeing his pants," according to Holzman. More than once, John Densmore would throw down his drumsticks and storm out of the recording studio in response to Morrison's drunken antics. During one afternoon at the recording studio for the *L.A. Woman* sessions, Doors manager Bill Siddons witnessed Morrison drink thirty-six beers. When not in the recording studio, Morrison could often be found drinking himself into a stupor at his favorite bars such as the Phone Booth, the Palms, and Barney's Beanery, where he once got so drunk that he stood up on the bar and urinated. Even when Morrison posed for the famous "young lion" photos in 1967, he was "totally plastered," according to photographer Joel Brodsky. At the end of the shoot, Brodsky claimed that Morrison was so drunk that "he was stumbling into the lights."

Busted

Morrison's alcohol abuse frequently got him into trouble with the law. As a student at Florida State University on September 23, 1963, Morrison was arrested for the first time en route to a football game and charged with petty larceny, disturbing the peace, resisting arrest, and public drunkenness. On January 28, 1968, Morrison (along with his friend Robert Gover) was charged with vagrancy and public drunkenness in front of the Pussycat A Go Go in Las Vegas. On February 7, 1969, Morrison was charged with drunk driving and driving without a license in Los Angeles. On November 11, 1969, Morrison and Tom Baker were arrested after a flight to Phoenix for drunk and disorderly conduct and interfering with a flight crew.

Freak Show

During the late 1960s, many fans became attracted to Doors concerts just for the promise of a spectacle or freak show, and Morrison most often obliged them with his damaging consumption of alcohol that would nearly always lead to unpredictable and destructive behavior. Morrison would often show up totally inebriated before concerts and continue drinking during the performance. In fact, the Doors' most notorious concerts such as the University of Michigan (October 20, 1967) and the Dinner Key Auditorium (March 1, 1969) all had one thing in common—a drunken Morrison onstage. During a concert at the Cleveland Public Auditorium on August 3, 1968, Morrison reportedly walked onstage with a bottle of whisky and flipped off the crowd. Before the Doors took the stage at the Isle of Wight Festival on August 29, 1970, Roger Daltrey of the Who claimed that he and Morrison knocked back two bottles of Southern Comfort.

The year 1969 started out on a positive note for the Doors as they took the stage at Madison Square on January 24, 1969, in a concert *Variety* referred to as the band's "triumphant return to New York." However, over a month later, the debacle in Miami signaled the beginning of the end for the Doors.

Courtesy of Logan Janzen/mildequator.com

29

Once I Had a Little Game

The Real Story of the Miami Concert

Let's just say I was testing the bounds of reality. I was curious to see what would happen. That's all it was: curiosity.

—Jim Morrison

During the infamous Miami concert on March 1, 1969, at the Dinner Key Auditorium (a sweltering former seaplane hangar packed way beyond capacity), the Doors took the stage with disastrous results. Drunk, belligerent, fueled with ideas from experimental theater, and totally out of his mind, Jim Morrison tried to spark a revolution (or at least a riot!) during the sixty-five-minute performance, the band's first appearance in Morrison's home state of Florida. To top it off, the audience that night was made up primarily of restless teenagers who had paid $6 to $7 and simply wanted to hear "Light My Fire."

The Living Theatre

It all started back in Los Angeles a week earlier when Morrison attended every performance of the radical Living Theatre at USC's Bovard Auditorium based upon the recommendation of his friend, Beat poet Michael McClure. Founded by Julian Beck and his wife, Judith Malina, in 1947 and based in New York City, the avant-garde Living Theatre utilized the ideas of Antonin Artaud, who was known for his concept of the "Theatre of Cruelty." The Living Theatre remains the oldest experimental theater group still existing in the United States.

Prelude to Disaster

In Los Angeles on the day of the concert, Morrison got into a huge fight with Pamela Courson, who was supposed to travel with him. Morrison missed his scheduled flight to Miami and spent the time waiting for the next flight drinking in the airport lounge with Doors manager Bill Siddons. He continued drinking heavily on the plane. During a stopover in New Orleans, Morrison missed his flight again and continued drinking. Needless to say, he was extremely drunk when he reached Miami.

Dinner Key Auditorium

The Dinner Key Auditorium was located at the Pan American Airways seaplane base at Dinner Key in Miami, Florida. Seats at the Dinner Key Auditorium were removed to accommodate 12,000 to 13,000 fans, packing the hall far beyond capacity (it was built to hold 6,900 people). According to Manzarek in liner notes for *The Doors Box Set*, "Miami! Live, crazy, out of control! Prelude to a riot. A hot, southern Tennessee night when swamp madness prevailed." In *Follow the Music*, Doors road manager Vince Treanor referred to the venue as "An abandoned building. Dry-rotted, grayed out, rickety, a concrete floor, and a wretched smell, the most godawful stench. It had been used by derelicts in every possible way for quite some time. A cesspool. They literally had to hose it out."

"You're All a Bunch of Fuckin' Idiots"

A bearded Morrison stumbled on the stage wearing a leather hat with a skull and crossbones. As the concert began, the Doors started playing "Back Door Man," but Morrison had no interest in singing. Instead, he started addressing the crowd: "I ain't talking about no revolution. And I'm not talking about no demonstration. I'm talkin' about having a good time." According to Krieger, Morrison was just "storming around the stage, screaming and yelling." The band tried to play "Five to One," hoping to get Morrison singing again. After slurring the first two stanzas, Morrison started berating the audience:

"You're all a bunch of fuckin' idiots. Let people tell you what you're gonna do. Let people push you around. How long do you think it's gonna last? How long are you gonna let it go on? How long are you gonna let them push you around? Maybe you like it. Maybe you like being pushed around. Maybe you love it. Maybe you love getting your face stuck in the shit . . . You're all a bunch of slaves. Bunch of slaves. Letting everybody push you around. What are you gonna do about it? What are you gonna do about it? . . . What are you gonna do?" As Krieger played a solo on "Five to One," Morrison kneeled in front of his guitar. Morrison would later be charged with "feigning oral copulation."

Throughout the concert, the band continually tried to get Morrison refocused on the concert by playing such songs as "Touch Me," "When the Music's Over," and "Light My Fire," but to no avail. At one point in the concert, Morrison brought up his experience with the Living Theatre the week before: "Now listen, I used to think the whole thing was a big joke. I used to think it was something to laugh about. And then the last couple of nights I met some people who were doing something. They're trying to change the world, and I want to get on the trip. I wanna change the world." Morrison also brought up the fact that he was born in Melbourne and that he attended a "little junior college" in St.

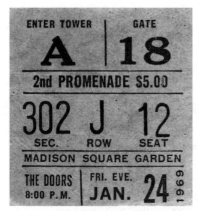

ENTER TOWER | GATE

A | 18

2nd PROMENADE $5.00

302 J 12

SEC.   ROW   SEAT

MADISON SQUARE GARDEN

THE DOORS | FRI. EVE. **24** 1969
8:00 P.M. | JAN.

After a "triumphant return" to New York for a concert at Madison Square Garden, the Doors headed to Miami a little over a month later for the disastrous Dinner Key Auditorium show.
Courtesy of Ida Miller/idafan.com

Petersburg and then "went up to a little college in Tallahassee. Then I got smart and I went out to a beautiful state called California."

In one of the more surreal moments of the night, Morrison was handed a lamb onstage, which he held for a couple of minutes. It turned out that an eccentric named Lewis Marvin (of Moonfire) was traveling with a lamb to symbolize his philosophies of nonviolence and vegetarianism.

At some point during the end of his extended rant, Morrison indicated that he might pull his pants down. Manzarek yelled at Doors road manager Vince Treanor to stop him. Treanor grabbed the waistband of Morrison's leather pants to make sure he wouldn't pull them down. Meanwhile, an oblivious Morrison continued his dialogue with the crowd: "Ain't nobody gonna love my ass? C'mon, I need ya." Soon fans were climbing all over the stage. Although some fans in the crowd would later say that Morrison exposed himself, no one in the band or the road crew witnessed it.

Snake Dance

The police and security started throwing kids off the stage. In the midst of all the confusion, the promoter's brother (a karate expert) mistakenly threw Morrison off the stage, thinking he was a fan. Morrison started to snake dance through the crowd "with ten thousand people following him," according to Densmore. With the stage starting to collapse, both Densmore and Krieger made a hasty retreat backstage, while Manzarek continued to flail away at the keyboards.

Aftermath

According to Krieger in *The Doors by the Doors*, "Everybody had a good time. After the show the cops came up and had some beer with us. If something had happened we would've been arrested." All four of the Doors headed to the Caribbean for a vacation getaway, unaware of the storm clouds that were brewing in Miami. Less than a week later, an arrest warrant was issued for Morrison.

In a later interview, Morrison remarked, "I think that was the culmination, in a way, of our mass performing career. Subconsciously, I think I was trying to get across in that concert—I was trying to reduce it to absurdity, and it worked too well. I was just fed up with the image that had been created around us . . . It just got too much for me to really stomach, and so I just put an end to it in one glorious evening."

30

It Hurts to Set You Free

Negative Consequences Stemming from the Miami Concert

This whole thing started with rock 'n' roll, and now it's out of control.
—*Jim Morrison*

The devastation wrought from the Miami concert debacle on March 1, 1969, led to a chain of increasingly nightmarish events for the Doors, including an arrest warrant for Jim Morrison, cancelled tour dates, lack of airplay, a poorly received fourth album (*The Soft Parade*), the infamous *Rolling Stone* magazine "Wanted in Miami" poster, a forty-day obscenity trial, and ultimately the death of "the Lizard King" in Paris on July 3, 1971. According to Robby Krieger in *The Doors by the Doors*, "[Morrison] really didn't do anything that wrong, except being too drunk and doing a bad show. But it ruined our career for at least a year, and probably was one of the contributing factors to the demise of The Doors."

Fueling the Flame

The *Miami Herald* fueled the flame by publishing an article, "Rock Group Fails to Stir a Riot," by staff writer Larry Mahoney, who had attended the concert. Mahoney, who was in his twenties and a former FSU student like Morrison, wrote,

> It was the night of the riot that did not happen. The Doors, a theatrical rock group, and singer Jim Morrison pulled out all stops in an abortive effort to provoke chaos among a huge crowd of Miami young people packed into the Dinner Key Auditorium at $6 a head. The hypnotically erotic Morrison, flouting the laws of obscenity, indecent exposure, and incitement to riot, could only stir a minor mob scene toward the end of his Saturday night performance . . . Morrison appeared to masturbate

in full view of his audience, screamed obscenities, and exposed himself. He also got violent, slugged several Thee Image officials, and threw one of them off the stage before he himself was hurled into the crowd.

Arrest Warrant

Less than a week after the disastrous concert, an arrest warrant was issued for Morrison. An article titled "Warrants Issued in 'Doors' Concert," that appeared in the *Miami News* stated, "The self-styled 'King of Orgasmic Rock' reportedly simulated masturbation and unzipped his pants during the blue-language performance."

Doors concerts were quickly cancelled in Jacksonville, Pittsburgh, Philadelphia, Providence, Toronto, Kent State University, Detroit, Cleveland, Cincinnati, Dallas, Houston, Boston, Buffalo, Syracuse, and St. Louis. In fact, the Doors did not perform again until a June 14, 1969, concert at the Chicago Auditorium Theater. Most commercial radio stations also banned the Doors' records from the airwaves. According to Doors manager Bill Siddons, the Miami incident cost the Doors at least half a million dollars and "almost caused the band to break up."

Rally for Decency

Community outrage over the concert (based mostly on newspaper reports) led to the organization of a "Rally for Decency" that was held at the Orange Bowl in Miami on March 23, 1969. Spearheaded by seventeen-year-old student Mike Levisque, a senior at Miami Springs High School, the Rally for Decency drew approximately 30,000 attendees and featured such celebrities as Jackie "Ralph Kramden" Gleason, Kate "God Bless America" Smith, Anita Bryant, the Lettermen, Roslyn Kind, and the Miami Drum and Bugle Corps. Gleason was quoted in the *New York Times*, stating "I believe this kind of movement will snowball across the United States and perhaps around the world."

The impact of the Miami concert lingered over a year later as the Doors' performance at Fairfield University scheduled for May 9, 1970, was cancelled after an emergency meeting by the university's board of trustees. The board released a statement saying it was not in the school's best interest to "have as its star attraction at spring weekend a person such as Mr. James Douglas Morrison."   *Courtesy of Robert Rodriguez*

Four days after the rally, President Richard Nixon sent a letter of congratulation to the organizers: "I was extremely interested to learn about the admirable initiative undertaken by you and the 30,000 other young people at the Miami Teenage Rally for Decency held last Sunday. This very positive approach, which focused attention on a number of critical problems confronting society, strengthens my belief that the younger generation is our greatest natural resource and therefore of tremendous hope for the future."

On May 26, 1969, Levisque helped organize another rally in Baltimore that erupted into a race riot when James Brown failed to appear. The disastrous Baltimore rally did not deter Levisque, who organized additional rallies in Columbus, Ohio, and Enterprise, Alabama (which caused more controversy by featuring Governor George Wallace).

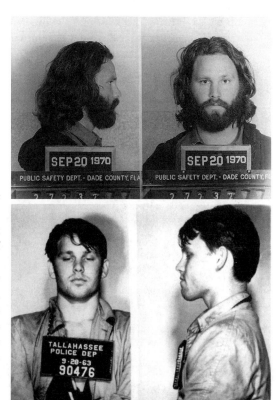

Jim Morrison had various brushes with the law over the years starting with an arrest at FSU in 1963 and culminating with his forty-day Miami trial in 1970.

Author's Collection

"Jim Morrison Exposed!"

The media also jumped into the fray with reckless abandon. For example, an article called "Jim Morrison Exposed!" by John Burks that appeared in the April 5, 1969, issue of *Rolling Stone* magazine stated, "The Doors are shut down by the Miami-Dade police when Jim unleashes his lizard onstage." *Rolling Stone* also published a notorious "wanted" poster that featured the Lizard King photo of Morrison and read: "WANTED IN THE COUNTY OF DADE FOR: Lewd and Lascivious Behavior in Public by Exposing His Private Parts and by Simulating Masturbation and Oral Copulation, A Felony."

In a later interview, Morrison remarked, "I think it was really the life-style they were going after. I don't think it was me personally. I just kind of stepped into a hornet's nest. I had no idea that the sentiment down there was so tender. The audience that was there seemed to enjoy it. I think that the people who read about it in the paper in this distorted version created a climate of hysteria. A few weeks later they had an antidecency—I mean anti-indecency rally at the

Orange Bowl with a famous fat comedian . . . The President congratulated the kid that started this rally. They had him all over the country."

The Legacy of Miami

Everything changed after Miami for the Doors. Morrison ditched his leather pants along with his Lizard King persona. He started to devote himself to projects outside the band such as his experimental film, *HWY*, and getting his poetry published. According to Danny Sugerman in *Wonderland Avenue*, the Miami incident proved to be a mixed blessing: "While it was a major curse in terms of lost concerts and court costs, it also slowed things down; the band could rehearse, working up material in a manner they hadn't time for since the very early days before their first rush of success. They luxuriated in the process, growing confident and tight. Gone were the horns and strings. They'd returned to the roots, back to the randy carnivalesque classic Doors sound of yore."

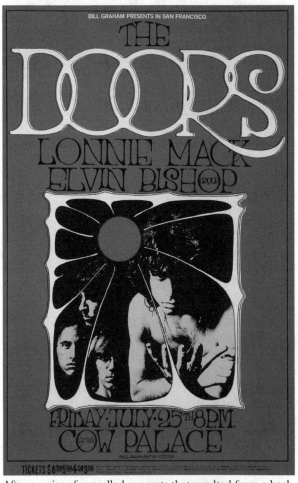

After a series of cancelled concerts that resulted from a backlash from the Miami incident, the Doors made a triumphant return to the stage at the Aquarius Theater followed by a well-received performance at the Cow Palace in San Francisco on July 25, 1969.   *Courtesy of Robert Rodriguez*

31

Witnessing the Wild Breeze

Morrison's Arrest on a Flight from Los Angeles to Phoenix

They were just trying to hang me because I was the only one that had a well-known face.

—*Jim Morrison*

In a bizarre series of circumstances, Jim Morrison was arrested after a flight to Phoenix, Arizona, on November 11, 1969, and eventually acquitted in April 1970. Morrison and his drinking buddy Tom Baker (an actor who appeared in Andy Warhol's *I, A Man*), as well as Frank Lisciandro and Doors publicist Leon Barnard, were on their way to catch a Rolling Stones concert at the Phoenix Veterans Coliseum. Ironically, just two days earlier, Morrison had been in Miami where he entered a formal "not guilty" plea to the charges stemming from the infamous Dinner Key Auditorium concert on March 1, 1969.

Interference with a Flight Crew

Sitting in first-class seats, Morrison and Baker had been drinking heavily even before they boarded the airplane. However, it was Baker who actually got rowdy—demanding that the stewardesses get drinks quicker and later throwing peanuts at them. Although Morrison laughed at Baker's antics, he apparently did not participate. After Baker allegedly touched one of the stewardesses, she told the captain, who issued a warning to both Baker and Morrison. Baker kept up the rowdy behavior, which included grabbing bars of soap from the lavatory and throwing them around the cabin. One of the bars of soap landed in Morrison's drink. Craig A. B. Chapman, the captain of Flight 172, reportedly had to go back to the cabin three times to try to calm the unruly, intoxicated passengers. Once the plane landed, Chapman requested police assistance. The Phoenix police, as well as the FBI, were waiting for the flight and upon landing in Phoenix, Morrison and Baker were arrested at the Sky Harbor International Airport on charges of "drunk and disorderly conduct" and "interference with a flight crew"

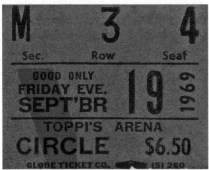

The Doors turned in a powerful performance at the Philadelphia Arena on September 19, 1969. Less than two months later, Jim Morrison was arrested in Phoenix.
Courtesy of Ida Miller/idafan.com

(a federal crime that at the time could result in a ten-year prison sentence and $10,000 fine). Lisciandro and Barnard, who were not charged with anything, headed to the Stones concert while Morrison and Baker spent the night in jail.

The following day, Morrison and Baker appeared in court and pled not guilty to the charges. The arraignment was set for December 2. However, a hastily convened federal grand jury indicted them on the felony counts of "assault, intimidation and threatening a flight attendant on an interstate flight." Bail was set at $2,500 each, and an arraignment was scheduled for November 24. A *Miami News* article, "Morrison Nabbed in Phoenix," stated, "Police said that the two used vulgar language on a Continental Airlines plane and threw glasses across the aircraft while it was in flight."

Mistaken Identity

On November 24, Morrison and Baker appeared before U.S. District Court Judge William P. Copple, under representation of attorney Craig Mehrens and entered a plea of not guilty. Copple informed them that they could face prison terms of up to twenty years and a $10,000 fine for each of the charges. Bail was set at $25,000 each, and the trial was then scheduled for February 17, 1970, at the federal court in Phoenix. On March 26, 1970, Morrison and Baker appeared in federal court. The key witness in the trial, stewardess Sherry Mason, testified that she was confused over which of the men was Morrison. On April 20, 1970, Morrison was acquitted. Ten days later, the Doors were back on tour at the Spectrum in Philadelphia.

In a later interview, Morrison remarked, "Well, it came under a law that was created because of hijacking, but it wasn't really a hijacking. It was just a little over-exuberant kind of playing. It wasn't a threat to safety or anything. Actually we were acquitted because the stewardesses mistook me for someone who I was with . . . They were just trying to hang me because I was the only one that had a well-known face."

"Seedy Junk-House"

Morrison and Baker had a falling out from the incident but later reinitiated their friendship shortly before Morrison left for Paris in the spring of 1971. Morrison reportedly told Baker that his "rock 'n' roll days are over." Baker, who wrote a memoir, *Blue Centre Light*, died of a drug overdose in a "seedy junk-house for heroin addicts" on New York City's Lower East Side in 1982 (just a little over a week after his forty-second birthday). At the time, several media outlets mistakenly reported that British actor Tom Baker, most famous for portraying *Doctor Who* on BBC TV, had passed away. Michael Madsen portrayed Baker in Oliver Stone's 1991 film, *The Doors*, while Jay Jeff Jones's 1991 play *The Lizard King*, highlighted the turbulent relationship of Baker and Morrison. In addition, Kinky Friedman dedicated his novel *Elvis, Jesus & Coca-Cola* to Baker.

32

No One Left to Scream and Shout

The Atmosphere During the Forty-Day Miami Trial

I thought there might be a possibility of it becoming a major, ground-breaking kind of case, but it didn't turn out that way.

—*Jim Morrison*

J im Morrison's forty-day Miami trial, which started on August 12, 1970, resulted from his arrest for lewd and lascivious behavior, indecent exposure, open profanity, and drunkenness following the infamous Dinner Key Auditorium concert on March 1, 1969.

Cast of Characters

The eclectic cast of characters for the Miami trial included Morrison's defense lawyer Max Fink; Morrison's Miami attorney, Robert Josefsberg; the prosecuting attorney, Terrence McWilliams (who was actually a Doors fan!); and Judge Murray Goodman, who just happened to be up for reelection. The cards were stacked against Morrison from the beginning since the age of the youngest juror was forty-two (while Morrison at the time was twenty-six). The State of Florida vs. James Douglas Morrison (Case #69-2355) began with jury selection on August 12, 1970, at the Metropolitan Dade County Justice Building in Miami. The jury eventually consisted of four men and two women.

Contemporary Standards

Fink requested that contemporary works such as *Midnight Cowboy* (the only X-rated film to win an Academy Award for Best Picture); *I Am Curious, Yellow*, *Tropic of Cancer*, *Woodstock*; and *Hair* be introduced in court so that Morrison might be judged according to community standards. "A rock concert is an expression of dissent," stated Fink. In *The Miami News* ("Doors' Morrison in

Court as Jury Selection Begins"), Fink stated, "We have to accept the generation gap. People like Morrison's group, The Doors, are protesting the problems created by their forebears." Fink also pointed out the irony of the trial being held in South Florida, "considering Miami Beach is one of the most immoral cities in the U.S." On August 20, Judge Goodman dealt a strong blow to the defense by denying the request for admission of evidence pertaining to "community standards."

Prosecution Witnesses

On August 17, the State started presenting its case and brought forth two witnesses who testified that Morrison exposed himself. However, the Doors' attorney successfully pointed out inconsistencies in their testimony compared to sworn statements they had made just two months before. Two days later, jurors viewed more than one hundred photographs taken by Jeffrey Simon, who was standing no more than five feet from the stage. None of the photos indicated that Morrison had exposed himself. In addition, Simon testified that he did not see any evidence of indecent exposure. On August 25, a policewoman took the stand and testified that the reason Morrison was not arrested on the night of the concert was because the police feared retaliation from the crowd. Fink responded that they could have waited until Morrison was backstage and then arrested him. According to Fink, the arrest warrant was issued only after the "news

In the last Doors concert before the forty-day Miami trial, the band played the P.N.E. Coliseum in Vancouver with Albert King as the opening act.   *Courtesy of Derek Pattison/mildequator.com*

media fueled a hysteria." On August 27, the jury listened to a tape of the concert; however, Morrison made no remarks about exposing himself. The following day, the Doors flew to England to perform at the Isle of Wight Festival, where an exhausted Morrison turned in a rather lackluster performance. The prosecution rested its case on September 2.

Defense Witnesses

The defense had requested to present sixty witnesses, but Judge Goodman ordered them to restrict the number to just seventeen. An eleven-day recess was called on September 3, and Morrison and his drinking buddies, Babe Hill and Frank Lisciandro, attended an Elvis Presley concert in Miami and then took a fishing trip to the Bahamas with Fink. After the defense resumed on September 14, Morrison and all three of the other Doors testified. Morrison, who was questioned for approximately four hours, denied exposing himself and also claimed that he was "feeling good, but not drunk" during the concert. The defense rested on September 18 (the same day that Jimi Hendrix died in London at the age of twenty-seven). The following day, both the prosecution and the defense gave their closing arguments. Morrison took extensive notes during the trial and planned to write a book on the experience. He told Manzarek that the title would be *Observations on America, While on Trial for Obscenity.*

Jury Verdict

On September 20, the jury returned with not guilty on the felony charges of "lewd and lascivious behavior" and "public drunkenness," while convicting Morrison of two misdemeanors: "open profanity" and "indecent exposure" (unaware that in recess, Judge Goodman had stated that it was "already proven beyond a shadow of a doubt that Mr. Morrison didn't expose himself"). Sentencing was scheduled for October 30. As Morrison was exiting the courtroom, he told reporters, "This trial and its outcome won't change my style, because I maintain that I did not do anything wrong."

On October 2, Admiral Morrison wrote a letter at the request of Robert Disher of the Florida Probation and Parole Commission, describing his son as an "intellectual rebel" who nevertheless "always obeyed and respected authority." In the letter, the elder Morrison admitted not having seen his son since his senior year at UCLA five years before, blaming it on his having severely criticized him for wanting to pursue a career in rock music and "strongly advising him to give up any idea of singing." He did state that he had spoken to his son once over the phone during that period in which he "congratulated him on his first album" and that he viewed "his success with pride." Admiral Morrison concluded the letter by stating, "Based on my knowledge of Jim through his 21st year, I firmly believe that his performance in Miami was a grave mistake and not in character."

Sentencing

On October 30, Morrison returned to Miami and was given the maximum sentence of two months for "profanity" and six months for "indecent exposure" to be served in the Dade County Jail. Judge Goodman addressed Morrison, "To admit that this nation accepts as a community standard the indecent exposure and the offensive language spoken by you would be to admit that a small minority who spew obscenities, who disregard law and order, and who display utter contempt for our institutions and heritage have determined the community standards for all." Morrison was released on $50,000 bail, and Fink immediately filed an appeal with the U.S. District Court. The convictions were still in appeal when Morrison left for Paris in the spring of 1971.

The court proceeding was so drawn out that it really drained Morrison's energy and creativity. In an interview with Bob Chorush of the *L.A. Free Press*, Morrison remarked,

> I wasted a lot of time and energy with the Miami trial. About a year and a half. But I guess it was a valuable experience because before the trial I had a very unrealistic schoolboy attitude about the American judicial system. My eyes have been opened up a bit. There were guys down there, black guys, that would go on each day before I went on. It took about five minutes and they would get twenty or twenty-five years in jail. If I hadn't had unlimited funds to continue fighting my case, I'd be in jail right now for three years. It's just if you have money you generally don't go to jail.

Given permission to attend the Isle of Wight Festival during a break from the Miami trial, an exhausted Jim Morrison turned in a mediocre, lackluster performance before the estimated crowd of 600,000 attendees. *Courtesy of Mark Smigel/mildequator.com*

Pardoned

The case received renewed attention in the fall of 2010 when outgoing Florida Governor Charlie Crist stated his intention of pardoning Morrison for the 1970 conviction. Crist told *Rolling Stone* magazine, "After reviewing the case, it seems like a real injustice was done . . . It would be a tragedy to have this be the lasting legacy of his life."

On December 9, 2010, one day after Morrison's birthday (he would have been sixty-seven years old), Florida's Clemency Board unanimously agreed to pardon Morrison for the two misdemeanor convictions. However, on December 22, 2010, the three surviving Doors, along with Morrison's family, issued a press release stating that an apology would be more appropriate than a pardon:

> In 1969, the Doors played an infamous concert in Miami, Florida. Accounts vary as to what actually happened onstage that night.
>
> Whatever took place that night ended up with the Doors sharing beers and laughter in the dressing room with the Miami police, who acted as security at the venue that evening. The next day we flew off to Jamaica for a few days' vacation before our planned 20-city tour of America.
>
> That tour never materialized. Four days later, warrants were issued in Miami for the arrest of Morrison on trumped-up charges of indecency, public obscenity, and general rock-and-roll revelry. Every city the Doors were booked into canceled their engagement.
>
> A circus of fire-and-brimstone "decency rallies," grand jury investigations and apocalyptic editorials followed—not to mention allegations ranging from unsubstantiated (he exposed himself) to the fantastic (the Doors were "inciting a riot" but also "hypnotizing" the crowd).
>
> In August, Jim Morrison went on trial in Miami. He was acquitted on all but two misdemeanor charges and sentenced to six months' hard labor in Raiford Penitentiary. He was appealing this conviction when he died in Paris on July 3, 1971. Four decades after the fact, with Jim an icon for multiple generations—and those who rallied against him now a laughingstock—Florida has seen fit to issue a pardon.
>
> We don't feel Jim needs to be pardoned for anything.
>
> His performance in Miami that night was certainly provocative, and entirely in the insurrectionary spirit of the Doors' music and message. The charges against him were largely an opportunity for grandstanding by ambitious politicians—not to mention an affront to free speech and a massive waste of time and taxpayer dollars. As Ann Woolner of the *Albany Times-Union* wrote recently, "Morrison's case bore all the signs of a political prosecution, a rebuke from the cultural right to punish a symbol of Dionysian rebellion."
>
> If the State of Florida and the City of Miami want to make amends for the travesty of Jim Morrison's arrest and prosecution forty years after

the fact, an apology would be more appropriate—and expunging the whole sorry matter from the record. And how about a promise to stop letting culture-war hysteria trump our First Amendment rights? Freedom of Speech must be held sacred, especially in these reactionary times.

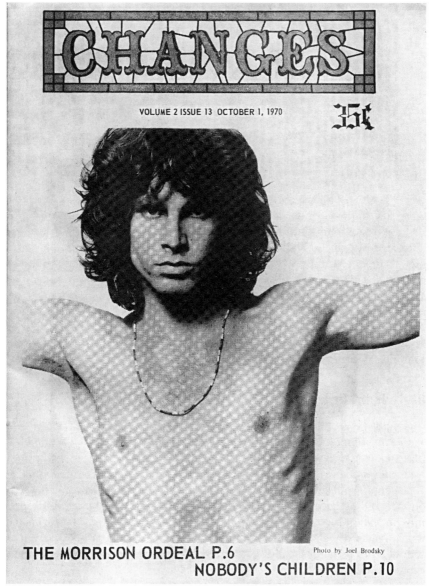

VOLUME 2 ISSUE 13 OCTOBER 1, 1970

35¢

THE MORRISON ORDEAL P.6

Photo by Joel Brodsky

NOBODY'S CHILDREN P.10

In an October 1, 1970, cover story in *Changes* magazine, "The Morrison Ordeal," the Doors' lead singer is portrayed as a scapegoat during the forty-day Miami trial.

Courtesy of Robert Rodriguez

33

Night Is Drawing Near

The Doors' Last Concert as a Quartet

That fateful last concert in New Orleans, where the bayou and the voodoo conjoined to snuff out Jim's spirit.

—*Ray Manzarek*

Jim Morrison's last performance with the Doors took place four days after his twenty-seventh birthday on December 12, 1970, at the Warehouse at 1820 Tchoupitoulas Street in New Orleans. By all accounts, it was a disastrous night for the band, and a totally exhausted Morrison had to be literally dragged off the stage halfway through the set. The Doors' sixth studio album, *L.A. Woman*, was released just four months later, and Manzarek always said one of his main regrets was that the band never got the opportunity to do a tour promoting all of the great songs on *L.A. Woman* such as the title track, "Riders on the Storm," "Love Her Madly," "Been Down So Long," "Cars Hiss by My Window," and "The WASP (Texas Radio and the Big Beat)," as well as the John Lee Hooker cover "Crawlin' King Snake."

State Fair Music Hall

The night before the Doors' gig at the Warehouse, the band had put on two successful sellout shows at the 6,000-seat State Fair Music Hall in Dallas and even performed "Riders on the Storm" for the first and only time, as well as several other songs that would appear on *L.A. Woman* such as "Love Her Madly," "The Changeling," and "L.A. Woman." A rather sedate Morrison appeared exhausted onstage and sang with his back to the audience for most of the set. Reviewing the concert for the *Dallas News*, critic Pat Pope remarked, "Their performance was casual, informal. No encore was played, but the set was a satisfying one that rounded out their music, giving it an electronic blues dimension that doesn't come through as strongly on record."

Lame Jokes

John Densmore in *Riders on the Storm* remarked, "It was great, and it was terrible
... one night great, the next awful—the worst. We played 'Riders on the Storm'
for the first time, and the audience loved it. The next night, Jim was as drunk
as hell, telling bad jokes on stage. It was horrible. Pathetic." About halfway
through the New Orleans concert, Morrison began to forget song lyrics; then
he just leaned against the microphone stand and told a few lame jokes. He took
the microphone stand and repeatedly smashed it into the stage, splintering the
boards. He then threw the stand into the stunned audience. The owners of the
Warehouse, who recognized the significance of the concert, refused to repair
the damage to the stage until years later. According to Manzarek in *Light My Fire*,
Morrison's "vital force, his chi, just left him." In *The Doors by the Doors*, Densmore
called the concert "pathetic" and "completely lame." According to Densmore,
the Doors only got through about half of the set: "Everything caught up with
[Morrison]. He was tired. There was no passion."

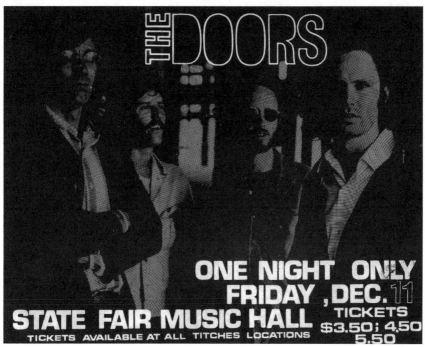

Just one night before the Doors' final performance with Jim Morrison at the Warehouse in
New Orleans, the band took the stage at the State Fair Music Hall in Dallas on December
11, 1970, and performed several songs from their album in progress, *L.A. Woman.*

Courtesy of Mark Smigel/mildequator.com

End of the Road

Appropriately, the song that started it all, "Light My Fire," ended the set and became the last song the Doors ever played live as a quartet. After the disastrous concert in New Orleans, the band unanimously agreed to stop touring indefinitely and focus exclusively on studio work. They returned to the studio to work on what would turn out to be their last studio album with Morrison, *L.A. Woman.*

However, in early 1971, the group considered scheduling one last performance at the Whisky A Go Go before Morrison headed to Paris. All of the band members were nostalgic for the intimate atmosphere of the Whisky, where they performed some of their best early shows before hitting it big and moving onto the bigger arenas and stadium-size venues (where trouble tended to erupt at venues like the New Haven Arena in 1967; the Singer Bowl in New York City in 1968; and, of course, the Dinner Key Auditorium in Miami in 1969). In an interview with Bob Chorush of the *L.A. Free Press* (January 15, 1971), Morrison remarked, "A few years ago I wanted to do live performances. I was trying to get everyone to do free surprise spots at the Whisky, but no one wanted to. Now everyone wants to, and I totally lost interest. Although I know it's a lot of fun, I just don't have the desire to get up and sing right now." So Morrison said goodbye to the rest of the band and headed for Paris in mid-April 1971. In late April, the Doors released *L.A. Woman*, which achieved gold status on July 22 of that year.

History of the Warehouse

The No. 1 venue for rock music in New Orleans, the Warehouse was a former cotton warehouse built in the 1850s that opened its doors on January 30, 1970, with Fleetwood Mac, followed by the Grateful Dead the next night. The Dead immortalized their arrest for marijuana possession in their hotel that weekend in their classic hit "Truckin'": "Busted, down on Bourbon Street, set up, like a bowling pin."

Other acts to take the stage at the Warehouse over the years included Pink Floyd, the Who, Yes, Rush, Kiss, ZZ Top, Bob Marley, Chicago, Joe Cocker, Bob Dylan, Elton John, Led Zeppelin, Rod Stewart, the Clash, and many others. The Allman Brothers performed at the Warehouse so frequently they were known as the 30,000-square-foot venue's unofficial house band. The Warehouse was also notorious for its outrageous, all-night New Year's Eve shows. On September 10, 1982, the Talking Heads were the last band to perform at the club, which was torn down in 1989.

34

I Need a Brand New Friend

Morrison's Attempt to Shed His Rock Star Image

If my poetry aims to achieve anything, it's to deliver people from the limited ways in which they see and feel.

—Jim Morrison

After the debacle at the Miami concert, Jim Morrison seemed to lose interest in live performances and started to turn most of his attention to poetry, screenplays, and other artistic endeavors. At the legendary Aquarius Theater concerts July 21–22, 1969, Morrison distributed his poem "Ode to L.A. While Thinking of Brian Jones—Deceased" to the audience at his own expense. Jones had drowned in his pool under mysterious circumstances on July 3, 1969, two years to the day before Morrison himself would die with equal mystery in Paris.

Morrison also drastically changed his appearance. Out were the leather pants and the "Lizard King" persona as he switched to loose-fitting shirts, grew a scraggly beard, and wore dark sunglasses everywhere. It was also around this time that Morrison began working on his experimental film, *HWY*, assisted by his three drinking buddies—Babe Hill, Frank Lisciandro, and Paul Ferrara. The premiere of *HWY* took place at the "Jim Morrison Film Festival" at Orpheum Theater in Vancouver, Canada, on March 27, 1970.

Elektra Records President Jac Holzman later recalled sitting with Morrison at a bar near the recording studio and the Doors singer telling him "how he wanted to be remembered as a poet—how this rock 'n' roll thing had gotten far beyond his ability to control the public's perception of him. He was acutely uncomfortable, hiding behind unkempt hair, a thick beard, and an excess of avoirdupois. With a mischievous snicker he talked about the great joy in life of being 'out there'—on the very edge . . ."

In a foreshadowing of things to come, a somewhat bewildered audience at the Doors concert at the Berkeley Community Theatre on February 10, 1968, heard Jim Morrison reading poetry instead of performing the usual Doors hits.

Courtesy of Robert Rodriguez

Cinematheque Performances

In May 1969, Morrison made his debut as a solo spoken-word performer, reading "An American Prayer" at a benefit for Norman Mailer's New York mayoral campaign at the Cinematheque Theater in Los Angeles. Other performers included Beat poet Michael McClure, Tom Baker, Seymour Cassel, Michael C. Ford, Mary Woronov, and Jamie Sanchez. Joined by Robby Krieger on guitar, Morrison sang a few songs, including Elvis Presley's "I Will Never Be Untrue" (which would resurface on the 1978 album *An American Prayer*). The Doors' documentary, *Feast of Friends*, was also aired for the audience during a midnight film screening.

Also in 1969, Morrison collaborated with McClure on several writing projects and readings, including an appearance at Sacramento State College Gallery on May 1, 1969. They also collaborated on a screenplay called *The Adept* that was based on one of McClure's unpublished novels. An influential member of the Beat Generation, McClure had joined Allen Ginsberg, Phil Whalen, Philip Lamentia, and Gary Snyder at a legendary poetry reading at the Six Gallery in 1955 to launch the so-called San Francisco Renaissance. McClure once referred to Morrison as "the best poet of his generation."

US #1 A Paperback Magazine

Morrison's poetry also appeared in *US #1 A Paperback Magazine*, which was edited by rock critic Richard Goldstein (a longtime Doors enthusiast) and published in June 1969. Taken from *The New Creatures*, the poems were billed as "Selections from a volume of verse by America's oedipal nightingale." In the biography section, it incorrectly stated that Morrison "holds a master's degree in film making from UCLA" (he had earned a bachelor's degree). The eclectic paperback also contained poetry by Ed Sanders (of the Fugs), drawings by R. Crumb, an essay by rock critic Paul Williams, and more.

The Lords and The New Creatures

In 1969, Morrison self-published two volumes of his poetry: *The Lords/ Notes on Vision* and *The New Creatures*. *The Lords* contained Morrison's reflections on cinema that dated back to his days in the UCLA Film School, while *The New Creatures* featured newer poetry that was heavy on the lizard and snake imagery. Not surprisingly, *The New Creatures* was dedicated to "Pamela Susan." The first printing of a combined volume, *The Lords and the New Creatures*, was published by Simon and Schuster in April 1970 under his full name: James Douglas Morrison. It was McClure who was instrumental in encouraging Morrison to publish his poetry.

The original published poetry of **Jim Morrison.**

The Lords. The New Creatures.

Jim Morrison the poet achieved one of his dreams when he self-published two volumes of poetry, *The Lords/Notes on Vision* and *The New Creatures* in 1969. *Courtesy of Ida Miller/idafan.com*

Poetry Recording Session

On December 8, 1970, Morrison's twenty-seventh birthday, he went to Village Recorders in West Los Angeles with engineer John Haeny to record a four-hour session of his poetry that is commonly referred to as the *An American Prayer* poetry reading (since the 1978 spoken-word album contains a mixture of recordings from this session and another poetry reading Morrison recorded in March 1969 that Haeny had also recorded). Many of the poems Morrison recited during this session can be read in *Wilderness* (1988) and *The American Night* (1990). Morrison invited several close friends to the recording session such as Alain Ronay and Florentine Pabst, as well as Frank and Kathy Lisciandro. The group passed around a bottle of Old Bushmills Irish Whiskey (a gift from Haeny) while Morrison read his poetry. At one point, Morrison announced he was ready to take a break, so the group headed to the Lucky U Cafe for tacos.

A testament to Jim Morrison's enduring popularity, two popular collections of his poetry appeared in the decades following his death: *Wilderness* (1988) and *The American Night* (1990).   *Courtesy of Kerry Humpherys/doors.com*

35

Out Here on the Perimeter

The Reasons Paul Rothchild Quit as Producer of *L.A. Woman*

Paul didn't really have anything more to say that we didn't already think of ourselves, so he wasn't really a necessary factor any more.

—*Robby Krieger*

Paul Rothchild, who had produced the Doors' first five studio albums, quit early in the production of *L.A. Woman*. He had just finished producing the final Janis Joplin album, *Pearl*, which was completed after she died of a heroin overdose on October 4, 1970, and included the hit single "Me and Bobby McGee." Producing *Pearl* was a "labor of love" for Rothchild. In contrast, according to Rothchild, the rehearsals with the Doors were "a joke." Half the time, Morrison would not even bother to show up. The rest of the Doors showed no enthusiasm about the material and were "drugged on their own boredom," according to Rothchild, who was totally disgusted by the atmosphere at the recording sessions.

"Cocktail Music"

According to Rothchild, the band had only developed rough versions of four or five songs that he thought were awful such as "Riders on the Storm," which sounded to him like "cocktail music." However, Rothchild later remarked in a 1981 interview with *BAM* magazine that his main problem was with the Krieger-penned "Love Her Madly." According to Rothchild, "Love Her Madly" was "the song that drove me out of the studio. That it sold a million copies means nothing to me." Last but not least, Rothchild had grown tired of "dragging the Doors from one album to another" and dealing with a drunken Morrison, who would often intentionally disrupt the recording sessions for his own amusement. Rothchild finally told engineer Bruce Botnick that he just didn't have the desire to "get it up again" and make the new album. After Rothchild's departure, Botnick agreed to coproduce the album with the Doors. According to John

Densmore in *Riders on the Storm*, "We hadn't played the songs very well, and they weren't rehearsed enough, but I knew we had some good ones . . . They were more blues-based, and the blues takes you to the root of your angst."

A Makeshift Recording Studio

After Rothchild's departure, the Doors and Botnick transformed the two-story Doors Office at 8512 Santa Monica Boulevard into a makeshift recording studio. The Doors Office, which had been used as a rehearsal studio for the first five Doors albums, featured unpainted walls, dirty carpets, and empty beer bottles littered on the floor, as well as copies of music magazines such as *Jazz & Pop* strewn about, recording equipment everywhere, and an old Doors poster unceremoniously tacked to one wall. The Doors installed a jukebox, pinball machine, and couch in the recording studio. The laid-back surroundings contributed to the relaxed feel of the album.

Album Tracks

Since the Doors were totally out of material, they had to once again come up with songs in the recording studio. The lyrics for "Cars Hiss by My Window" were actually taken from Morrison's Venice notebooks. "L'America" was originally supposed to appear on the soundtrack of Michelangelo Antonioni's 1969 film *Zabriskie Point*, but the director rejected the song. "Been Down So Long" was inspired by Richard Farina's cult novel. Morrison came up with "Riders on the Storm" after the band started playing "Ghost Riders in the Sky" for fun in the studio one day. Another song, "Paris Blues," which featured the prophetic lines "Goin' to the city of love, gonna start my life over again" and "Once I was warm, now I feel cold," was recorded during the *L.A. Woman* sessions but never released. In a letter to Dave Marsh, editor of *CREEM* magazine, Morrison remarked, "This is a blues album. We've even included a John Lee Hooker cut called Crawling King Snake which was part of our set in the earliest club days. The songs have a lot to do w/America & what it's like to live these years in L.A.—& by extension—the United States."

Recording Session

The Doors hired Elvis Presley's bassist Jerry Scheff and well-known rhythm guitarist Marc Benno for the *L.A. Woman* recording sessions. Scheff played bass on every song except "L'America." In an interview with *Classic Rock* magazine, Densmore commented, "Jerry was incredible; an in-the pocket man. He allowed me to communicate rhythmically with Morrison, and he slowed Ray down, when his right hand on the keyboards got too darn fast." Benno played on four of the songs on the album, including "L.A. Woman." The Doors would come up with the tunes "on the spot," according to Benno, and did very few takes, resulting in a "very spontaneous album."

In fact, the entire *L.A. Woman* album was recorded in just six days (in contrast to *The Soft Parade*, which took nine months to complete). Most of the songs for *L.A. Woman* were recorded live except for a few overdubbed keyboard parts by Manzarek. According to Botnick, "The overall concept for the recording session was to go back to our early roots and try to get everything live in the studio with as few overdubs as possible."

Doors producer Paul Rothchild later admitted that it was the Robby Krieger song "Love Her Madly" that drove him from the studio during the early *L.A. Woman* studio sessions. The Doors ended up completing the album with the help of audio engineer Bruce Botnick.   *Courtesy of Robert Rodriguez*

Thirty-Six Beers

Excited by the music, Morrison for the most part showed up on time for the recording sessions and cut back on his alcohol consumption somewhat. However, Siddons did recall Morrison drinking thirty-six beers one day during rehearsal. In addition, Doors road manager Vince Treanor has remarked that Morrison began snorting cocaine regularly during the *L.A. Woman* sessions. However, Manzarek, in *Light My Fire*, paints a totally different picture of the recording sessions: "A few beers, that was all . . . We were all happy . . . And it was beginning to feel like *L.A. Woman* was going to be one of our best albums ever. Maybe even a 'comeback' album." The finished product had a bluesy sound, which suited Morrison just fine. He later remarked in an interview that "Our music has returned to the earlier form, just using the four instruments. We felt that we had come too far in the other direction, i.e., orchestration, and wanted to get back to the basic format." To Densmore, the *L.A. Woman* recording sessions had the same feel as when the Doors started out as "a garage band." In addition, the band decided to drop the individual writing credits and have all songs written by the Doors just like on the first three albums.

Critical Reaction

Released in April 1971, *L.A. Woman* peaked at No 9 and spent thirty-four weeks on the charts. In addition, "Love Her Madly" skyrocketed to No. 11 on the charts. The single's B-side, Willie Dixon's "(You Need Meat) Don't Go No Further," was sung by Manzarek and did not appear on the album. *L.A. Woman* generally received high praise from the critics, including R. Meltzer of *Rolling Stone* magazine, who remarked, "You can kick me in the ass for saying this (I don't mind): this is the Doors' greatest album and (including their first) the best album so far this year. A landmark worthy of dancing in the streets." *Playboy* remarked that "the usual irritating pretentiousness that's part of any Doors album is kept to a minimum here" and referred to "L'America" as the album's one clunker, "an unsuccessful apocalyptic melange of Thirties German mock opera, Fifties rock and Seventies doom." Elektra Records president Jac Holzman remarked, "I had been worried about the material because of [Rothchild's] negative comments, but the album knocked me out, song after song."

In 2003, *Rolling Stone* magazine ranked *L.A. Woman* No. 362 on its list of the "500 Greatest Albums of All Time." A new version of the album, *L.A. Woman (40th Anniversary Mixes)*, was released in 2007 and featured two bonus tracks: "Orange County Suite" and "(You Need Meat) Don't Go No Further."

36

Smooth as Raven's Claws

Some Common Myths About Morrison's Death

Jim Morrison—it's a strange story—that he died in a bathtub in Paris. It seemed a Goddamned odd thing to happen. I never believed it for a minute.
—William S. Burroughs

Jim Morrison died under mysterious circumstances in his Paris apartment at 17 rue Beautreillis on July 3, 1971. Did he overdose on heroin? Suffer a heart attack? Was he murdered? Did he stage his own death? Morrison had gone to Paris to escape the rigors of the rock 'n' roll lifestyle. Just before he left for Paris, he told his old friend Tom Baker that "My rock 'n' roll days are over." In the lyrics to "Paris Blues," a song that was recorded for *L.A. Woman* but not released, Morrison sang, "Goin' to the city of love, gonna start my life all over again." According to Danny Sugerman in *The Doors Illustrated History*, "In Paris he found new friends, more bars, more fans, and without a focus for his enormous talents and his strident search he became bored, depressed, and confused. And he drank." Since Morrison's death was shrouded in mystery, many myths have arisen over the years to try to explain the series of events that led to his tragic death at the age of twenty-seven.

Death of the Lizard King

On July 3, 1971, Jim Morrison reportedly died of "heart failure" in the bathtub of a spacious Paris apartment, which was located in the Marais *arrondissement* on the Right Bank. During his last few months, Morrison had decided to quit the band, retire to Paris, and become a serious poet.

When Doors manager Bill Siddons showed up in Paris, he was greeted by Morrison's girlfriend, Pamela Courson, with a sealed coffin and a death certificate that listed the cause of death as a heart attack. No autopsy had been performed since there was no indication of foul play. The State Department released a "Report of the Death of An American Citizen" that mistakenly claimed Morrison was born in Clearwater, Florida. The report listed the time of death as 5 a.m. on July 3, 1971, and the cause of death as "Heart Failure," which was certified by Dr. Max Vassille. Morrison was buried rather unceremoniously in Pere Lachaise Cemetery on July 7, 1971. In its August 5, 1971, obituary for Morrison, *Rolling Stone* magazine stated, "The Doors frontman exits under mysterious circumstances; his death is made public two days after his burial in Paris."

Pamela's Version

According to Courson, she and Morrison went to see a movie, *Pursued*, a film noir-style Western starring Robert Mitchum, on the evening of July 2. After the film, they stopped to eat at a Chinese restaurant. When they returned to their apartment, Morrison started coughing up blood. About 3 a.m., the couple went to bed. An hour later, Courson was awakened by Morrison's coughing and gurgling. She woke him up and suggested he take a bath. Morrison started throwing up, but later told her he felt better. She returned to bed and left him in the bathtub. About an hour later, she went to check on him, and he was dead. Courson later told Siddons that he "had a half-smile on his face."

Heroin Overdose Rumor

Rumors spread throughout Paris that Morrison had actually overdosed on heroin at a nightclub called "The Circus." However, according to Ray Manzarek, "To my knowledge, Jim had never tried heroin. Certainly not in the States." Others claim that it was the mind-numbing quantity of booze Morrison consumed that led to his hasty demise. In *The Lizard King*, Doors biographer Jerry Hopkins stated, "I am certain that Jim died of an overdose of heroin, complicated by the alcohol level in his bloodstream." Meanwhile, a Scandinavian magazine published an article suggesting Morrison was actually assassinated by French intelligence agents for unknown reasons. What is known to be true is that Morrison had a respiratory ailment and was reportedly coughing up blood for nearly two months in Paris.

Faked Death Rumors

Long before he was famous, Morrison had suggested faking his own death to get some publicity for the Doors. Did Morrison actually fake his death and head to Africa, following in the footsteps of his hero Rimbaud? Courson took the secret with her to the grave, overdosing on heroin on April 25, 1974. The Morrison-faked-his-own-death rumors intensified in 1980 with the phenomenal success of Jerry Hopkins and Danny Sugerman's Morrison biography *No One Here Gets Out Alive*. The authors suggest at the end of the book that "if there was ever a man who was ready, willing, and able to disappear," it was Morrison. In addition, they conclude that "it would be perfectly in keeping with his unpredictable character for him to stage his own death as a means to escape his public life."

Phantom's Divine Comedy

In 1974, Capitol Records released a mysterious album called *Phantom's Divine Comedy* that was full of mysticism and wizards or as one critic described it, "The Doors on a Tolkien binge." Rumors quickly spread that it was actually Jim Morrison singing vocals backed by an anonymous band that featured Drummer X, Bassist Y, and Keyboardist Z. Other rumors spread that it was actually Iggy Pop singing on the album. As it turns out, the lead singer, "Arthur Pendragon," was reportedly an eccentric musician from Michigan. Some of the band members regrouped for a second album in 1978 under a new name, the Happy Dragon Band. Album tracks included "Tales of a Wizard," "Devil's Child," "Calm Before the Storm," "Half a Life," "Spiders Will Dance (On Your Face While You Sleep)," "Black Magic/White Magic," "Merlin," "Stand Beside My Fire," and "Welcome to Hell."

"Morrison is still alive" rumors were reinvigorated when a mysterious album called *Phantom's Divine Comedy* was released in 1974 that featured a lead singer that some believers insisted was Jim Morrison.   *Courtesy of Kerry Humpherys/doors.com*

The Bank of America of Louisiana

One of the strangest post-Morrison artifacts was a book called *The Bank of America of Louisiana*, which was published in 1975 and opened with the line: "This is the story of the reappearance on earth of a dead Hollywood rock star as super hippie, disguised as a mild-mannered Louisiana banker." In the legendary "He's hot, he's sexy and he's dead" issue of *Rolling Stone* magazine (September 17, 1981), Doors biographer Jerry Hopkins wrote, "The 200 pages of prose that followed were described accurately by one of the few book reviewers who paid it any attention as 'either prenatal or post-Quaalude.'" The author was reportedly an eccentric from an influential family in Louisiana who changed his name to Jim Morrison after claiming the spirit of the Lizard King entered his body during an acid trip. His so-called revelation inspired him to fight the establishment by subverting its financial institutions. Finding *The Bank of America of Louisiana* is pretty difficult these days, and a used copy usually sells for $75 or more on Amazon.

The Poet in Exile

"Was it all an elaborate ruse to free the Poet from his worldly entanglements . . . and send him off to ports unknown where he could pursue his craft unencumbered?" Ray Manzarek's first novel, *The Poet in Exile* (2001), deals with the myth of Morrison staging his own death. "Roy" traces "the Snake Man" to a remote island in the Indian Ocean, where he is the happily married father of two children. Roy and the Snake Man, whose real name is "Jordan," discuss the possibility of reuniting the band. In the novel, Manzarek refers to Robby Krieger simply as "the guitar player" and John Densmore as "the drummer." The thinly disguised story also features a studio album called *Angel Woman* (*L.A. Woman*), an epic poem known as "Sacrifice of the Reptile" ("Celebration of the Lizard"), and a spoken-word poetry album called *A Prayer for the American Century* (*An American Prayer*).

37

Ancient Shapes Were All Around Us

Jim Morrison's Final Resting Place

"Que Devient Le Rere Quand Le Rere Est Fini" ("What becomes of the dream when the dream's over")

—*Epitaph inscribed on the grave of Italian dancer Serge Peretti at Pere Lachaise Cemetery*

Jim Morrison's grave in the Cemetery of Pere Lachaise (Cimetiere du Pere-Lachaise) is still one of the most visited sites in Paris, and the cemetery also serves as the final resting place of Frederic Chopin, Honore de Balzac, Marcel Proust, Edith Piaf, Isadora Duncan, Heloise and Abelard (the original Romeo and Juliet), Moliere, Oscar Wilde, Max Ernst, Guillaume Apollinaire, Colette, Max Ophuls, Gertrude Stein and Alice B. Toklas, Richard Wright, Maria Callas, and Sarah Bernhardt, among many other famous people.

Morrison had visited the cemetery approximately one month before his death and reportedly told a friend he would like to be buried there someday. In *The Doors by the Doors*, Morrison's father commented, "I was impressed with the fact that here was my son getting into a great cemetery in Paris. I thought it was quite an honor for him and the

This "Unknown Soldier" ad stating "It's All Over" and featuring Jim Morrison striking a crucifixion pose eerily foreshadowed the Lizard King's death in Paris on July 3, 1971. *Courtesy of Robert Rodriguez*

family to have a man in that position where he's side-by-side with the great literary people of the past century."

When he returned from Paris, Doors manager Bill Siddons released the following statement to the media:

> I have returned from Paris, where I attended the funeral of Jim Morrison. Jim was buried in a simple ceremony, with only a few friends present. The initial news of his death and funeral was kept quiet because those of us who knew him intimately and loved him as a person wanted to avoid all the notoriety, and circuslike atmosphere that surrounded the deaths of such other rock personalities as Janis Joplin and Jimi Hendrix. I can say that Jim died peacefully of natural causes—he had been in Paris since March with his wife, Pam. He had seen a doctor in Paris about a respiratory problem and had complained of this problem on Saturday—the day of his death. I hope that Jim is remembered not only as a rock singer and poet, but as a warm human being. He was the most warm, most human, most understanding person I've known.

History of Pere Lachaise Cemetery

At 118.6 acres, Pere Lachaise (known affectionately by Parisians as "la cite des morts" or the city of the dead) is the largest cemetery in Paris and reputedly the world's most visited. It is located in the 20th *arrondissement* on Boulevard de Menilmontant. Established by Napoleon I in 1804, Pere Lachaise takes its name from the confessor to Louis XIV, Pere Francois de la Chaise (1624–1709). Pere Lachaise is also the site of three World War I memorials. It is said that Pere Lachaise, with approximately 1.5 million visitors annually, is the fourth most visited site in the Paris area—after Versailles, the Louvre, and the Eiffel Tower.

Graveside Ceremony

The funeral service took place on a Wednesday afternoon (July 7, 1971). Morrison's graveside ceremony has been described as "pathetically inadequate" at best. Attended by Pamela Courson, Alain Ronay, Agnes Varda, Robin Wertle, and Bill Siddons, the ceremony involved the attendees bowing their heads and throwing dirt on the cheap wooden coffin. A Frenchwoman, Madame Colinette, who was visiting a nearby grave, found the observances at Morrison's grave "disgraceful." Quoted in *Stairway to Heaven*, Colinette remarked, "Everything was done in a hurry . . . No priest was present, everybody left quickly. The whole scene was piteous and miserable."

Tenth Anniversary

The three surviving Doors visited the grave on the tenth anniversary of Morrison's death (July 3, 1981). They were accompanied by a Boston film-maker. According to reports, Manzarek made a speech, questioning aloud if Morrison was actually buried there. Manzarek later remarked, "I'd love to have a celebration going on at my grave every day like Jim has." Throughout the years, Morrison's grave has attracted graffiti artists and stoned groupies. On the twelfth anniversary of Morrison's death in 1983, the police used tear gas to break up a group of mourners. Two people were once nabbed trying to dig up Morrison's coffin. The bust of the Lizard King adorning his Paris plot was vandalized before being stolen in 1990.

Jim Morrison's grave as it appeared in 1986, complete with a bust created by sculptor Mladen Mikulin (the bust was stolen in 1988). *Courtesy of Susan Bourdin/jimmorrisonsparis.com*

Twentieth Anniversary

On July 3, 1991, the twentieth anniversary of Morrison's death, thousands rioted at the grave when guards tried to close the cemetery at night. After they were expelled from the cemetery, they continued to demonstrate on the street, late at night, chanting and setting cars on fire. French police used tear gas to disperse the crowd.

"True to His Own Spirit"

A bronze plaque on Morrison's tombstone reads "KATA TON DAIMONA EAYTOY," Greek for "True to his own spirit." Morrison's father came up with the quote. Security guards (paid for by the estate), closed-circuit cameras, and nighttime floodlights now protect Morrison's grave.

Some of the more colorful Morrison-related graffiti to appear in the cemetery over the years includes "Acid Rules," "Morrison This Way," "Jim was a Junkie," "This is Not the End," "Jim Lives," "Nietzsche was right, Jim Morrison is dead," "Jim, Welcome to the Severed Garden," and "Stoned Immaculate."

Many celebrities have visited Morrison's grave to pay their respects, including Patti Smith, Iggy Pop, Jim Carroll, Bono, Ian Astbury of the Cult, Billy Idol, Axl Rose, and others. In addition, American punk rocker Stiv Bators's ashes were spread over Morrison's grave by his girlfriend, according to legend. Bators (the Dead Boys, the Lords of the New Church) was struck by a taxi and killed in Paris in 1990 at the age of forty. However, cult director John Waters claims that Bators's girlfriend actually snorted his ashes.

38

Wandering in Hopeless Night

Other Musicians Who Died at the Age of Twenty-Seven

Castles made of sand fall in the sea, eventually.
— *Jimi Hendrix*

After Jimi Hendrix and Janis Joplin died within weeks of each other in the fall of 1970, Jim Morrison told his friends, "You're drinking with No. 3." Hendrix, Joplin, and Morrison all died at the age of twenty-seven. Along with Brian Jones of the Rolling Stones and Kurt Cobain of Nirvana, they are the most prominent members of the notorious "27 Club." In addition, Morrison's "cosmic mate," Pamela Courson, followed the "Lizard King" to the grave three years later, overdosing on heroin on April 25, 1974, at the age of 27. According to Ray Manzarek in an interview that appeared in the *St. Petersburg Times* (June 7, 2005), "It was success . . . [Morrison] was the same age as Janis Joplin and the same age as Kurt Cobain. They couldn't make it past that hurdle into adulthood. The people worship you . . . you become godlike. And they just couldn't handle that weight without intoxication."

Other notable members of the 27 Club include Rudy Lewis of the Drifters, Malcolm Hale of Spanky and Our Gang, Arlester Christian of Dyke and the Blazers, Amy Winehouse, Gary Thain of Uriah Heep and Keef Hartley Band, Roger Lee Durham of Bloodstone, Helmut Köllen of Triumvirat, Chris Bell of Big Star, D. Boon of Minutemen, Pete de Freitas of Echo & the Bunnymen, Mia Zapata of Gits, Kristen Pfaff of Hole, Raymond "Freaky Tah" Rogers of Lost Boyz, Sean McCabe of Ink & Dagger, Jeremy Michael Ward of De Facto and the Mars Volta, Bryan Ottoson of American Head Charge, and others.

Robert Johnson (1911–38)

Both Robert Johnson and Jim Morrison shared a love of the blues and died under mysterious circumstances at the age of twenty-seven. In fact, details of Johnson's entire life remain sketchy. Known as the "King of the Delta Blues

Singers," Johnson was born out of wedlock on May 8, 1911, in Hazelhurst, Mississippi. Johnson, who roamed from town to town performing in juke joints, recorded just twenty-nine songs, never performed outside of the South, achieved little commercial success during his lifetime, and died in relative obscurity.

Johnson started playing guitar as a teenager, learning the ropes from such blues legends as Charlie Patton, Son House, and Willie Brown. According to legend, Johnson sold his soul to the devil one night at a country crossroads in exchange for his guitar talent. During his brief lifetime, he recorded such blues classics as "I Believe I'll Dust My Broom," "Sweet Home Chicago," "Love in Vain," "Cross Road Blues," "Stones in My Passway," "Terraplane Blues," "Me and the Devil Blues," and "Hellhound on My Trail."

The events of Johnson's death on August 16, 1938, in Greenwood, Mississippi, are shrouded in mystery. According to legend, he was poisoned by a jealous husband in a Mississippi juke joint. However, his death certificate stated that he died of syphilis. Johnson's songs have been covered by Elmore James, Cream, the Rolling Stones, Captain Beefheart, and many others. Eric Clapton called Johnson "the most important blues singer that ever lived." In 1986, Johnson was inducted into the Rock and Roll Hall of Fame as an "Early Influence." He is ranked No. 5 on *Rolling Stone* magazine's list of the "100 Greatest Guitarists of All Time."

Jesse Belvin (1932–60)

A popular R&B singer and songwriter during the 1950s, Jesse Belvin was born in Texarkana, Texas, and moved with his family to Los Angeles at the age of five. Belvin, who joined saxophonist Big Jay McNeely's backing vocal quartet, Three Dots and a Dash, in 1950, signed with Specialty Records two years later. In 1953, his album *Dream Girl*, which featured Marvin Phillips on saxophone, reached No. 2 on the R&B charts.

Belvin cowrote "Earth Angel" with Curtis Williams of the Penguins. The song became a major hit for the Crew-Cuts in 1955, reaching No. 2 on the charts. Belvin's biggest hit was "Goodnight My Love," which reached No. 7 on the R&B charts. He also had a Top 40 hit in 1959 with "Guess Who," which was written by his wife, Jo Anne. Tragically, Belvin and his wife were killed in a head-on collision after a raucous concert (the first-ever integrated concert in the area) in Hope, Arkansas, in 1960. Before the concert, Belvin had received several death threats, and there has been speculation over the years that his car was tampered with, but those allegations have never been proven. Belvin is buried at Evergreen Memorial Park in Boyle Heights, California.

Brian Jones (1942–69)

Rolling Stone Brian Jones died on July 3, 1969, exactly two years to the day before Jim Morrison's own death in Paris. Morrison penned a tribute to Jones in the form of a poem titled "Ode to L.A. While Thinking of Brian Jones—Deceased," and distributed it at the Doors' Aquarius Theatre performances on July 21, 1969. The poem can be found in *Wilderness: The Lost Writings of Jim Morrison, Volume 1*, which was published in 1988.

Jones was born on February 28, 1942, learned how to play the guitar (his influences were Muddy Waters, Jimmy Reed, Howlin' Wolf, and Willie Dixon), and formed the Rolling Stones in 1962. He reportedly named the band after picking up a copy of *The Best of Muddy Waters*, which featured "Rollin' Stones Blues." The Rolling Stones made their debut at the Marquee Club in London on July 12, 1962. In its August 1969 obituary for Jones, *Rolling Stone* magazine stated, "If Keith and Mick were the mind and body of the Stones, Brian was clearly the soul." However, by 1969, Jones was mired in drug addiction, and Mick Jagger and Keith Richards asked him to leave the group. Less than a month later, Jones was discovered floating in the swimming pool of his country estate, Cotchford Farm, the former home of A. A. Milne, the creator of Winnie the Pooh. During a Rolling Stones concert three days after Jones's death, Jagger recited Shelley's "Adonais" in tribute to him, and thousands of butterflies were released.

Although Jones's drowning was ruled "death by misadventure," speculation of foul play has continued to this day. In fact, Anna Wohlin, his girlfriend at the time of death, penned a book called *The Murder of Brian Jones*, claiming that one of the builders working on Jones's house murdered him.

Alan "Blind Owl" Wilson (1943–70)

Born on July 4, 1943, in Boston, Massachusetts, Alan Wilson was nicknamed "Blind Owl" for his extreme nearsightedness. In 1966, Wilson cofounded with Bob "the Bear" Hite the white blues band Canned Heat, one of the Doors' favorite groups. Canned Heat performed at both the Monterey Pop Festival in 1967 and Woodstock in 1969, and scored two Top 20 hits: "On the Road Again" and "Going up the Country." Wilson, who suffered from bouts of depression, died of a drug overdose on September 3, 1970. A "fanatical conservationist" who often slept outdoors, he was discovered in a sleeping bag behind Hite's Topanga Canyon home. Hite himself would die of a drug overdose after a gig at the Palomino in 1981 at the age of thirty-eight.

Jimi Hendrix (1942–70)

Widely regarded as the greatest electric guitarist in rock history, Jimi Hendrix was born on November 27, 1942, in Seattle, Washington. After serving a stint as a paratrooper in the 101st Airborne Division, Hendrix backed musicians such as James Brown, Little Richard, B. B. King, and Jackie Wilson. In June 1967, Hendrix caught a performance by the Doors at the Scene in New York City while he was en route to the Monterey Pop Festival, where he performed a riveting version of "Wild Thing," doused his guitar with lighter fluid, and set it on fire.

Morrison caught Hendrix's first gig at the Whisky A Go Go the following month. On another notorious night at the Scene, an extremely inebriated Morrison crawled on stage while Hendrix was performing with the Chambers Brothers, grabbed him around the legs, and yelled, "I want to suck your cock."

Hendrix formed the Jimi Hendrix Experience with bassist Noel Redding and drummer Mitch Mitchell and recorded three classic albums: *Are You Experienced* (1967), *Axis: Bold as Love* (1968), and *Electric Ladyland* (1968). In an interview with the *Record Mirror*, Hendrix stated, "We don't want to be classed in any category. If it must have a tag, I'd like it to be called 'Free Feeling.' It's a mixture of rock, freak-out, blues, and rave music." Hendrix performed at the 1970 Isle of Wight Festival along with the Doors several weeks before his death. He died after suffocating on his own vomit on September 18, 1970, in London. In its October 15, 1970, obituary for Hendrix, *Rolling Stone* magazine stated, "The world's greatest guitarist dies in a hotel room after an apparent sleeping pill overdose." He is buried at Greenwood Memorial Park and Cemetery in Renton, Washington. The grave receives approximately 15,000 visitors annually. Hendrix was ranked No. 1 on *Rolling Stone's* list of the "100 Greatest Guitarists of All Time."

Janis Joplin (1943–70)

Born on January 9, 1943, Janis Joplin grew up as a true outsider in her hometown of Port Arthur, Texas, and she was voted "Ugliest Man on Campus" in a college poll. She soon headed to California and made her debut with Big Brother and the Holding Company at the Avalon Ballroom in San Francisco on June 10, 1966. Joplin's energetic performance at the Monterey Pop Festival helped to establish her legend. In 1968, the band released *Cheap Thrills*, which reached No. 1 on the charts, featured famous cover art by R. Crumb, and contained the hit "Piece of My Heart," which reached No. 12 on the U.S. charts. Joplin left Big Brother and the Holding Company and formed her own group, Kozmic Blues Band, which later became Full Tilt Boogie.

Two months before her death, Joplin discovered that one of her musical idols, Bessie Smith, the "Empress of the Blues," was buried in an unmarked grave in Sharon Hill, Pennsylvania. Joplin bought an expensive headstone for Smith that read "The Greatest Blues Singer in the World Will Never Stop Singing." Joplin, who always carried a pint of Southern Comfort around with her, died of a heroin overdose alone in room 105 at the Landmark Hotel (7407 Franklin Avenue, Hollywood) on October 4, 1970. It was just three days after Hendrix's funeral. In its October 29, 1970, obituary for Joplin, *Rolling Stone* magazine stated, "Rock's foremost female voice is silenced during the recording sessions for *Pearl*. Joplin was 27."

Joplin's posthumous album, *Pearl*, was produced by the "fifth Door" himself, Paul Rothchild, and featured her only No. 1 single, "Me and Bobby McGee" (written by Kris Kristofferson). It was only the second posthumous No. 1 single in history (Otis Redding's "Dock of the Bay" being the first). Joplin's ashes were scattered in the Pacific Ocean. The 1979 film *The Rose*, which starred Bette

Midler, was loosely based on Joplin's life. Joplin was posthumously inducted into the Rock and Roll Hall of Fame in 1995, following the Doors by two years. Ranked No. 46 on *Rolling Stone* magazine's list of the "100 Greatest Artists of All Time," Joplin was awarded a Grammy Lifetime Achievement Award in 2005.

Ron "Pigpen" McKernan (1945–73)

A rarity among the Grateful Dead, which he cofounded in 1965, Ron "Pigpen" McKernan eschewed LSD in favor of mind-numbing quantities of booze (frequently in the form of cheap wine). According to Grace Slick in her 1998 memoir *Somebody to Love?*, McKernan had a brief affair with Janis Joplin and was "the one who introduced her to Southern Comfort." Born on September 8, 1945, in San Bruno, California, McKernan was drawn to the blues at an early age. In 1964, McKernan helped form Mother McCree's Uptown Jug Champions, which morphed into the Warlocks and later the Grateful Dead.

After years of alcohol abuse, McKernan was diagnosed with advanced liver disease in 1971, forcing him to leave the Grateful Dead. On March 8, 1973, he was discovered by his landlord lying on the floor next to his bed in his Corte Madero, California, apartment. He had been dead for two days. The official autopsy concluded that McKernan died of a "massive gastrointestinal hemorrhage" resulting from his liver disease. He had withered to just over 100 pounds and looked at least twice his twenty-seven years. According to *Rolling Stone* magazine in its April 12, 1973, obituary for McKernan, "The Grateful Dead's 'dirty' keyboard player, 27, is found dead from liver disease in his apartment."

Pete Ham (1947–75)

Born on April 27, 1947, in Swansea, Wales, Pete Ham was a member of Badfinger (originally known as the Iveys), which became the first band signed by the Beatles' Apple label. In fact, Paul McCartney wrote their first hit, "Come and Get It," and George Harrison produced their biggest hit, "Day After Day." Ham cowrote "Without You," which was covered by Harry Nilsson in 1972 and years later became a hit for Mariah Carey.

Ham, who struggled with financial difficulties, hanged himself in the garage of his Surrey, England, home on April 23, 1975, just four days before his twenty-eighth birthday. His blood alcohol level at the time of his death was .27 percent. Ham's suicide letter read "I will not be allowed to love and trust everybody. This is better." In 1983, band member Tom Evans, who reportedly never got over his friend's death, hanged himself in his backyard.

David Michael Alexander (1947–75)

A native of Michigan who was born on June 3, 1947, David Michael Alexander served as the original bassist for the Stooges, a proto-punk band led by Iggy Pop, who first caught the Doors in 1967 at the notorious University of Michigan concert. Alexander met brothers Ron and Scott Asheton at Pioneer High School in Ann Arbor. The trio befriended Iggy Pop in 1967 and formed the Stooges. Alexander played bass on the Stooges' first two albums: *The Stooges* (1969) and *Fun House* (1970). He also reportedly wrote the songs "We Will Fall," "Little Doll," "Dirt," and "Fun House." In 1970, Alexander was fired from the band after showing up too drunk to take the stage at the Goose Lake International Music Festival. Alexander died of pulmonary edema in 1975 in Ann Arbor after being admitted to a hospital for pancreatitis, which was linked to his heavy drinking. In the spoken intro to "Dum Dum Boys" on his solo album *The Idiot*, Pop remarks, "How about Dave? OD'd on alcohol."

Kurt Cobain (1967–94)

Kurt Cobain was born in Aberdeen, Washington, and attended his first punk rock show—Black Flag at the Mountaineer Club in Seattle, in August 1984. Reflecting on the concert, Cobain remarked, "What really changed my attitude, my idea of punk rock, was my first Black Flag concert. It was incredible. I was paralyzed and, at the same time, completely drawn to it with all my being. It was simply the most extraordinary thing I had ever seen. There was this passion, this hatred, this energy that I understood that I could never make any kind of music but that kind." Cobain also fell under the spell of Aberdeen punk band the Melvins.

During the mid-1980s, Cobain formed a succession of pre-Nirvana bands, including Fecal Matter, Brown Towel, and Stiff Woodies. Nirvana formed in late 1986, and their first album, *Bleach*, cost just $606.17 to record and was released in 1989. The band featured Cobain on vocals/guitar, Chris Novoselic on bass, and eventually Dave Grohl on drums.

In his journal, Cobain wrote, "NIRVANA is a trio who play Heavy Rock with Punk overtones. They usually don't have jobs. So they can tour anytime. NIRVANA has never jammed on Gloria or Louie Louie. Nor have they ever had to rewrite these songs and call them their own." Cobain also referred to his lyrics as "a big pile of contradictions" that were "split down the middle between very sincere opinions and feelings that I have and sarcastic and hopefully humorous rebuttles [*sic*] towards cliche-bohemian ideals that have been exhausted for years." In addition, Cobain listed both the Stooges (citing *The Stooges*, *Raw Power*, and *Fun House* among his favorite albums) and Black Flag (*Damaged*) among Nirvana's musical influences. Both the Stooges (especially lead singer Iggy Pop) and Black Flag (particularly Henry Rollins) were influenced strongly by the Doors.

In 1991, Nirvana signed a record deal with Geffen Records and released their masterpiece, *Nevermind*, which featured the hit "Smells Like Teen Spirit." The arrival of Nevermind and the birth of the "grunge" music scene caused a revolution, overshadowing heavy metal as exemplified by such groups as Poison,

Mötley Crüe, Guns N' Roses, and Metallica. In 1992, Cobain married Courtney Love, the lead singer of Hole. The couple had one child, Frances Bean.

In March 1994, Cobain nearly died in Rome after mixing depressants with alcohol. Cobain flew to Los Angeles and checked into a rehab facility but walked out after just forty-eight hours. On April 5, Cobain committed suicide with a shotgun. His body was discovered several days later by an electrician who came to install an alarm system. Cobain's suicide note quoted from Neil Young's "My My, Hey Hey": "It's better to burn out than fade away." Cobain's mother reportedly remarked, "Now he's gone and joined that stupid club." Many conspiracy theorists have speculated that Cobain was actually murdered. In the "documentary" *Kurt and Courtney*, Love's father commented on the death of Cobain: "I don't think he killed himself. I think somebody killed him. I'm not saying Courtney did it. I don't really know, but the evidence is so strong."

39

We Linger Alone

Studio Albums That Were Released After Jim Morrison's Death

Morrison's passing stamped The Doors with a seal of legend and immortality. There was no opportunity for the band to go into the seventies intact. Perhaps that's a good thing. I can't imagine The Doors in the era of disco.
—Henry Rollins

The three surviving Doors did a lot of soul searching during the immediate post-Jim Morrison period. Robby Krieger believed that the band should change their name since they were no longer really the Doors without Morrison, while Ray Manzarek lightheartedly suggested they change their name to "And the Doors." In addition, the Doors reportedly asked both Joe Cocker and Paul McCartney to become the band's new lead singer. Iggy Pop's name also came up as a possibility. Meanwhile, Elektra Records president Jac Holzman had generously offered the band members a recording contract for five albums, of which they only completed two: *Other Voices* in 1971 and *Full Circle* in 1972. In March 1973, the Doors called it quits for good.

Other Voices—Released in October 1971

The first post-Morrison album, *Other Voices*, was recorded in the summer of 1971 and released in October of that year. Bruce Botnick coproduced the album, which featured vocals by both Manzarek and Krieger. The Doors also brought in some studio musicians, including Jerry Scheff, who had played bass on the *L.A. Woman* recording sessions, and Ray Neapolitan, who had worked on the *Morrison Hotel* album. *Other Voices* featured several bright spots such as the energetic "Tightrope Ride" (which peaked at No. 71 on the charts) and the Krieger-penned novelty song "I'm Horny, I'm Stoned." In addition, "Down on the Farm" was allegedly written at the time of the *L.A. Woman* recording sessions, but Morrison rejected it for unknown reasons. Other songs on the album included "In the Eye of the Sun," "Variety is the Spice of Life," "Ships w/Sails," "Wandering Musician," and "Hang on to Your Life."

The Doors launched the new record with a sellout concert at Carnegie Hall and embarked on a short tour in smaller venues across the United States to promote the material. One of the tour dates, Pirates World in Dania on March 10, 1972, returned the band back to South Florida for the first time since the notorious Dinner Key Auditorium concert in 1969, but this performance was considerably less eventful. *Other Voices* reached No. 31 on the U.S. charts, but none of the singles charted.

In a review of *Other Voices* that appeared in *Rolling Stone* magazine, critic Ben Gerson wrote, "The material is weak, the singing colorless, the playing irrelevantly consistent. They are still The Doors, but they are Doors without a cause or a passion, however awkward and uncommunicative those passions could sometimes be." Steve Gattinger of the *Salem Capital Journal* remarked that Morrison's "talents as a lyricist are sorely missed. It would appear that it was his lyrics which provided the impetus for the others' intense psychological instrumentation, for the whole album here seems to lack guts." In addition, rock critic Robert Christgau stated, "This record has some terrific moments, starting with the first hook riff, and the musicians deserve their reputations. But even a good singer couldn't do much with a line like 'To roam is my infection,' and this band could use a good singer." In a 1993 interview that appeared in *The Doors Collectors Magazine*, Manzarek singled out "Tightrope Ride" and "Ships w/Sails" as his personal favorites from *Other Voices.*

Released in October 1971, the Doors' first post-Jim Morrison album reached No. 31 on the charts and failed to produce a hit single.

Courtesy of Stev Bauske/mildequator.com

Full Circle—Released in July 1972

The Doors' last studio album, *Full Circle*, was recorded at A&M Recording Studios in Hollywood in the spring of 1972 and released in July of that year. It was produced by the Doors without Bruce Botnick. One of the album's few highlights was a cover of Roy Brown's "Good Rockin' Tonight" sung by Manzarek. Other songs included "Get Up and Dance," "4 Billion Souls," "Verdillac," "Hardwood Floor," "The Mosquito," "The Piano Bird," "It Slipped My Mind," and "The Peking King and the New York Queen."

According to Doors biographer Greg Shaw in *The Doors on the Road, Full Circle* "was released with a zoetrope of the cover designed to display a moving image of a fetus that progresses to an old man and returns to a fetus when played on a turntable." The album limped into the charts, reaching No. 68 before fading away. *Full Circle* included "The Mosquito," the last hit single by the Doors. Densmore later reflected that "*Full Circle* was a bit of a disaster, but at the time, we had our hearts in it."

The Doors' Final Performance

The Doors' final performance took place at the Hollywood Bowl in Los Angeles on September 10, 1972. The set list featured material from *Other Voices* and *Full Circle* with the addition of crowd pleasers "Love Me Two Times and "Light My Fire." Tim Buckley opened the show, followed by the Doors and headliner Frank Zappa, who premiered his twenty-piece orchestra, the Grand Wazoo, and performed contemporary jazz and classical pieces to the bewildered audience.

The Doors' set included "Tightrope Ride," "In the Eye of the Sun," "The Mosquito," "Love Me Two Times," "Piano Bird," "Verdillac," "I'm Horny, I'm Stoned," "Ships with Sails," and "Light My Fire." Manzarek dedicated "Light My Fire" to Morrison, remarking, "I know you're out there somewhere man, so get ready for it 'cause here it comes!"

Interestingly, Manzarek failed to even mention the Doors' final performance or the last two studio albums in his autobiography *Light My Fire*. For his part, Densmore in *Riders on the Storm* brought up the two post-Morrison albums in passing, commenting that *Other Voices* "wasn't bad." In fact, neither *Other Voices* nor *Full Circle* has ever been released on CD in the United States. In addition, the albums are conspicuously absent from both *The Doors Box Set* (1997) and *The Complete Studio Recordings* (2000).

Jim Morrison Memorial Disappearance Party

On July 3, 1974, the third anniversary of Morrison's death, Manzarek helped organize a "Jim Morrison Memorial Disappearance Party" at the Doors' old stomping ground, the Whisky A Go Go. Iggy Pop joined the three Doors onstage and sang a couple of Doors songs. Pop had dyed his hair black and wore a Jim Morrison T-shirt for the occasion. He also sported a pair of Morrison's black leather pants supposedly given to him by Manzarek. During a rendition of "L.A. Woman," Pop added these lyrics: "Jim Morrison died today, Jim Morrison was more beautiful than any girl in this town, and now he's dead, now I cry."

40

Death Not Ends It

Factors That Led to the Doors' "Resurrection"

I see myself as a huge fiery comet, a shooting star. Everyone stops, points up and gasps "Oh, look at that!" Then whoosh, and I'm gone . . . and they'll never see anything like it ever again . . . and they won't be able to forget me—ever.
—*Jim Morrison*

In the early 1970s, with the rise of singer-songwriters such as Carole King and James Taylor, followed by the era of disco, the Doors started falling off the radar—with minimal airplay on commercial radio. However, by the end of the decade a startling renaissance of interest in the band took place through albums like *An American Prayer* and *The Doors Greatest Hits*, movies such as Francis Ford Coppola's Vietnam War epic *Apocalypse Now*, which featured the haunting ballad "The End," and the bestselling Jim Morrison biography *No One Here Gets Out Alive*. A whole new generation of teenager Doors fans arose, proving that the group's sound was timeless. In fact, over the years the Doors have sold more than 75 million albums worldwide, and new generations of fans continue to discover the band and their enigmatic lead singer.

Rise of Punk Rock

Doors record sales plummeted during the peak years of disco fever between 1974 and 1976, averaging approximately 100,000 sales a year, but started to rise again in the late 1970s along with the emergence of punk rock. In "The Legacy of Jim Morrison and The Doors," which appeared in the April 4, 1991, issue of *Rolling Stone* magazine, writer Mikal Gilmore remarked, "As punk rose, it brought with it a reevaluation of rock history, and as a result, some of the tougher-minded bands of the late 1960s—such as the Doors, the Velvet Underground, MC5 and the Stooges, all of which had explored some difficult and often unpopular themes during their short-lived careers—enjoyed a new currency that transformed them into some of American rock's more enduring and pervasive influences."

Certainly punk pioneer Iggy Pop of the Stooges owes much of his early image to Jim Morrison's influence, which can be traced to Pop's attendance at the notorious Doors concert at University of Michigan on October 20, 1967. The Stooges, in turn, influenced many of the early punk bands performing at CBGB's ("country, bluegrass, blues") on New York's Lower East Side as early as 1974 such as the Ramones, Patti Smith (a disciple of both Morrison and Arthur Rimbaud), the Heartbreakers, Television, Suicide, and Richard Hell and the Voidoids.

Punk music was loud and raw, while the attitude was total rebellion against mainstream society. The influential *Punk* magazine made its debut in 1976, giving a name to the movement, which soon spread overseas to London with bands such as the Sex Pistols and Generation X, which featured Billy Idol. Los Angeles punk bands like X and Black Flag (specifically Henry Rollins) were strongly influenced by the Doors' sound. Ray Manzarek even produced X's stunning debut album, *Los Angeles.* The aptly titled *Back Door Man*, an early Los Angeles zine started by Phast Phreddie (Fred Patterson), covered the early punk scene as it evolved on the West Coast.

An American Prayer (1978)

The first sparks of a renewed interest in the Doors were ignited with the release of *An American Prayer* in November of 1978. An album of Morrison's spoken poetry accompanied by newly recorded music by the surviving Doors, *An American Prayer* was billed as "Poems, lyrics and stories by James Douglas Morrison." It was released as a "Jim Morrison Album" with "Music by the Doors" and sold approximately 250,000 copies, making it the biggest-selling album of spoken-word verse in history. *An American Prayer* peaked at No. 54 on the charts and was the first and only Doors album to be nominated for a Grammy Award in the "Spoken Word" category.

According to Ray Manzarek in a *Los Angeles Times* interview from November 19, 1978, "We did this album to show the side of Jim which has been underrated all these years. As far as we were concerned, Jim was a poet. But being the Lizard King has overshadowed the fact that he did some incredible poetry." According to Manzarek, the first part of the album covered Morrison's childhood, the second part his high school years, the third part "the young poet, stoned on a rooftop with acid dreams," the fourth part his time in the Doors, and the fifth part "a final summation in a way, of the man's entire life and his philosophy."

Morrison had recorded much of the poetry on his twenty-seventh birthday at Village Recorders in Los Angeles on December 8, 1970, as well as at an earlier poetry session in March 1969. One review referred to the album as sounding like a "porn-movie soundtrack" for the inclusion of such lines as "Her cunt gripped him like a warm, friendly hand." However, *An American Prayer* had at least one prominent critic: Doors producer Paul Rothchild called the album "a rape" that was similar to "taking a Picasso and cutting it into postage stamp-sized pieces and spreading it across a supermarket wall . . . it was the first commercial sell-out of Jim Morrison." In *Riders on the Storm*, Densmore responded, "Ray, Robby and I worked incredibly hard on the record, trying to make it a 'movie for the ears,' even though we knew that its concept wasn't commercial." In 1995, *An American Prayer* was remastered and rereleased as a CD with bonus tracks.

Apocalypse Now (1979)

John Milius, screenwriter of Coppola's *Apocalypse Now*, once remarked, "When I want some good pagan carnage, I put on the Doors." The inspired use of "The End" at the beginning and end of *Apocalypse Now* was one of the main factors in the Doors' resurrection. In

An American Prayer was released in 1978 and became the first and only Doors album to be nominated for a Grammy Award (in the spoken-word category).   *Author's Collection*

fact, Doors music was extremely popular with U.S. soldiers serving in Vietnam, as author Michael Herr detailed in his 1977 memoir *Dispatches*: "Whenever one of us came back from an R&R we'd bring records, sounds were as precious as water: Hendrix, the Airplane, Frank Zappa and the Mothers, all the things that hadn't even started when we'd left the States . . . the Doors, with their distant, icy sound. It seemed like such wintry music; you could rest your forehead against the window where the air-conditioner had cooled the glass, close your eyes and feel the heat pressing against you from outside."

Coppola, who had attended UCLA film school at the same time as Morrison and Manzarek, was quoted in Peter Cowie's *The Apocalypse Now Book*: "[T]hey fought this war to 'Light My Fire.' They had loudspeakers, this is true, they had loudspeakers and they would play acid rock and roll during the battles and be stoned on dope when the flares went across the sky . . . I mean, it was the most absurd war that has ever been fought and I want to get that imagery. Can you imagine playing 'Light My Fire' on loudspeakers as the enemy is approaching?"

A very loose adaptation of Joseph Conrad's novella *Heart of Darkness*, *Apocalypse Now* was originally titled *The Psychedelic Soldier*. In fact, Coppola intended to use "Light My Fire" in "some kind of cathartic way" at the end of the movie or during the Do Lung Bridge scenes. Milius preferred using "Light My Fire" over "The End" during the opening sequence but was overruled by Coppola. "Break on Through (to the Other Side)," "I Can't See Your Face in My Mind," "Summer's Almost Gone," "When the Music's Over," and "People Are Strange" were also incorporated into the film but missed the final cut. According to Densmore in *Riders on the Storm*, "Vietnam vets were in an insane war, and Jim sang 'all the children are insane.' This lyric section opened *Apocalypse Now*. Jim connected to people on the edge because they could sense that he, too, was on the edge."

Promoter Bill Graham, who had first booked the Doors in early 1967 at the Fillmore Auditorium in San Francisco, appeared in the film during the Playboy Bunny sequence; Morrison's old buddy Dennis Jakob served as special assistant to Coppola; and Harrison Ford, a former Doors roadie, appeared in a bit role as an officer who briefs Willard on Kurtz.

No One Here Gets Out Alive (1980)

The Doors' resurrection a decade after Morrison's death would not have been possible without the success of the first Jim Morrison biography, *No One Here Gets Out Alive*, which was cowritten by Jerry Hopkins and Danny Sugerman. The book made the rounds of publishers for years before finally being accepted by Warner Books (who had originally rejected it) through the diligence of Sugerman. The book, which included the famous "Lizard King" image of Morrison on its cover, took its name from a line in "Five to One," which appeared on the Doors' third album, *Waiting for the Sun*. The book also perpetuated a lot of myths about Morrison such as the idea that he may have faked his own death. In fact, Hopkins had originally wanted to release two versions of the biography: one in which the lead singer died in Paris and the other where he faked his death to escape the pressures of rock stardom. Phenomenally successful, *No One Here Gets Out Alive* spent nine months on the bestseller list. In 1995, an audio version of the book was released and read by Sugerman himself.

Lower Record Prices

Despite rather pedestrian record sales during the disco era, by 1980 every album in the Doors catalog had doubled or tripled its sales over the previous year. Elektra Records made the decision to lower prices on three Doors albums—*The Doors*, *Waiting for the Sun*, and *The Soft Parade*—from $8.98 to $5.98. The records in turn started flying off the shelves, resulting in approximately 2.5 million albums sold in 1981 alone. In the September 17, 1981, issue of *Rolling Stone* magazine, Bryn Bridenthal, vice president of Elektra/Asylum Records, remarked, "The group is bigger now than when Morrison was alive. We've sold more Doors records this year than in any year since they were first released." The renewed interest in the band led to more airplay on FM stations and the development of a new fan base of teenagers who were just toddlers when Morrison died in 1971.

The Doors Greatest Hits (1980)

The Doors released their fourth compilation album, *The Doors Greatest Hits*, in 1980, and it sold almost a million copies in that year alone, making it the band's all-time bestselling album. The cover included a huge image of Morrison in the heyday of his "Lizard King" persona with no sign of the other band members until you flipped it over. The album featured a solid introduction to the Doors sound, with each of the band's six studio albums represented, including "Hello, I Love You," "Light My Fire," "People Are Strange," "Love Me Two Times," "Riders on the Storm," "Break on Through (to the Other Side)," "Roadhouse Blues," "Not to Touch the Earth," "Touch Me," and "L.A. Woman."

Released in 1980, *The Doors Greatest Hits* was a significant factor in the band's resurrection and helped to introduce the music to a whole new generation of fans nearly ten years after Jim Morrison's death.   *Author's Collection*

CREEM Special Edition on the Doors (Summer 1981)

Overshadowed by *Rolling Stone* magazine's subsequent tribute to the Doors in its September 17, 1981, issue (perhaps simply because of the sensational "He's hot, he's sexy and he's dead" cover), *CREEM's Special Edition on The Doors* stands on its own. Billed as a "Special Ten Year Commemorative Issue," the magazine (which sold for $2.95) featured "Tongues of Knowledge in the Feathered Night (The Blue Bus is Double Parked): The Doors on Record" by Richard Riegel; "Jim Morrison: Ten Years Gone" by Lizze James; "Jim Morrison, Oafus Laureate" by Lester Bangs; "A Shaman's Sojourn Through the Doors" by Danny Sugerman; "Morrison in Miami: Flesh and Memories" by Dave DiMartino; and "Jukebox Cruci-Fix" by Patti Smith, as well as other articles, interviews with the three surviving Doors, full-color pull-out posters, and rare photos.

In his classic piece on the band, Bangs commented, "The Beats meant to bring poetry back to the streets and the gutter-mind of the people at large, and they succeeded: they gave birth to Jim Morrison, a giant resplendent in the conviction that stardom may guarantee Chivas Regal till you drown, but to clown is divine and ultimately sexy." Sugerman in turn declared, "Jim had to stand directly in front of Hell before he could storm its gates." Billed as "America's Only Rock 'n' Roll Magazine," *CREEM*, based in Detroit, was first published in March 1969.

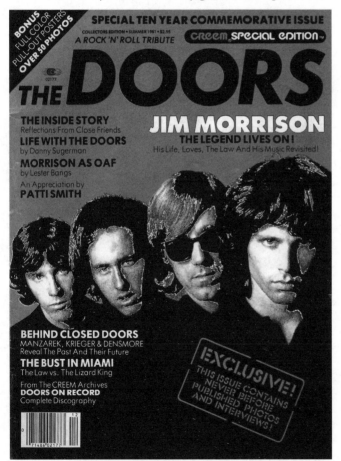

CREEM magazine's *Special Edition on the Doors* was published in the summer of 1981 and featured a gold mine of eclectic features on the band such as Lester Bangs's "Jim Morrison, Oafus Laureate."

Author's Collection

Rolling Stone (September 17, 1981)

The infamous *Rolling Stone* cover for September 17, 1981, featured a huge image of Jim Morrison in his prime along with the title "Jim Morrison. He's hot, he's sexy and he's dead" and the subtitle "More than a decade after his death, The Lizard King is bigger than ever. What is his hold on modern pop culture?" The main story, "Jim Morrison, 1981: Renew My Subscription to the Resurrection (Teenage Morrison Mania)" by Rosemary Breslin, highlighted the popularity of Morrison and the Doors among a new generation of teenage fans. According to Breslin, "Most of these teenagers couldn't care less whether Morrison actually exposed himself or not; they simply adore the fact he would even think of doing it. The new generation of Doors fans, many of whom were in kindergarten when the band peaked in the late Sixties, is attracted to Morrison's unabashed sexiness, the lure of his voice and the hot, ornery lyrics."

Breslin's article also quoted Manzarek praising the new generation of Doors fans: "I think the kids are getting the message. I think they understand the words and the music . . . I'm proud of them. They're not a bunch of little idiots. All hope is not lost. Morrison introduced them to a bit of literature."

In addition, rock critic Jerry Hopkins, the coauthor of *No One Here Gets Out Alive*, weighed in with an article titled "Jim Morrison is Alive and Well All Over the Place," discussing the Morrison-faked-his-own-death myth. Finally, *Crawdaddy!* founder Paul Williams broke down four popular Doors songs ("Light My Fire," "The End," "Riders on the Storm," and "When the Music's Over") in the article "Music Without the Myth." Other articles featured in this issue included "Did the Colonel Cheat Elvis?," "Democrats in Decline," and "The Go-Go's: Girl Group for the Eighties." Interestingly, the top five albums listed on September 17, 1981, were Pat Benatar's *Precious Time*, Stevie Nicks's *Bella Donna*, Foreigner's *4*, Rickie Lee Jones's *Pirates*, and Journey's *Escape*.

Alive, She Cried (1983)

Produced by Paul Rothchild, *Alive, She Cried* was released in November 1983 as the Doors' eleventh album and featured live recordings between 1968 and 1970 from concerts in Los Angeles, New York, Detroit, and Copenhagen. The album's title was taken from a line in "When the Music's Over." *Alive, She Cried* contained plenty of highlights to please Doors fans. For instance, Morrison's macabre "Graveyard Poem" (actually recited during a Boston concert in April 1970) was incorporated into an extended version of "Light My Fire," while "Horse Latitudes" appeared within a hypnotic version of "Moonlight Drive."

Other songs on *Alive, She Cried* included "You Make Me Real," "Texas Radio and the Big Beat," and "Love Me Two Times." The album also boasted lively covers of Willie Dixon's "Little Red Rooster," featuring John Sebastian of the Lovin' Spoonful on harmonica and recorded at the Felt Forum in 1970, and Them's "Gloria," which was recorded during a soundcheck to an empty hall at the Aquarius Theatre in July 1969.

In the album's liner notes, critic Benjamin Edwards wrote "The Van Morrison classic ["Gloria"] was one of the first songs the band had worked up as they invented themselves in a makeshift Venice rehearsal room, and a presence that would snake through their entire history. They used it to flesh out their earliest sets, jamming on it with Van himself when the Doors opened for his group Them at the Whisky A Go Go. It was central to the late 1966 performances at the New York club Ondine that helped win the band its influential East Coast following, and a song they would continue to call upon every so often until their final shows in 1971." *Alive, She Cried* was discontinued in 1991 after the release of *In Concert*, which included all the songs from the album, as well as *Absolutely Live* and some bonus tracks.

The Doors: The Illustrated History (1983)

Danny Sugerman, who cowrote (with Jerry Hopkins) *No One Here Gets Out Alive*, the first biography about Jim Morrison, had an instrumental role in the Doors' resurrection. As a young teenager, Sugerman began hanging out at the Doors office and eventually started answering fan mail and compiling a comprehensive scrapbook of the band that would later evolve into *The Doors: The Illustrated History*, which was published in 1983. The 204-page book contained concert reviews (both positive and negative), features on the Doors, and illustrations covering every page, as well as the original Elektra Records biographies for all four band members. The only drawback to *The Illustrated History* is that the articles are not dated.

In the book's introduction, Sugerman exclaims, "Jim was obsessed with discovery: finding meaning, understanding why we are and where we are going. He searched compulsively for the pulse of the world." Highlights of *The Doors: The Illustrated History* include Digby Diehl's "The Doors' Story," which appeared in *Eye* magazine and provides early background details of the band; Richard Goldstein's critical appraisal of the band, "The Doors Open Wide," from *New York Magazine*; Fred Powledge's "Wicked Go the Doors," a firsthand account for *Life* magazine of the notorious New Haven Arena concert; Lizze James's entertaining interview with a philosophical Morrison ("I think people resist freedom because they're afraid of the unknown . . ."); Joan Didion's "Waiting for Morrison," which captures conflicts between Morrison and the other band members during the turbulent *Waiting for the Sun* recording sessions); and Larry Mahoney's *Miami Herald* article "Rock Group Fails to Stir a Riot," which fueled the flame after the Miami concert.

41

You've Seen This Entertainment Through and Through

The (In)Accuracy of *The Doors*

The portrayal of Jim Morrison as this crazed, drunken poet spouting his poetry on the streets and on the beach . . . It was a fantastical look at a poet, and I always thought it was Oliver Stone in leather pants. That's what that movie is. It's not Jim.

—Ray Manzarek

Oliver Stone's highly entertaining, if historically inaccurate, film *The Doors* opened to decidedly mixed reviews on March 1, 1991, exactly twenty-two years to the day after the band's infamous concert at the Dinner Key Auditorium in Miami. Although titled *The Doors*, the film is actually a highly fictionalized portrayal of Jim Morrison. In an interview that appeared in *The Doors Collectors Magazine* (Fall 1993), Doors biographer Jerry Hopkins remarked, "About 40% of the scenes were made up, chronology was ignored, and characters were merged."

"Stuck in a Bar with an Obnoxious Drunk"

The cast of *The Doors* included Val Kilmer as Jim Morrison, Meg Ryan as Pamela Courson, Kyle MacLachlan as Ray Manzarek, Frank Whaley as Robby Krieger, and Kevin Dillon as John Densmore. In addition, Stone had a cameo as Morrison's film professor, Densmore appeared as the recording engineer during Morrison's solo poetry session on December 8, 1970, and Krieger can be seen briefly in a scene at the London Fog.

Film critic Roger Ebert of the *Chicago-Sun Times* stated, "Watching the movie is like being stuck in a bar with an obnoxious drunk when you're not drinking." Promoter Bill Graham, who served as executive producer on the film but had little input into the final product, was also reportedly less than pleased with the result. However, by far the biggest critic of *The Doors* was Manzarek, who wanted

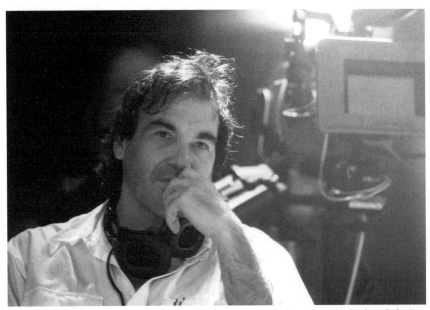

A self-described Doors fanatic, Oliver Stone became fascinated with the band during his stint as a soldier in Vietnam. The first time he heard "Light My Fire" was a "fucking revolution," according to Stone.   *Author's Collection*

the film to focus on all four band members rather than just on Morrison. In an interview with *The Doors Collectors Magazine*, Manzarek called the film "a pathetic portrayal of an alcoholic and not the Jim Morrison that I knew." Manzarek was disgusted by the fact that the film did not include scenes that reflected Morrison's "lyrical or musical genius." Manzarek even criticized MacLachlan's portrayal as "too wooden" and advised him to loosen up and "get a membership in the hemp brigade."

Responding to the avalanche of criticism, Stone stated, "[Morrison] was everything to everybody, and no one will quite agree on all the events." In a *Rolling Stone* magazine interview, Kilmer reiterated "[I]f you interviewed 100 people about Jim Morrison, you came away with 135 versions of the guy. The people I was directly involved with convinced me I was on the right track, and what else can you ask for as an actor?"

However, even Krieger and Densmore were impressed with Kilmer's total immersion into the Morrison character. According to Krieger in *The Doors by the Doors*, "I thought Val Kilmer did a great job, and I thought, 'Hell, it could have been a lot worse.' Kilmer even pulled a De Niro, gaining thirty-five pounds to portray Morrison in decline.

Background of *The Doors*

Plans for a Doors film had languished in Hollywood for more than ten years, with various directors such as Francis Ford Coppola, Brian De Palma, William Friedkin, and Martin Scorsese expressing interest. Meanwhile, the diverse lineup of actors rumored for the part of Morrison over the years included John Travolta, Richard Gere, Tom Cruise, Michael O'Keefe, Timothy Hutton, Kevin Costner, Gregory Harrison, Steven Bauer, Michael Ontkean, Christopher Lambert, Bono from U2, Michael Hutchence from INXS, Timothy Bottoms, Jason Patric, Keanu Reeves, and Ian Astbury of the Cult (and later lead singer of the Doors of the 21st Century).

Stone had been fascinated with the Doors since he enlisted in the Army in 1967. As an infantryman in the 2nd Platoon of Bravo Company, 3rd Battalion, 25th Infantry, Stone was stationed on the Cambodian border for 15 months starting on September 16, 1967 (a day before the Doors performed "Light My Fire" on *The Ed Sullivan Show*). In a 1988 interview with *Playboy* magazine, Stone remarked, "I remember the first time we heard 'Light My Fire.' It was a fucking revolution!" Stone, who was wounded twice and received a Purple Heart and Bronze Star, was discharged in November 1968. When Morrison died in Paris in 1971, Stone remarked, "it was like the day Kennedy died." By the time he took on the Doors biopic, Stone had compiled an impressive list of screenwriting and directing credits such as *Midnight Express* (1978), *Scarface* (1981), *Salvador* (1986), *Platoon* (1986), *Wall Street* (1987), and *Born on the Fourth of July* (1989). He has revealed that the character of Sgt. Elias (portrayed by Willem Dafoe) in

The famous peyote scene in *The Doors* was totally fabricated. In fact, none of the Doors ever reportedly even dropped acid together.   *Author's Collection*

Although riddled with historical inaccuracies, Oliver Stone's 1991 film *The Doors* featured an intense performance by Val Kilmer as Jim Morrison. Robby Krieger later remarked that Kilmer should have received an Academy Award nomination for the role.

Author's Collection

his 1986 Oscar-winning film *Platoon* was based on Morrison: "He was a free spirit, a Jimmy Morrison in the bush. Handsome . . . he was our god."

During the production of *The Doors*, Stone relied heavily on *No One Here Gets Out Alive* and Densmore's autobiography, *Riders on the Storm*, as well as some minor memoirs such as Judy Huddleston's *This is the End . . . My Only Friend: Living and Dying with Jim Morrison*, which prominently featured blurbs on its cover from both Stone ("An extremely important book that put Jim Morrison into perspective for the film") and Kilmer ("The book was my bible for the film"). Huddleston even served as an advisor on the film.

Historical Inaccuracies

According to Manzarek, Morrison was portrayed in the movie as an "out-of-control sociopath," while omitting the sensitive poet with a great sense of humor that he knew. Manzarek also stated that Stone totally misinterpreted Morrison's student film at UCLA (which has unfortunately been lost to history), making it seem like a "fascist statement." According to Manzarek in *Light My Fire*, "Oliver tried to re-create Jim's film based on what I told him . . . Of course, he went completely over the top."

One of the most interesting parts of the film was early on when the band members bond by taking peyote in the desert. Of course, the scene is purely fiction. In fact, though all of the Doors took LSD in the mid-'60s, there are no reports that they dropped acid together. Stone also has the band signing with Elektra Records immediately after they got fired from the Whisky A Go Go, when in fact they signed their record contract while still working as house band at the nightclub. In another scene, involving the Doors' first visit to New York City, Stone has the band being mobbed by fans and identifying themselves for a television camera. However, they were virtually unknown in New York City at the time, and the camera incident took place over a year later during their 1968 European Tour.

A number of live performances in the film were also fictionalized, including the Doors' appearance on *The Ed Sullivan Show*. Although Morrison did defy the show's producer during "Light My Fire," Stone has him shouting the word "higher" defiantly into the camera when in fact he sang the lyrics the same way he had countless times before. Before the New Haven Arena concert (which Stone labels as 1968 when it was actually 1967), Stone portrays Morrison as getting maced backstage as he chats with Patricia Kennealy. In fact, he was backstage with a coed from a nearby college whom he had just picked up. In addition, the Kennealy character mentions that Morrison attended the University of Florida when in fact he went to Florida State University. Stone later admitted that the Kennealy character was actually a composite and should have been given a fictional name in the film.

The portrayal of Pamela Courson in *The Doors* was softened in the film and she became "a cartoon girlfriend," according to Doors biographer Ben Fong-Torres. Courson's parents reportedly insisted that there be no suggestion that Courson, a heroin addict who overdosed in 1974, had anything to do with Morrison's death. Morrison first meets Courson after crashing a house party when in fact the two reportedly met for the first time at the London Fog. The movie also depicts Morrison locking Courson in a closet and setting it on fire, an incident that apparently never happened.

42

Can't Remember Where I've Been

Other Films That Feature the Doors

[M]aking a film is one of the hardest artistic endeavors anyone could ever undertake, and I'm not so sure the actual filming process is even artistic at all. I think it's akin to Hannibal moving elephants over the Alps.

—Ray Manzarek

As graduates of the UCLA Film School, both Jim Morrison and Ray Manzarek were fascinated with the prospect of combining their interest in films and filmmaking with the world of rock 'n' roll. In fact, the Doors created one of the first pre-MTV music videos when they dramatized "The Unknown Soldier" in a three-minute film shot on Venice Beach. In addition, the Doors enlisted a film crew to create a documentary of the band on tour that would become *Feast of Friends* and feature some lively footage such as the infamous Singer Bowl concert in 1968 that devolved into a full-scale riot. Also, in the wake of cancelled tour dates that followed the notorious Miami concert in 1969, Morrison got the opportunity to work on his experimental film *HWY*, which detailed the exploits of a murderous hitchhiker (played by the "Lizard King" himself). The several video compilations of Doors performances released over the years are definitely hit or miss. However, *The Doors Collection* (released in 1999) is a must-have for any hardcore Doors fan—consisting of *Dance on Fire*, *Live at the Hollywood Bowl*, and *The Soft Parade*, as well as bonus material such as two of Manzarek's UCLA Film School projects (*Evergreen* and *Induction*) and Henry Diltz's photojournal tour of the *Morrison Hotel* album sessions.

HWY (1969)

In the spring of 1969, Morrison embarked on a film project called *HWY* (originally titled *Hitchhiker*) with his drinking buddies Paul Ferrara (cinematography), Frank Lisciandro (editor), and Babe Hill (sound)—the same crew that worked on the Doors' documentary, *Feast of Friends*. Ironically, it was the fallout from the Miami concert, which included a string of cancelled tour dates, that gave

Morrison time to work on the project. Based in part on his screenplay *The Hitchhiker*, which can be found in *The American Night: The Writings of Jim Morrison, Volume 2*, the experimental film with little dialogue features a bearded Morrison wandering desert highways, encountering a dead coyote, hitchhiking, and apparently murdering the driver who gives him a ride. Portions of the film were shot at the Alta Cienega Motel, which served as Morrison's primary residence during the late 1960s. Morrison also does a dance atop the low wall on the roof of the 9000 Sunset Building. The mysterious call Morrison makes from a pay phone ("I wasted him") during the film was made to poet Michael McClure. *HWY* was featured at the Vancouver Film Festival and the "Jim Morrison Film Festival" in Toronto. Portions of *HWY* can be viewed in the 2010 Doors documentary *When You're Strange*.

Feast of Friends (1970)

In the spring of 1968, the Doors agreed to produce a documentary film that would include live concert footage along with behind-the-scenes footage of the band on tour. Morrison assembled a film crew from his friends Paul Ferrara, Babe Hill and Frank Lisciandro (all of whom would later assist him with his experimental film *HWY* the following year). Filming began while the Doors toured in April 1968 and concluded with the band's final performances before embarking on their European tour in September of that year. Whenever the film crew showed up at concerts, Morrison would do his best to incite the crowd to get some footage (most evident during the Singer Bowl concert debacle on August 2, 1968).

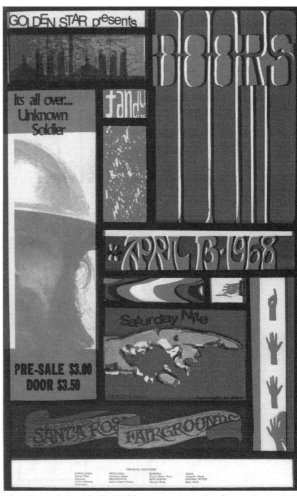

The Doors' April 13, 1968, concert at the Santa Rosa Fairgrounds featured a production crew for *Feast of Friends* for the first on-location shooting of the documentary.

Courtesy of Mark Smigel/mildequator.com

The fifty-minute film's soundtrack features live performances of "Strange Days," "Wild Child," "Moonlight Drive," "Five to One," "Not to Touch the Earth," and a legendary rendition of "The End," where Morrison does an elaborate shamanistic dance, which was recorded at the Hollywood Bowl on July 5, 1968. According to Lisciandro in his memoir *Jim Morrison: An Hour for Magic*, "Jim's appearance at the Hollywood Bowl in 1968 was a triumphant acclamation of the success the Doors had achieved. The cavernous Bowl was packed to capacity with fans and celebrities. Jim was never more playful, or more generous with his audience. He danced, sang, joked and recited poems. He had a good time and we captured a lot of it on film for *Feast of Friends*." Behind-the-scenes footage in *Feast of Friends* includes Morrison performing "Ode to Friedrich Nietzsche" while banging on a piano, a weird conversation between Morrison and Pastor Fred L. Stegmeyer, and Morrison attempting to comfort an injured fan (who had been hit with flying debris) backstage at the notorious Singer Bowl concert.

In 1969, Morrison and Lisciandro attended the Atlanta International Film Festival, where they were awarded a Gold Medal for *Feast of Friends*. According to Lisciandro, Morrison got insanely drunk at the award ceremony and "grabbed an empty wine bottle, shoved it under the draping, white table cover, unzipped his fly and enjoyed the relief of emptying his bursting bladder. Finished, he returned the now almost filled green wine bottle to the table, placing it among the empty ones." *Feast of Friends* was never officially released, although portions can be viewed in other videos, including the documentary, *When You're Strange*.

No One Here Gets Out Alive (1981)

A companion video to the bestselling 1980 Morrison biography, *No One Here Gets Out Alive* is a true artifact that features fascinating interviews with the three surviving Doors members, authors Jerry Hopkins and Danny Sugerman, producer Paul Rothchild and Elektra Records president Jac Holzman, as well as clips of interviews with Morrison. Although the production values come off like a cheap wedding video of the time, *No One Here Gets Out Alive* includes some rare footage, and was the first video released by the band. It also featured full-length performances of "Touch Me," "The Changeling," and "L.A. Woman," as well as clips from performances of "Five to One," "Back Door Man," "Celebration of the Lizard," "The End," "Moonlight Drive," "Crawlin' King Snake," "The Unknown Soldier," "People Are Strange," "Light My Fire," and "When the Music's Over." Along with the bestselling book that spent nine months on the bestsellers list, the video helped rekindle interest in the Doors.

Dance on Fire (1985)

Directed by Ray Manzarek, *Dance on Fire* premiered at the Roxy in Los Angeles on April 11, 1985. The film's title was taken from "When the Music's Over," the Doors' epic on *Strange Days*: "For the music is your special friend/Dance on fire as it intends." Essentially a compilation of concert footage, music videos, promo films, and live TV performances strung together, *Dance on Fire* features the original Elektra Records promotional clip for "Break on Through (to the Other Side)," "People Are Strange" from *The Ed Sullivan Show* and the *Murray the K Special*, "Light My Fire" from *The Ed Sullivan Show*, "Wild Child" from an Elektra recording session, an "L.A. Woman" video directed by Manzarek, "The Unknown Soldier" promotional film, "Roadhouse Blues" from 1968 concert footage, "Texas Radio and the Big Beat" and "Love Me Two Times" from the Danish TV special, "Touch Me" from *The Smothers Brothers Comedy Hour*, "Horse Latitudes"/"Moonlight Drive" from *The Jonathan Winters Show*, "The End" from the July 5, 1968, Hollywood Bowl concert, "The Crystal Ship" from *American Bandstand*, and "Adagio"/"Riders on the Storm."

Live at the Hollywood Bowl (1987)

Filmed and recorded on July 5, 1968, *Live at the Hollywood Bowl* features a surprisingly sedate performance by Morrison, who later revealed that he had dropped acid before the show. Morrison, who wore a weird blue and gold vest, rarely strayed from the microphone stand and chain-smoked cigarettes during most of the concert, which began with an extended version of "When the Music's Over." At one point, Morrison even belched loudly into the microphone to the amusement of the crowd before launching into the "We want the world" phase of the song. The rather lackluster set included "Alabama Song," "Back Door Man" (which briefly morphed into "Five to One"), "Moonlight Drive"/"Horse

Latitudes," "Go Insane" and "The Hill Dwellers" (both from Morrison's epic poem, "Celebration of the Lizard"), "Spanish Caravan," "Wake Up," and "Light My Fire."

Perhaps the most interesting aspect of the performance was the finale, which featured the band's original epic "The End." It started with Morrison chiding "Mr. Light Man" to "turn the

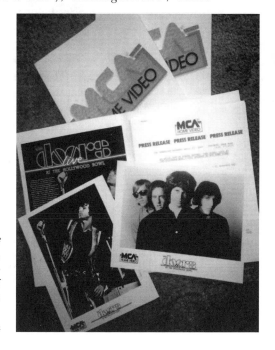

MCA Home Video released *Live at the Hollywood Bowl* amid much fanfare in 1987, although the actual show was not that memorable except for a mesmerizing rendition of "The End" that featured the humorous "Ode to a Grasshopper."

Courtesy of Ida Miller/idafan.com

lights down." In the middle of the song, Morrison then embarked on a story (about an accident involving "six bachelors and their bride"). Then Morrison spotted what he thought was a grasshopper on the stage and recited "Ode to a Grasshopper" (later discovering it was a moth). Finally, he embarked on a bizarre shamanistic dance. According to Manzarek in *Canyon of Dreams*, "You saw Jim Morrison possessed and become the shaman in 'The End.' The last ten minutes of that show were visually intense, an insane performance."

One interesting sidelight of the Hollywood Bowl concert was that future Hollywood superstar Harrison Ford worked on the crew. In addition, the Rolling Stones' Mick Jagger and his then-girlfriend, Marianne Faithfull, had a front-row seat for the Doors concert and later remarked to his producer that he had found the show "boring." The *Feast of Friends* crew was also on hand at the concert. Built in 1929, the Hollywood Bowl had a storied history and hosted many memorable acts over the years such as the Beatles, Bob Dylan, and Janis Joplin. Jimi Hendrix even opened for the Monkees there in 1967.

The Doors Are Open (1991)

The Doors Are Open was first broadcast on UK television on October 6, 1968, as part of the "Pioneer Artist Concert Film Series." Filmed in black and white, the documentary captured the Doors' electric performance at the Roundhouse in London during their European Tour on September 6, 1968. Interspersed with scenes from the Vietnam War and footage of protests in the United States to give it a political edge, *The Doors Are Open* features powerful renditions of some of the band's most popular songs: "Light My Fire," "When the Music's Over," "Five to One," "Hello, I Love You," "The Unknown Soldier," and "Spanish Caravan," as well as their cover of Willie Dixon's "Back Door Man." Quoted in a *Rave* magazine article ("The Explosive Jim Morrison"), the Doors' lead singer reflected on the Roundhouse concert: "They were one of the best audiences we've ever had. Everyone seemed to take it so easy. It was like going back to the roots again and it stimulated us to give a good performance. They were fantastic."

The Doors' performance at Asbury Park Convention Hall on August 31, 1968, was filmed for *Feast of Friends* and featured an extended encore of "The End."

Courtesy of Ida Miller/idafan.com

The Doors: Soundstage Performances (2002)

Soundstage Performances highlights three totally diverse Doors performances at different stages of their career in Toronto, Denmark, and New York City. In 1968, the band performed "The End" on a Toronto soundstage. Later that year, they performed in Denmark as part of their European Tour. Finally, they took the stage in New York City in 1969. According to Danny Sugerman, "Even without an audience, the Doors mesmerize, playing for nothing but the cameras. Morrison still delivers electrifying performances. Whether reciting poetry in Denmark preceding 'Love Me Two Times' or getting it on during 'The Soft Parade'—Jim Morrison's charisma, beauty and brilliance shine during all."

Live in Europe 1968 (1989)

Filmed during the Doors' only European Tour in the fall of 1968, *Live in Europe 1968* features rare live performances in London, Stockholm, Frankfurt, and Amsterdam. The video features an introduction and narration by Paul Kantner and Grace Slick of Jefferson Airplane, who shared the bill with the Doors during the tour. Highlights include Kantner and Slick discussing Morrison's notorious drug-fueled collapse onstage in Amsterdam, the famous footage of each band member introducing themselves, the "firing squad" skit during "The Unknown Soldier," and Morrison's improvisation during "Back Door Man" ("Ya love me don't cha baby . . . Climb all over me baby . . . touch me . . . play with me . . . "), as well as footage of the Doors at Morrison's grave upon the tenth anniversary of his death in 1981. Other performances featured in the fifty-eight-minute, black-and-white video include "Light My Fire," "Love Me Two Times," "Spanish Caravan," "Hello, I Love You," "When the Music's Over," and "Alabama Song."

Classic Albums: The Doors (2008)

A fascinating documentary about the Doors' groundbreaking debut album, *Classic Albums: The Doors* features interviews with Manzarek, Densmore, Krieger, Bruce Botnick, Jac Holzman, Bill Siddons, Ben Fong-Torres, Michael McClure, Paul Ferrara, and legendary Los Angeles DJ Jim Ladd.

Billed as "the definitive authorized story of the album," the documentary features rare footage, live performances, and musical demonstrations, including Krieger performing a riveting "Light My Fire" guitar solo. Each song on the album is dissected during the documentary, and even songs that didn't make the cut such as "Moonlight Drive," the first song the Doors recorded (which would later appear on the *Strange Days* album), are analyzed. Fascinating anecdotes abound, such as an LSD-fueled Morrison returning to the Sunset Studio Recorders late at night after the band recorded "The End" and hosing down the studio with a fire extinguisher. The album took just six days to record since the band had honed the material at Sunset Strip bars for almost a year before hitting the recording studio. "The first album is basically the Doors live," according to Manzarek, while Botnick refers to "Break on Through" as "probably the most definitive song of their work in what made the Doors different than anybody else."

Classic Albums: The Doors also features discussion of the early days in Venice Beach, organizing the band, recording the demo, rehearsing, performing at the London Fog and Whisky A Go Go, and signing a record deal with Elektra Records. Songs performed in the documentary include "Break on Through," "The Crystal Ship," "Back Door Man," "Alabama Song," "Light My Fire," "End of the Night," and "The End."

The Doors from the Outside (2009)

An interesting perspective on the Doors from a group of rock journalists and writers familiar with the band's history, *The Doors from the Outside* also features rare footage as well as classic live and studio performances. Those interviewed in the documentary, which was "not authorized by The Doors or their management," include Robert Christgau, Johnny Rogan, Dave DiMartino, Ritchie Unterberger, Doug Sundling, James Riordan, Richard Goldstein, and Patricia Kennealy Morrison, among others. In addition, *The Doors from the Outside* includes interviews with Billy James ("the man who 'discovered' Jim Morrison") and Marc Benno, a legendary session musician who played guitar on *L.A. Woman*.

43

The Ceremony Is About to Begin

The Doors' Induction into the Rock and Roll Hall of Fame

I think we're the band you love to hate. So I, it's been that way from the beginning, you know. We're universally despised. I kind of, I kind of relish the whole situation.

—*Jim Morrison*

Just one year after they were eligible, the Doors were inducted into the Rock and Roll Hall of Fame on January 12, 1993, in front of a crowd of 1,400 at the Century Plaza Hotel in Los Angeles, along with Cream, Creedence Clearwater Revival, Van Morrison, Etta James, Sly & the Family Stone, Ruth Brown, and Frankie Lymon and the Teenagers. Not only was it the first induction ceremony held in Los Angeles, but it was also the beginning of a new tradition of enlisting young artists to play the music of inductees—including the Counting Crows performing Van Morrison's "Caravan," Boyz II Men singing a Frankie Lymon and the Teenagers tune, and Eddie Vedder of Pearl Jam standing in for Jim Morrison alongside the Doors.

Induction Ceremony

At the induction ceremony, Vedder gave a brief speech that started with him joking about dropping acid back stage to calm his nerves. Next he told a humorous anecdote about how each member of the Doors got out of the draft: Ray Manzarek swallowed foil so it would look like he had an ulcer, John Densmore simply acted psychotic, and Robby Krieger said he was homosexual. However, Jim Morrison received a "Z" classification, and "no one even knows what that means," joked Vedder. Vedder then recited a list of all the Doors' biggest hits and then remarking, "It's amazing to me that all of these songs and all of the records were in this period of '67 to '71. Six records. It makes me real proud and honored to induct them into the Rock and Roll Hall of Fame."

The enduring legacy of the Doors continues from merchandising to various awards and honors such as the band's 1993 induction into the Rock and Roll Hall of Fame.

Courtesy of Ida Miller/idafan.com

Standing in for Jim Morrison was his sister, Anne Cherney, who simply stated, "On behalf of my family I would like to thank you for honoring Jim tonight. Thank you very much." Next up was Robby Krieger, who thanked his parents, who were in attendance. Krieger stated that when the band first started out they were "kind of broke," and "we need to borrow $300 for a piano bass. And my parents loaned us $300. And believe it or not, they never asked for it back." Ray Manzarek spoke next, injecting some politics into the evening by stating: "We are theoretically the class of 1967. Lest we forget 1967 was the Summer of Love. So please now that the '90s are here, now that a new administration has taken over, from my perspective now that the fascists are no longer in office . . . We're gonna try to reinstitute into the '90s the feeling, the spirit, of the '60s." Manzarek then cited Morrison's influences as the Beat Generation—particularly Lawrence Ferlinghetti, Jack Kerouac, Allen Ginsberg, and Michael McClure—"while Robby, John and I were into jazz." Manzarek also read a selection from Morrison's poem "An American Prayer." Finally, Densmore took the podium and thanked his parents "for eventually coming to terms with the lyric, 'Father? Yes, son? I want to kill you. Mother, I want to . . .' I want to send my love to Ray and Robby and, most importantly, I want to thank Jim."

Performance

The band performed "Roadhouse Blues," "Break on Through," and "Light My Fire," with Vedder handling vocal duties. Vedder even injected Morrison's "Dead Cats, Dead Rats" poem into "Break on Through." At the end of "Light My Fire," Manzarek shouted "Keep the fire alive!" as the crowd gave the band a standing ovation.

The lead singer of alternative rock band Pearl Jam, Vedder was born Edward Louis Severson III in 1964. He grew up in Southern California but moved to Seattle in 1990 to join the band, which was initially called Mookie Blaylock. Pearl Jam signed with Epic Records in 1991 and released their debut album, *Ten*, which became one of the bestselling alternative albums in the 1990s and placed the band at the forefront of the so-called "grunge" movement along with Nirvana, Soundgarden, and Alice in Chains. The album featured a slew of hits such as "Jeremy," "Black," and "Alive." In 2007, Vedder released his first solo album, the soundtrack for *Into the Wild*. That same year, John Densmore stated that he would rejoin the band for a fortieth anniversary concert tour only if someone of Vedder's caliber could be enlisted as lead singer. In an interview with *Classic Rock* magazine (Summer 2007), Densmore remarked, "I'm not dissing Ian Astbury, but if you want to talk about greatness then there's Eddie Vedder."

History of the Rock and Roll Hall of Fame and Museum

The Rock and Roll Hall of Fame Foundation was created in 1983. The inaugural class of inductees in 1986 included Chuck Berry, James Brown, Ray Charles, Sam Cooke, Fats Domino, the Everly Brothers, Buddy Holly, Jerry Lee Lewis, Little Richard, and Elvis Presley. The decision to locate the Rock and Roll Hall of Fame in Cleveland, Ohio, stemmed from the fact that legendary Cleveland DJ Alan Freed was widely credited with promoting the term "rock and roll" back in the 1950s (it also helped that the city pledged $65 million in public money to fund the museum's construction). The groundbreaking and building plans for the Rock and Roll Hall of Fame and Museum in Cleveland were announced at the 1993 induction ceremony. On June 7, 1993, a groundbreaking ceremony for the museum was held with Pete Townshend of the Who and Chuck Berry doing the honors.

The Rock and Roll Hall of Fame and Museum officially opened on September 2, 1995, on the shores of Lake Erie in downtown Cleveland (Yoko Ono and Little Richard were among the celebrities who helped perform the ribbon-cutting ceremony). From May 25, 2007, to September 1, 2008, the Rock and Roll Hall of Fame and Museum featured an exhibit called "Break on Through: The Lasting Legacy of the Doors," in honor of the band's fortieth anniversary. In addition, the museum features a Jim Morrison exhibit that contains the original lyrics to "Not to Touch the Earth," as well as Morrison's Cub Scout uniform, first poem ("The Pony Express"), a jacket that belonged to Pamela Courson, baby book, baptism certificate, report cards, high school diploma, drawings, cards, letters, last will and testament, and photos of his grave at Pere Lachaise Cemetery in Paris.

44

Follow Me Down

Musicians Who Have Been Influenced by the Doors

The key to The Doors is the culture behind the myth.

—*Iggy Pop*

With their timeless, innovative music combined with the cult fascination surrounding rock icon Jim Morrison, the Doors have inspired countless musicians over the past forty years such as proto-punk legends Iggy Pop and Patti Smith, punk rock bands like X and Black Flag (particularly lead singer Henry Rollins), post-punk bands such as the Cult and Echo & the Bunnymen, and alternative rock bands that include Jane's Addiction and Stone Temple Pilots. Today, musical artists like Chester Bennington continue to reveal the Doors' widespread influence—the lead singer of Linkin Park handled vocal duties on a cover of "Riders on the Storm" that appeared on Carlos Santana's 2010 album, *Guitar Heaven* (which also featured Ray Manzarek on keyboards).

Iggy Pop

Acknowledged in some circles as the "Father of Punk Rock," James Newell Osterberg Jr. was born on April 21, 1947, and grew up in a trailer park in Ypsilanti, Michigan. Embarking on his musical career as a professional drummer, Osterberg backed several Motown groups such as the Four Tops and later formed a band called Megaton Two, which morphed into the Iguanas (Osterberg rechristening himself "Iggy").

Osterberg attended the Doors' infamous concert at the University of Michigan on October 20, 1967. In a March 25, 2010, interview with *SPIN* magazine, he described the scene as something out of the prom dance in *Carrie*:

> When the dude appeared, Morrison, he lurched onto the stage, and people probably thought he was drunk. But I knew that cat had three or four hits of acid. His pupils were totally dilated, and he had on a sort of Hedy Lamarr-as-Delilah outfit, and when he opened his mouth, he sang only in falsetto baby talk. There was no applause. No approval.

No comprehension. It was a visibly unsuccessful evening, and that's what I loved about it in retrospect. Afterwards, I was vibrating with this feeling that I have no excuse not to get our miserable, good-for-nothin' band out on the stage.

On March 3, 1968, the Stooges (orginally known as the Psychedelic Stooges and named in honor of Moe, Larry, and Curly) performed their first gig opening for Blood, Sweat & Tears at Detroit's Grande Ballroom. With the Stooges, Pop soon took Morrison's stage antics to a new level—rubbing peanut butter, hamburger meat, and raw steaks all over his body; slicing his chest open with broken glass; and hurling himself into the audience. In "Toking Down with the MC5," a January 4, 1969, *Rolling Stone* magazine article, Pop was described as having "the potential to make Jim Morrison look like a tame puppy." In an interview with Salli Stevenson that appeared in *Circus* magazine (Winter

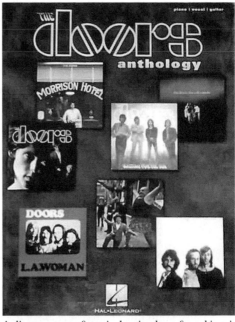

A diverse array of musical artists have found inspiration in the Doors' small but influential catalog of albums such as Iggy Pop, Patti Smith, Henry Rollins, Axl Rose, and Perry Farrell, among many others.   *Courtesy of Ida Miller/idafan.com*

1970), Morrison was asked what he thought of groups likes the Stooges and Alice Cooper and he answered, "I like people who shake other people up and kind of make them uncomfortable. A young friend of mine [presumably Danny Sugerman] thinks Iggy is great." Music critic Lester Bangs of *CREEM* magazine called Pop the "most intense performer" he had ever seen.

Miraculously, in 1968 the Stooges landed a deal with the Doors' label, Elektra, and recorded two albums—*The Stooges* (1969), which was produced by the Velvet Underground's John Cale, and *Funhouse* (1970)—that failed miserably but have since been acknowledged as proto-punk classics. Mired in drug addiction, the band broke up and later re-formed as Iggy & the Stooges for *Raw Power* (1973), one of the most influential punk rock albums of all time. Once again, the album failed to sell, the band broke up, and Pop sank into the abyss of heroin addiction. In the 1970s, the Stooges' musical influence extended to such punk bands as Suicide, the New York Dolls, the Sex Pistols, the Damned, the Germs, and Black Flag. According to the *Rolling Stone Album Guide*, "During the Stooges' brutal and brief career, more people heard about the antics of singer Iggy Pop than ever heard the band's music. His lizard charisma still is undeniable, but these albums have endured beyond all expectations. Punk, glitter, shock-rock, thrash-metal: this is where it begins—and ends up."

Patti Smith

A disciple of both Arthur Rimbaud and Jim Morrison, Patti Smith was born on December 30, 1946, the daughter of a New Jersey factory worker. A former writer for *CREEM* magazine, Smith published two books of poetry, *Witt* and *Seventh Heaven*, before embarking on a singing career.

In June 1975, Smith's article "Jukebox Cruci-Fix," appeared in *CREEM* magazine, chronicling her visit to Morrison's grave at Pere Lachaise Cemetery in Paris:

> I went to Jim Morrison's grave . . . I sat there like some jack ass sobbing in the mud all alone in paris . . . but there was nothing . . . I remembered this dream I had. I came in a clearing and saw a man on a marble slab. it was Morrison and he was human. but his wings were merging with the marble. he was struggling to get free but like Prometheus freedom was beyond him.

In November 1975, Smith released her stunning debut album, *Horses*, which included a rendition of Them's "Gloria" strongly influenced by the Doors' live performances of the song. Smith also did guest vocals on Ray Manzarek's second solo album, *The Whole Thing Started with Rock & Roll*. No less an authority than Beat legend William S. Burroughs was a big fan of Smith's performing abilities, remarking: "It isn't the poetry itself, it's the way she puts it across. She's a terrific performer, a great stage presence." Smith could whip herself into a total frenzy onstage and once confessed, "All I know is that in some moment every night, I'm so committed that I piss myself or come on stage."

Smith married Fred "Sonic" Smith of the MC5 in 1980, and the couple settled in Detroit with their two children. She was inducted into the Rock and Roll Hall of Fame in 2007. In 2010, Smith won the National Book Award in the nonfiction category for her memoir *Just Kids*, which details her life in New York City in the 1960s and 1970s, as well as her relationship with controversial artist Robert Mapplethorpe.

Henry Rollins of Black Flag

Born Henry Garfield on February 13, 1961, Rollins was the manager of a Washington, D.C. Haagen-Dazs ice cream shop and Black Flag "superfan" when the Los Angeles-based hardcore punk band invited him to be their new lead singer in 1981. Originally known as Panic, Black Flag was founded by guitarist Greg Ginn in 1977 in Hermosa Beach, California. Black Flag scored their first gig at an outdoor Parks Department concert at Hollywood Park by claiming they were a Fleetwood Mac cover band.

In November 1981, Black Flag released *Damaged*, an album full of such hits as "Spray Paint," "Police Story," "TV Party," and "Six Pack." In an early interview, Rollins described his intense performance style: "I feel pain every day of my life. When you see me perform, it's that pain you're seeing coming out. I put all my emotions, all my feelings, and my body on the line." In his diary, Rollins described Black Flag's live shows as "the ultimate soundtrack to a full-scale riot."

Rollins also wrote a foreword to *The Doors by the Doors*, the band's official biography that was published in 2006. In it he admitted that "Break on Through" was a "revelation" to him when he first heard the song, calling it "intense, revolutionary music." In addition, he claimed that "People Are Strange" helped him understand his own feelings of alienation during his teenage years: "Like many young people, I did not fit in and had no backup, no corner man. The Doors became that for me." He also described Morrison as "a dangerous mind . . . an intellectual and artistic anarchist." Currently, Rollins hosts IFC's *The Henry Rollins Show* and runs his own publishing company, 2-13-61.

Perry Farrell of Jane's Addiction

Known as "the Godfather of Alternative Rock," Perry Farrell was born Peretz Bernstein on March 29, 1959. Farrell formed Jane's Addiction in 1986. Jane's Addiction paved the way for such bands as Nirvana, Pearl Jam, Alice in Chains, and Stone Temple Pilots. The band featured Farrell on vocals, Dave Navarro (guitar), Eric Avery (bass), and Steve Perkins (drums). *Nothing's Shocking* (1988) contained the hit single, "Jane Says." In addition, in 1991 Farrell organized the first Lollapalooza Tour, which featured his new band, Porno for Pyros, accompanied by a diverse lineup of supporting artists such as Henry Rollins, Living Colour, and Ice-T.

In the 2000 Doors tribute album *Stoned Immaculate*, Farrell and Exene (of the Los Angeles punk band X) performed "Children of Night" (backed by the surviving Doors). In 2006, Farrell wrote a foreword to *The Doors by the Doors*, acknowledging his debt to the band: "As a boy, the music—and the musicians—formed my identity. Lighting my passion, they guided me through life's great adventure."

The Cult

Originally known as Southern Death Cult, then Death Cult, and finally just the Cult, this band featured a lineup that included Ian Astbury (vocals), Billy Duffy (guitar), Jamie Stuart (bass), and a succession of drummers that variously included Ray Mondo, Nigel Preston, and Mark Brzezicki. In 1984, the Cult released *Dreamtime*, an album that *The Rough Guide to Heavy Metal* described as follows: "The ghosts of Morrison and Hendrix were lurking within the grooves of *Dreamtime* but the fusion of Astbury's spiritual yelping and Duffy's guitar lines had yet to reach a convincing critical mass." The *Rolling Stone Album Guide* described the band as "essentially a heavy-metal band for folks who think they're above such things" with a "sound out of equal parts post-punk guitar aggression and neo-hippy mysticism, a combination that quite naturally results in some of the most pompous and silly music rock has seen since the heyday of the Doors."

The band embarked on a headlining tour with Guns N' Roses that featured such lowlights as Astbury frequently trashing the band's equipment in an alcoholic stupor during concerts. Astbury organized the Gathering of the Tribes in October 1990 with a diverse bill that included Ice-T, Soundgarden, Public Enemy, Iggy Pop, and the Charlatans.

The Cult performed "Wild Child" on the 2000 Doors tribute album *Stone Immaculate*. In addition, Astbury sang "Touch Me" on the album. In the liner notes, Astbury wrote, "The Doors, more than any other group, had the unique chemistry of blues, jazz, classical, and pop fed through the mojo filter to create the high-minded anarchic, angel-headed rock to which all in their wake aspired." In 2002, Astbury joined the Doors of the 21st Century as lead singer, along with surviving Doors members Ray Manzarek and Robby Krieger.

Echo & the Bunnymen

An English post-punk group formed in Liverpool, England, in 1978, Echo & the Bunnymen consisted of lead singer Ian McCulloch, guitarist Will Sergeant, and drummer Pete De Freitas (who left the band in 1986 and died in a car crash in 1989). The *All Music Guide to Rock* described the band as a "dark, swirling fusion of gloomy post-punk and Doors-inspired psychedelia." Echo & the Bunnymen's critically acclaimed debut album, *Crocodiles*, was released in 1980 and followed by *Heaven Up Here* (1981), which reached No. 10 on the UK charts. Their third album, *Porcupine* (1984), reached No. 2 on the UK charts and was followed by *Ocean Rain* (1984), which spawned such hits as "The Killing Moon," "Silver," and "Seven Seas."

In 1987, Echo & the Bunnymen's cover of "People Are Strange" appeared on the soundtrack for *The Lost Boys*. That same year, McCulloch left the band to pursue a solo career. The band reappeared under a new incarnation in 1990 and released an album called *Reverberation*, which was poorly received by critics and fans alike. They disbanded in 1993 but have periodically reunited since then.

Chester Bennington of Linkin Park

An Arizona native born on March 20, 1976, Chester Bennington serves as lead singer of the rap metal band Linkin Park, which formed in Southern California in 1998. The band released their debut album, *Hybrid Theory*, in 2000. Bennington wrote a foreword to *The Doors by the Doors*, claiming to have first heard "Break on Through (to the Other Side)" at the age of thirteen. He soon formed a garage band that dropped a lot of acid and played Doors songs such as "People Are Strange." According to Bennington, "The Doors will always stand the test of time. Their story is truly a rock 'n' roll legacy, with beauty, ugliness, passion, and tragedy."

Axl Rose of Guns N' Roses

Born on February 6, 1962, in Lafayette, Indiana, Axl Rose (real name: William Bailey) endured a strict religious upbringing. As a teenager, he discovered *No One Here Gets Out Alive* and strongly identified with Jim Morrison: "I must have read *No One Here Gets Out Alive* seven times and I think everybody in my band's read it about three or four times. I sent a copy to my parents 'cause I figure they're trying to be nice and get along with me in the world I live in. So I sent them the book because it gets down to the real points and exposes a lot of things about my life." He was so inspired by Morrison's story that he even wrote a poem in his journal about the Doors' lead singer titled "Artistic Death."

Formed in Los Angeles in 1985, Guns N' Roses consisted of Rose (vocals), Izzy Stradlin (guitar), Duff McKagan (bass), Slash (guitar), and Steven Adler (drums). The band played their first gig at the Troubadour Club on June 6, 1985. *Appetite for Destruction* was released in 1987 and steadily rose to the top of the U.S. charts. The following year, their next album, *G N' R Lies*, generated controversy with the song "One in a Million," which included references to "niggers" and "faggots."

In "Bad to the Bone," a feature on Guns N' Roses by Danny Sugerman in the November 1990 issue of *SPIN* magazine, Rose discussed the time he made a pilgrimage to Morrison's grave: "I just sat down next to where he was lying, if he's even there. I was just thinking; I don't even remember how long I was there. It was one of those depressing gray days—Nobody recognized me. And you know, it was like a turning point. I just realized that I could sacrifice myself like Morrison did if I wanted. That was my turning point—realizing that it was up to me . . . If you die, the road of excess leads to a dirt plot in a foreign land that people pour booze on and put out cigarettes on." The following year, Sugerman published a biography of Guns N' Roses called *Appetite for Destruction: The Days of Guns N' Roses.*

In 1993, Guns N' Roses generated even more controversy by including a song penned by Charles Manson called "Look at Your Game Girl" on their album of covers called *The Spaghetti Incident.* Robert Hilburn of the *Los Angeles Times* compared Rose to Morrison: "Like Jim Morrison, Rose exhibits a fierce independence that sometimes leads to errors in judgment as he races in a somewhat romantic pursuit of artistic truth. He also shares Morrison's duality: exploring the dark side of man's nature while also possessing an almost old-fashioned yearning for innocence."

Scott Stapp of Creed

Born on August 8, 1973, Scott Stapp had a strict Christian upbringing with ultrareligious parents. According to Stapp, "I first heard Led Zeppelin in 1994 because rock 'n' roll wasn't allowed in my house. My dad used to say that electric guitars were the devil's music. One day my parents woke up and I wasn't there."

Formed in 1995 and originally called Naked Toddler, Creed featured Stapp (vocals), Mark Tremonti (guitar), Brian Marshall (bass), and Scott Phillips (drums). The band released *My Own Prison* in 1999, featuring the hits "Torn," "One," and "What's This Life For?" *Human Clay*, released the same year, topped the U.S. charts with the No. 1 hit single "With Arms Wide Open." Robby Krieger performed "Roadhouse Blues" and "Riders on the Storm" with Creed at Woodstock 99.

According to Stapp, "I've gotten death threats from right-wing Christian groups who think I'm leading their sons and daughters to hell, and Satan worshippers who think I talk about God too much in my music." At an infamous concert in Chicago in December 2002, Stapp appeared to be so intoxicated that he could barely stand, let alone sing. Some fans even filed a lawsuit that was later dismissed.

Scott Weiland of Stone Temple Pilots

Scott Weiland, who was born on October 27, 1967, met bass player Robert DeLeo at a Black Flag concert in Long Beach and formed a band called Mighty Joe Young, which morphed into the alternative rock band Stone Temple Pilots (a.k.a. STP) in 1991. The band's debut album, *Core*, was released in 1992 and featured such hits as "Sex Type Thing," "Plush," and "Creep." The follow-up album, *Purple*, in 1994 included "Interstate Love Song" and "Big Empty," which ended up on *The Crow* soundtrack.

Stone Temple Pilots recorded a memorable cover of "Break on Through (to the Other Side)" with Ray Manzarek and Robby Krieger that appeared on the Doors' tribute album *Stoned Immaculate* in 2000. In the liner notes, Weiland commented, "Being as there are many obvious parallels regarding my personal and artistic life and that of The Doors lead singer Jim Morrison it was eerie for me to be holed up in the infamous Ocean Way Studio on Sunset Blvd. in Hollywood looking out the vocal booth and seeing not only my brothers in Stone Temple Pilots but Robby Krieger and Ray Manzarek. The track seemed to come to life on its own, no tricks involved, just great players and a lot of raw emotion. That weekend will stand out for me as one of the highlights of my musical life."

Known for his battles with heroin and alcohol addiction over the years, Weiland served as the lead singer of the hard rock supergroup Velvet Revolver between 2003 and 2008. The band also consisted of former Guns N' Roses members Slash, Duff McKagan, and Matt Sorum, as well as Dave Kushner, former member of Wasted Youth.

45

Rage in Darkness by My Side

Artists Who Have Covered Doors Songs

Rock is going to become a dumb fad very soon.

—*Jim Morrison*

Doors covers over the years have proven to be a mixed bag, ranging from the good (Echo & the Bunnymen, "People Are Strange") to the bad (Adam Ant, "Hello, I Love You) to the ugly (Duran Duran, "The Crystal Ship"). The best covers are those that interpret Doors songs in the performer's own style such as Jose Feliciano's phenomenally successful cover of "Light My Fire," as well as Stone Temple Pilots' "Break on Through (to the Other Side)" and Aerosmith's "Love Me Two Times." Many interesting Doors covers—from artists as diverse as Creed, Stone Temple Pilots, Aerosmith, the Cult, John Lee Hooker, Train, Bo Diddley, Days of the New, and more—can be heard on the tribute album *Stoned Immaculate*, which was released in 2000.

Jose Feliciano—"Light My Fire" (1968)

In 1968, singer, guitarist, and composer Jose Feliciano (who was born one of eleven children in Lares, Puerto Rico in 1945) got together with producer Rick Jarrad and recorded "Light My Fire" in a Latin style. It sold more than one million copies and reached No. 5 on the Billboard Charts on August 17, 1968, behind the Rascals' "People Got to be Free," the Doors' "Hello, I Love You," Mason Williams's "Classical Gas," and Steppenwolf's "Born to Be Wild."

Released just a year after the Doors scored a No. 1 hit with the song, Feliciano's version (included on the album *Feliciano!*) is by far the best-known and most successful cover of "Light My Fire." Although the Doors actually liked the version, the *Rolling Stone Album Guide* called it a "slaughter" of the original tune, stating "Feliciano seemed to have believed that the song was only a weirder version of 'Girl from Ipanema.'" In an interview in the Summer 2007 issue of *Classic Rock* magazine, John Densmore remarked, "I really liked it. He did a good job. There's a little bit more saccharine in there but it's such a fresh approach."

For his part, Robby Krieger stated that he "owed a big debt" to Feliciano because once he covered the song "everybody started doing it. He did a whole different arrangement on it."

Feliciano, who won two Grammy Awards for Best New Artist of the Year and for Best Pop Song of the Year in 1969, went on to an illustrious career that included such hits as the 1970 holiday perennial "Feliz Navidad." He also wrote the popular theme song to the TV comedy *Chico & the Man*, which starred Freddie Prinze and Jack Albertson. During one episode, Feliciano made a guest appearance as Chico's cousin "Pepe Fernando" and sang "Light My Fire" while the cast members danced around the garage.

X—"Soul Kitchen" (1980)

One of Los Angeles' most influential punk bands, X, covered "Soul Kitchen" on their debut album, *Los Angeles*, which was released in April 1980 and produced by Ray Manzarek, who also worked on the band's subsequent three albums: *Wild Gift* (1981), *Under the Big Black Sun* (1982), and *More Fun in the New World* (1983). X consisted of lead singer Exene Cervenka, guitarist Billy Zoom, drummer DJ Bonebrake, and bassist John Doe. Classic X tunes include "Your Phone's Off the Hook, but You're Not," "Johnny Hit and Run Paulene," "Nausea," and "Los Angeles."

Manzarek witnessed one of X's live shows at the Whisky A Go Go during the late 1970s in which they sang an intense cover of "Soul Kitchen" at "a thousand miles per hour" and from then on the Doors' keyboardist was a huge fan of the band. According to Manzarek, "I saw [X] playing at the Whisky-A-Go-Go and thought they were fabulous. Walked up to them after the show, went backstage and said 'You guys are great, man . . . what a punk rock band.' It was really, really powerful. America's best punk rock band." Manzarek also remarked that X and the Doors "occupied that film noir Los Angeles represented by John Fante."

Los Angeles was ranked No. 24 on *Rolling Stone* magazine's list of "The Greatest Albums of the 80s" and No. 286 on the magazine's list of "The 500 Greatest Albums of All Time." X released a total of seven studio albums before disbanding in the mid-1990s. They reunited in the early 2000s and still tour periodically. In 2000, Exene teamed up with Perry Farrell to perform "Children of Night," which appeared on the Doors' tribute album, *Stoned Immaculate*.

Echo & the Bunnymen—"People Are Strange" (1987)

English post-punk group Echo & the Bunnymen formed in Liverpool in 1978 with an original lineup that included lead singer Ian McCulloch, guitarist Will Sergeant, and bassist Les Pattinson, supplemented by a drum machine. By 1980, Pete de Freitas was hired as the band's drummer. Echo & the Bunnymen's cover of "People Are Strange" appeared on the soundtrack of the 1987 film *The Lost*

Boys. Produced by Ray Manzarek, the song was also released as a single (with "Bedbugs and Ballyhoo" as the B-side) that reached No. 29 on the UK Singles Chart in February 1988.

Aerosmith—"Love Me Two Times" (1990)

Known as "the Bad Boys from Boston," Aerosmith covered "Love Me Two Times" for the soundtrack of the 1990 film *Air America*, which starred Mel Gibson and Robert Downey Jr., and also performed the song at their *MTV Unplugged* performance that year

English post-punk rock group Echo & the Bunnymen successfully covered "People Are Strange," which appeared on the soundtrack of the 1987 film *The Lost Boys.*   *Courtesy of Kerry Humpherys/doors.com*

(lead singer Steven Tyler dedicated the song to Morrison). Ironically, the performance took place at the Ed Sullivan Theater, where Morrison had defied the censors in 1967 by singing "higher" during "Light My Fire." Aerosmith's "Love Me Two Times" cover reached No. 27 on the U.S. charts. In addition, the group included "Love Me Two Times" on their 2001 greatest hits album, *Young Lust: The Aerosmith Anthology*, which was reissued in 2005 as *Gold*. Their version of "Love Me Two Times" also appears on the Doors tribute album *Stoned Immaculate.*

The Cure—"Hello, I Love You" (1990)

In 1990, a compilation album called *Rubáiyát* was released to commemorate the fortieth anniversary of Elektra Records. Contemporary Elektra artists were recruited to cover songs from the company's historic catalog for *Rubáiyát: Elektra's 40th Anniversary*. Two longtime Elektra artists, Jackson Browne and the Cure, covered songs (including "Hello, I Love You") and had songs covered by other artists for the album. Carly Simon and the Eagles were the only artists to have two songs covered in the album, which was produced by Lenny Kaye, guitarist of the Patti Smith group. Formed in 1976, the Cure (variously described as post-punk, New Wave, goth rock, and alternative rock) featured the highly talented Robert Smith as singer/songwriter. The band released their debut album, *Three Imaginary Boys*, in 1979. Their album *Pornography* (1982) featured such hits as "Let's Go To Bed," "Just Like Heaven," "Lovesong," and "Friday I'm in Love."

Billy Idol—"L.A. Woman" (1990)

From 1976 to 1981, Billy Idol (real name: William Broad) was lead singer for the British punk band Generation X. In 1982, Idol released a self-titled solo album that produced several hits, including "Dancing with Myself," White Wedding," and "Hot in the City." Idol covered "L.A. Woman" for his 1990 album *Charmed Life*, which reached No. 11 on the Billboard Charts. Released as a single, "L.A. Woman" rose to No. 52 on the charts. The *Rolling Stone Album Guide* referred to the cover as "a roaming, desperately uninspired version of 'L.A. Woman.'" The following year, Idol appeared in a small role in Oliver Stone's *The Doors* as "Cat," a drinking buddy of Jim Morrison's.

Duran Duran—"The Crystal Ship" (1995)

Best known for their many MTV-friendly hits during the 1980s such as "Rio" and "Hungry Like the Wolf," British New Wave band Duran Duran included "The Crystal Ship" on their all-covers album, *Thank You*, which was released in 1995. The album's cover features a collage of the artists whose songs were covered such as Bob Dylan, Iggy Pop, Flavor Flav of Public Enemy, Sly & the Family Stone, Lou Reed, and Jim Morrison representing the Doors. One of the most ludicrous songs on the album was a cover of Public Enemy's controversial rap anthem, "911 Is a Joke."

Although the album reached a very respectable No. 19 on the Billboard Charts, it was savagely attacked by the critics. For example, London-based *Q* magazine listed *Thank You* as the "Worst Album Ever" (with Spice Girls, *All Their Solo Albums!*; Various, *Urban Renewal: The Songs of Phil Collins*; Lou Reed, *Metal Machine Music*; and Billy Idol, *Cyberpunk*, rounding out the top five). The magazine described *Thank You* as "54 minutes and 29 seconds of pure hell." *Rolling Stone* magazine's review of *Thank You* slammed the whole concept: "[S]ome of the ideas at play here are stunningly wrongheaded, like the easy-listening arrangement given Elvis Costello's 'Watching the Detectives' or the version of Zeppelin's 'Thank You' that sounds like the band is covering Chris DeBurgh. But it takes a certain demented genius to recognize Iggy Pop's 'Success' as the Gary Glitter tune it was meant to be or redo '911 Is a Joke' so it sounds more like Beck than Public Enemy." Duran Duran later acknowledged that *Thank You* was "commercial suicide." However, at least one of the artists covered, Lou Reed, praised the band, referring to their version of his "Perfect Day" as "the best cover ever completed of one of my songs."

Amorphis—"Light My Fire" (2000)

Arguably the most bizarre Doors cover (discounting grindcore band Anal Cunt's 1993 version of "Hello, I Love You") has been the Finnish death metal band's version of "Light My Fire." Amorphis covered the song as a bonus track on the rerelease of their 2000 concept album, *Tales from the Thousand Lakes*. Formed in 1990, the band consists of Jan Rechberger, Esa Holopainer, and Tomi Koivusaari. Although Amorphis started out primarily as a death metal band, they have frequently incorporated elements of progressive, heavy metal, and even folk rock into their sound. The band often uses the Kalevala, the epic poem of Finland, as a source for their lyrics.

Marilyn Manson—"Five to One" (2000)

Shock rocker Marilyn Manson (real name: Brian Warner) released a cover of "Five to One" as a B-side to two singles, "Disposable Teens" and "The Fight Song," which appeared on his album *Holy Wood (In the Shadow of the Valley of Death)*. Manson's stage name was adapted from a juxtaposition of Marilyn Monroe and Charles Manson. The band formed in 1989 as "Marilyn Manson & the Spooky Kids" and quickly gained a cult following. Manson often performed with "Twiggy Ramirez" (Jeordie White) and "Madonna Wayne Gacy" (Stephen Gregory Bier). In 1994, Trent Reznor of Nine Inch Nails produced Marilyn Manson's debut album, *Portrait of an American Family*, on his Nothing Records label. The band's 1995 album *Smells Like Children* contained their first big hit, a cover of the Eurythmics' "Sweet Dreams (Are Made of This)." Subsequent albums included *Antichrist Superstar* and *Jack Off Jill*. Marilyn Manson's unique theatrical performances were designed for maximum shock value and heavily influenced by Alice Cooper. The band has sold more than 50 million albums worldwide.

Snoop Dogg—"Riders on the Storm" (2003)

Produced by Fredwreck, Snoop Dogg's remixed version of "Riders on the Storm" appeared in the 2003 game *Need for Speed: Underground 2*. The cover was dubbed over the original track and features lines such as "Goin off of this off of that with the Lizard King/Bumpin the back, how about that." A protégé of Dr. Dre, Snoop Dogg (real name: Calvin Broadus) is a rapper, record producer, and actor. He grew up as a member of the Crips in high school and spent six months in jail for cocaine possession shortly after he graduated. Snoop Dogg's debut album, *Over the Counter*, was released in 1991, followed by *Doggystyle*, which yielded the hit singles "What's My Name" and "Gin and Juice."

46

Let Them Photograph Your Soul

With each new film, a younger group of people gets exposed to the music and begins investigating The Doors.

—Ray Manzarek

In addition to appearing on the soundtrack of Oliver Stone's *The Doors*, Doors songs can be heard in a variety of films, most notably Coppola's *Apocalypse Now*. Other notable movies that feature Doors music include *Two-Lane Blacktop* ("Moonlight Drive"), *The Lost Boys* ("People Are Strange"), *Less Than Zero* ("Moonlight Drive"), *Forrest Gump* ("Soul Kitchen," "Hello, I Love You," "Break on Through," "People are Strange," and "Love Her Madly"), *The Waterboy* ("Peace Frog"), *School of Rock* ("Touch Me"), *Jarhead* ("Break on Through"), and several others. Significantly, the majority of these movies feature characters who are outcasts, oddballs, outsiders, and/or self-destructive individuals.

The Doors also served as the inspiration for *Eddie and the Cruisers* (1983), which depicts a fictional 1960s rock star (Michael Pare) who stages his own death and features a soundtrack by John Cafferty and the Beaver Brown Band. In addition, Robert Harmon, the director of *The Hitcher* (1986), has claimed that the whole idea for the thriller was inspired by "Riders on the Storm." "Jim Morrison" also makes a memorable appearance at "Waynestock" in *Wayne's World 2*. Last, and most certainly least, Lester Bangs (Philip Seymour Hoffman) in *Almost Famous* (2000) remarks despairingly, "The Doors? Jim Morrison? He's a drunken buffoon posing as a poet."

"Moonlight Drive"—*Two-Lane Blacktop* (1971)

"Performance and image, that's what it's all about." Released on July 7, 1971, just four days after Jim Morrison's death, *Two-Lane Blacktop* is an offbeat, existential road movie. Billed as "The Far-Out World of the High Speed Scene!," the film stars singer-songwriter James Taylor ("Fire and Rain") as "The Driver," Beach Boys drummer Dennis Wilson as "The Mechanic," Warren Oates as "GTO," and Laurie Bird as "The Girl," a hitchhiking teenager. In addition, Harry Dean Stanton appears in the film as a gay Oklahoma hitchhiker. *Two-Lane Blacktop* was the only time either Taylor or Wilson acted in a movie. The plot involves two street racers who live on the road in a 1955 Chevy 150, traveling from town to town challenging local residents to races. "Moonlight Drive" can be heard early in the film as The Driver and The Mechanic seek cars to race among endless small towns full of gas stations, cheap motels, and roadside cafes.

Two-Lane Blacktop was directed by Monte Hellman, who had previously directed a pair of existential Westerns: *Ride in the Whirlwind* (1965) and *The Shooting* (1967), both of which starred Jack Nicholson. Bird, who only acted in two other films, *Cockfighter* (1974) and *Annie Hall* (1977), committed suicide in the Manhattan apartment she shared with her boyfriend, Art Garfunkel, in 1979 at the age of twenty-five. Garfunkel dedicated his 1981 album,

In addition to Oliver Stone's 1991 film, *The Doors*, the band's music has appeared on the soundtracks of many movies starting with *Two-Lane Blacktop* (1971).   *Author's Collection*

Scissors Cut, to Bird. The only member of the Beach Boys who knew how to surf, Wilson drowned at the age of thirty-nine in 1983. He had been aboard a friend's boat in Marina del Rey and, after an afternoon of heavy drinking, dove into the icy water to retrieve items he had thrown from his own boat months earlier.

According to the director's commentary on the first DVD release of *Two-Lane Blacktop*, the reason the movie took so long to release on DVD was because the producers and Hellman initially had trouble securing permission from Morrison's estate to use "Moonlight Drive." The soundtrack also features "Me and Bobby McGee," written and performed by Kris Kristofferson; "Maybellene/ No Money Down," written by Chuck Berry and performed by John Hammond Jr.; and "Stealin'," written and performed by Arlo Guthrie. Billy James, who had signed the Doors to Columbia Records in 1965, served as music supervisor. Ironically, neither Taylor nor Wilson contributed to the film's soundtrack. Taylor's version of Carole King's "You've Got a Friend" reached No. 1 on the charts on July 31, 1971. *Two-Lane Blacktop* flopped at the box office but has since become a cult classic.

"The End"—*Apocalypse Now* (1979)

"Each time I looked around the walls moved in a little tighter." *Apocalypse Now* perfectly utilized "The End," both in the riveting opening sequence (with its hallucinatory blend of chopper blades and napalm accompanying the haunting ballad) and during the dramatic killing of Kurtz at the end. At the film's climax, Morrison can be heard chanting "kill, kill, kill" and "fuck, fuck, fuck," portions of the original recording that were previously mixed way down.

Francis Ford Coppola, who had directed the Academy Award-winning films *The Godfather* and *The Godfather II*, was a student at the UCLA film school at the same time that Ray Manzarek and Jim Morrison were there. In fact, Coppola had approached Manzarek about composing the film's score, but the Doors keyboardist was committed to working on the *An American Prayer* album at the time.

In addition to the effective use of "The End," the original script included a firefight accompanied by "Light My Fire" that was never filmed. Another scene deleted from the final film featured Kurtz teaching his army of native tribesmen "Light My Fire" in their own dialect.

Filmed in the Philippines, *Apocalypse Now* was a very loose adaptation of Joseph Conrad's 1902 novella *Heart of Darkness*, that starred Martin Sheen, Marlon Brando, Dennis Hopper, Robert Duvall, Frederic Forrest, Albert Hall, Sam Bottoms, and Laurence Fishburne. In addition, the film featured bit roles from former Doors roadie Harrison Ford as Colonel G. Lucas (a tribute to George Lucas, who gave Ford his big break in *American Graffiti*), legendary rock promoter Bill Graham (who booked the Doors at the Fillmore Auditorium in 1967) as the Playboy Bunnies' manager, and R. Lee Ermey (*Full Metal Jacket*) as a helicopter pilot.

The production (nicknamed *Apocalypse When?* for its numerous delays) was plagued with problems, including typhoons, the firing of Harvey Keitel, Martin Sheen's heart attack, and numerous financial issues. In 1979, Sheen hosted *Saturday Night Live* and appeared in a sketch featuring "The End" that satirized the troubled production of *Apocalypse Now*. Coppola famously remarked, "We were in the jungle, there were too many of us, we had access to too much money, too much equipment, and, little by little, we went insane."

Coppola shot a record 1.5-million feet of film for *Apocalypse Now*, and about twenty-three hours of film ended up on the cutting-room floor. Budgeted at $12 million, *Apocalypse Now* ended up costing $31 million. It earned $150 million worldwide. The film won the Palme d'Or, along with the *Tin Drum*, at the 1979 Cannes Film Festival. Like *An American Prayer*, the *Apocalypse Now* soundtrack was nominated for a Grammy Award in the Best Spoken Word category. The fascinating 1991 documentary *Hearts of Darkness: A Filmmaker's Apocalypse* chronicles the many difficulties faced by the cast and crew during the troubled shoot. In 2001, Coppola rereleased *Apocalypse Now* as *Apocalypse Now Redux*, restoring several sequences lost from the original 1979 cut of the film, thereby expanding its length to 200 minutes.

"Light My Fire"—*Altered States* (1980)

"We're all trying to fulfill ourselves, understand ourselves, get in touch with ourselves, face the reality of ourselves, explore ourselves, expand ourselves. Ever since we dispensed with God we've got nothing but ourselves to explain this meaningless horror of life." Unafraid of exploring the uncharted territory in the mind, a "psychopsychiatrist" named "Eddie Jessup" (portrayed by William Hurt in his film debut) takes his experiments in a sensory deprivation tank to the extreme and regresses into a primitive state. Madness to Jessup is "just another state of consciousness." Directed by Ken Russell, *Altered States* was adapted from a novel by Paddy Chayefsky, who based it on the pioneering work on sensory deprivation by renowned "psychonaut" and dolphin researcher John Lilly (1915–2001).

Although considered to be among the great psychedelic movies, *Altered States* actually represents one of Russell's more restrained directorial efforts (his credits include *Tommy, Lisztomania, Crimes of Passion, The Lair of the White Worm*, and *Whore*). In order to give viewers an idea of the time period, "Light My Fire" can be heard briefly at a party scene where Jessup meets his future ex-wife Emily (Blair Brown), who smokes a joint, thus demonstrating her hipness to the Harvard professor. As for Hurt, he gets the opportunity to spout such ludicrous lines as "I obviously regressed to some quasi-simian creature" and, somewhat more prophetically and Doors-like, "I want to break through."

In another scene, Jessup travels to Mexico, where he trips with Indians on Amanita muscaria and experiences some mind-blowing hallucinations reminiscent of the Doors' fictional peyote trip in Oliver Stone's *The Doors*. Arthur Penn (*Bonnie and Clyde*) was originally slated to direct the picture but quit after a dispute with Chayevsky. Curiously, Chayefsky, a three-time Oscar-winning screenwriter, demanded that his name be removed from the credits. Drew Barrymore made her film debut in *Altered States* as the Jessups' three-year-old daughter, Margaret.

"People Are Strange"—*The Lost Boys* (1987)

"Sleep all day. Party all night. Never grow old. Never die. It's fun to be a vampire." Directed by Joel Schumacher, this comedy/horror film about a gang of teenage vampires stars Jason Patric, the two Coreys (Haim and Feldman), Dianne Wiest, Edward Herrmann, Kiefer Sutherland, Alex Winter, Jamison Newlander, and Barnard Hughes. The soundtrack features "People Are Strange" as recorded by English post-punk band Echo & the Bunnymen. The song opens and ends the film. In addition, the Lost Boys' cave contains a huge poster of Jim Morrison as "The Lizard King." After Patric's character, "Michael," drinks blood, his face is superimposed with the Morrison poster and surrounded by fire.

The majority of the film was shot in Santa Cruz, California. *The Lost Boys* soundtrack also featured "Walk This Way" performed by Run-D.M.C., "Groovin'" by the Rascals, "Don't Let the Sun Go Down on Me" performed by Roger Daltrey, and "Good Times" performed by INXS. Patric was at one time considered for the part of Morrison in *The Doors* biopic. Ironically, Patric's grandfather, actor Jackie Gleason (*The Honeymooners*), was a central figure in the "Rally for Decency" in the Orange Bowl in 1969—a conservative reaction to the Doors' notorious March 1, 1969, appearance at the Dinner Key Auditorium in Miami that led to Morrison's arrest and trial.

"Moonlight Drive"—*Less Than Zero* (1987)

"Well, you're fucked up, you look like shit, but hey no problem, all you need is a better cut of cocaine." A shallow, overly stylized adaptation of Bret Easton Ellis's nihilistic 1985 bestselling novel of the same name (once hailed as the "first MTV novel"), *Less Than Zero* details the sordid lives of three aimless teens from wealthy Beverly Hills 90210 families who were best friends in high school but whose lives are now headed in totally opposite directions. Clay (Andrew McCarthy) returns home for the holidays from his freshman stint at an Ivy League college (his dorm room contains a bust of Jim Morrison and a Morrison poster) to find his former girlfriend, Blair (Jami Gertz), strung out on drugs and his best friend, the self-destructive Julian (Robert Downey Jr.), on the downward spiral toward total addiction. Worse still, Julian had been sleeping with Blair while Clay was away reading the Harvard classics.

Throughout the film, the gang get totally trashed, wander aimlessly from party to party, and half-heartedly attempt to bail Julian out of his troubles. James Spader turns in a sleazy performance as "Rip," one of the lamest drug dealers ever to hit the silver screen. It's also interesting in hindsight to realize that Downey was living the life of a drug-addled loser away from the camera as well. In addition, Brad Pitt can be seen briefly in an uncredited role as one of the drunken revelers, and Flea from the Red Hot Chili Peppers portrays "Musician #1."

"Moonlight Drive" can be heard at a club as Clay and Blair search for Julian, the mesmerizing tune contrasting with the phony, stuffy club loaded with superficial partygoers. The stellar *Less Than Zero* soundtrack also features "A Hazy Shade of Winter" performed by the Bangles, "Rock 'n' Roll All Night" by Poison, "Bring the Noise" by Public Enemy, "Life Fades Away" by Roy Orbison, "Bump 'n Grind" by David Lee Roth, "Rocking Pneumonia and the Boogie Woogie Flu" by Aerosmith, "Are You My Woman" by the Black Flames, "Going Back to Cali" by LL Cool J, "How to Love Again" by Oran "Juice" Jones and Alyson Williams, "Christmas in Hollis" by Run-D.M.C., "In-A-Gadda-Da-Vida" by Slayer, "Fight Like a Brave" by the Red Hot Chili Peppers, "Li'l Devil" by the Cult, "She's Lost You" by Joan Jett & the Blackhearts, and "Fire" by Jimi Hendrix.

The soundtrack peaked at No. 31 on the Billboard Charts and was certified gold in 1988. In addition, the Bangles' cover of Simon & Garfunkel's "Hazy Shade of Winter" reached No. 2 on the charts. The title "Less Than Zero" was taken from a song of the same name on Elvis Costello's 1977 debut album, *My Aim Is True.*

"Soul Kitchen," "Hello I Love You," "People Are Strange," "Break on Through," "Peace Frog," and "Love Her Madly"— *Forrest Gump* (1994)

"When I got tired, I slept, when I got hungry, I ate. When I had to go, you know, I went." Besides Oliver Stone's *The Doors, Forrest Gump* utilizes more Doors songs than any other movie (although only "Break on Through" appears on the film's soundtrack). Directed by Robert Zemeckis and loosely based on the 1986 Winston Groom novel of the same name, this comedy-drama stars Tom Hanks, Robin Wright Penn, and Gary Sinise. Doors songs that appear in the film include "Soul Kitchen" (Vietnam scene), "Hello, I Love You" (ping pong scene), "People Are Strange" (ping pong scene), "Break on Through" (ping pong scene), "Peace Frog" (New York City scene with Lt. Dan), and "Love Her Madly" (scene where Jenny leaves hotel with a black eye).

Music producer Joel Sill reflected on compiling the soundtrack, "We wanted to have very recognizable material that would pinpoint time periods, yet we didn't want to interfere with what was happening cinematically." Ironically, in spite of all the great '60s songs utilized throughout the film, *Forrest Gump* can definitely be viewed as an indictment of the 1960s counterculture movement. The hugely successful *Forrest Gump* soundtrack peaked at No. 2 on the Billboard Charts and eventually sold 12 million copies. In addition to "Break on Through," the soundtrack features "Blowin' in the Wind" by Bob Dylan, "Respect" by Otis Redding, "Sloop John B" by the Beach Boys, "Hey Joe" by the Jimi Hendrix Experience, and "Free Bird" by Lynyrd Skynyrd, among others.

"Riders on the Storm"—*The Basketball Diaries* (1995)

"I was just gonna sniff a bag but one guy says if you're gonna sniff you might as well pop it and another guys says if you gonna pop it you might as well mainline." Directed by Scott Kalvert and starring Leonardo DiCaprio, Lorraine Bracco, James Madio, and Mark Wahlberg, *The Basketball Diaries* captures all of the glory and depravity of the sordid, heroin-laced life of writer Jim Carroll, who makes a cameo in the film as a drug addict named "Frankie Pinewater." Based on Carroll's 1978 autobiographical novel of the same name, *The Basketball Diaries* documents the author's descent into the harrowing world of drug addiction. He attended Trinity High School in Manhattan on scholarship and was an All-City basketball star.

"Riders on the Storm" can be heard during a disastrous high school basketball game in which Carroll and two of his teammates are totally wasted. Carroll collapses onto the court after missing a foul shot and then quits the team, beginning his downward spiral. The soundtrack also includes "Star" by the Cult, "Catholic Boy" by Carroll (with Pearl Jam), "Blind Dogs" by Soundgarden, and "I've Been Down" by Flea. Controversy has shrouded the film's legacy because of a fantasy scene where DiCaprio's character shoots up the school that eerily recalls the Columbine tragedy.

In the late 1970s, Carroll was encouraged by his friend and roommate Patti Smith to form a New Wave/punk rock band called the Jim Carroll Band. His most memorable song, "People Who Died," appeared on the album *Catholic Boy*. Carroll showed up on Ray Manzarek and Michael McClure's 2006 DVD *The Third Mind*, along with poets Allen Ginsberg and Lawrence Ferlinghetti. According to the *Encyclopedia of Punk*, "Along with Richard Hell and Tom Verlaine, Carroll brought a literary sensibility to punk and was able to use his druggy past to evocative effect in chronicling a life almost wasted, but in which a true poetic talent was somehow nurtured through an opiate haze." Carroll died of a heart attack in 2009 at the age of sixty.

"Peace Frog"—*The Waterboy* (1998)

"A man with a serious drinking problem." One of the strangest uses of a Doors song in any soundtrack was the inclusion of "Peace Frog" in *The Waterboy*, a mediocre comedy directed by Frank Coraci and starring Adam Sandler, Henry Winkler, and Kathy Bates. Sandler portrays "Bobby Boucher" (pronounced "Boo-Shay"), a Cajun waterboy ("water distribution engineer") with hidden football talents who rallies a mediocre college football team, the South Central Louisiana State University Mud Dogs. Bates portrays Boucher's domineering mother, while Winkler plays the world's worst football coach.

"Peace Frog" can be heard during the first game, which takes place before a near-empty stadium and drunken cheerleaders. The eclectic soundtrack also includes "Born on the Bayou" by Creedence Clearwater Revival, "Tom Sawyer" by Rush, and "Small Town" by John Mellencamp. The film culminates with a trip to the "Bourbon Bowl," in which Boucher shows up at the stadium in an airboat at the last minute and saves the day. Yes, it's as bad as it sounds.

"Touch Me"—*School of Rock* (2003)

"God of Rock, thank you for this chance to kick ass . . . Please give us the power to blow people's minds with our high voltage rock." Directed by Richard Linklater (*Slacker*), *School of Rock* features Jack Black as "Dewey Finn," an unemployed musician (recently kicked out of the band "Maggotdeath") who assumes the identity of his roommate, "Ned Schneebly," a substitute teacher at an exclusive private school, and proceeds to tutor the kids in the ways of rock 'n' roll. The film features "Touch Me" in a scene where Finn teaches a student named Lawrence how to play the keyboard.

The scene where Finn stage dives and hits the floor was reportedly inspired by an incident witnessed by Black involving Ian Astbury of the Cult and later of the Doors of the 21st Century. According to Black, "I went to see a reunion, in Los Angeles, of The Cult; they were playing and Ian Astbury, the lead singer, took a dive. It was at The Viper Room, and it was just a bunch of jaded Los Angelinos out there, and they didn't catch him and he plummeted straight to the ground. Later I thought it was so hilarious. So that was put into the script." The stellar *School of Rock* soundtrack includes "Stay Free" by the Clash, "Back in Black" by AC/DC, and "Immigrant Song" by Led Zeppelin, among others.

"Break on Through (to the Other Side)"—*Jarhead* (2005)

"Every war is different, every war is the same." A powerful war film directed by Sam Mendes, *Jarhead* is based on U.S. Marine Anthony Swofford's 2003 Gulf War memoir of the same name and takes the characters from boot camp through Operation Desert Shield and Operation Desert Storm. The cast includes Jake Gyllenhaal as Swofford and costars Jamie Foxx, Peter Sarsgaard, and Chris Cooper.

"Break on Through (to the Other Side)" can be heard for about ten seconds near the end of the movie. The Marines are trekking through the desert as a helicopter flies overhead, blaring "Break on Through" over the speakers. Swofford exclaims, "That's Vietnam music, can't we get our own fuckin' music?" Other highlights of the film include the platoon cheering as they watch a video of the helicopter attack accompanied by the music of Wagner in *Apocalypse Now*, soldiers playing football with gas masks, and the hellish atmosphere of oil wells burning in the desert. In addition to "Break on Through," the Jarhead soundtrack includes "Fight the Power" by Public Enemy, "Something in the Way" by Nirvana, "O.P.P." by Naughty by Nature, "Soldier's Things" by Tom Waits, "Jesus Walks" by Kanye West, "Bang a Gong" by T-Rex, and "Ride of the Valkyries" by Richard Wagner.

47

So Sing a Lonely Song

The Controversy Caused by the Doors of the 21st Century

We're all getting older. We should, the three of us, be playing these songs because, hey, the end is always near. Morrison was a poet, and above all, a poet wants his words heard.

—*Ray Manzarek*

In 2002, Ray Manzarek and Robby Krieger reunited to produce a new version of the Doors called "the Doors of the 21st Century" that was surrounded with controversy and led to legal action that dragged on for years, pitting the two Doors against fellow Door John Densmore and the Morrison estate. In an interview in *Classic Rock* magazine (Summer 2007), Densmore remarked, "Jim Morrison was always very protective of The Doors name, and so am I."

However, the source of Densmore's anger with Manzarek can be traced to Manzarek's 1998 autobiography, *Light My Fire*, in which the keyboardist made the claim that Morrison had wanted to kick Densmore out of the band because he "couldn't stand him as a human being." Manzarek later reported that Densmore sent him a copy of the book "burnt up." After they were forced to drop the name "the Doors of the 21st Century," the band changed their name several times and now tour under the name Manzarek-Krieger. Dedicated to performing the music of the Doors, the group has been met with mixed reactions from fans and critics alike.

First Tour

It all started in 2002 when Manzarek and Krieger recruited Ian Astbury, lead singer of the Cult, to embark on a tour as the Doors of the 21st Century. It was reported that Densmore was invited to participate but declined since he suffered from tinnitus. (Densmore later denied that he was ever invited to join the band.) Manzarek and Krieger briefly hired Stewart Copeland of the Police (who quit after breaking his arm after falling off his bicycle) and then Ty Dennis to fill in for Densmore, and even added a bass player, Angelo

Just three years after the release of *The Doors: The Complete Studio Recordings*, two of the surviving band members, Ray Manzarek and Robby Krieger, formed the highly controversial group the Doors of the 21st Century.   *Courtesy of Kerry Humpherys/doors.com*

Barbera (who left the band in 2004 and was replaced by Phil Chen). One critic stated that even though Manzarek and Krieger looked "like a dentist and accountant, respectively," their jams were "blistering and hypnotic." As the Doors of the 21st Century, the band released a live DVD in 2003 titled *L.A. Woman Live*.

Permanent Injunction

Densmore filed an injunction in February 2003 to prevent his former band members from using the Doors name. After his injunction was denied in court, Densmore was soon joined by both Morrison's and Courson's families in his fight. Manzarek sarcastically remarked in an interview with the *St. Petersburg Times* (June 7, 2005) that the "people who Jim had completely cut out of his life have sided with the drummer who Jim wanted to fire. It's a Florida soap opera." In July 2005, Densmore and the Morrison/Courson estate won a permanent injunction, which led the band to rename themselves D21C and then Riders on the Storm (a real slap in the face to Densmore who had used that title for his 1990 autobiography). According to court papers, Manzarek and Krieger earned approximately $5,000 to $10,000 per show performing as solo acts but were offered anywhere from $150,000 to $200,000 for the band.

In a July 23, 2005, interview with Mike Bell of the *Calgary Sun*, Manzarek remarked, "I take it as a real insult for people to say, 'Well, you're just doing this for the money . . . God, can't we do it just to play the songs? Robby and I want to play. It's like, listen, I'm not going to be doing this for too much longer—don't you get it?" As for his part, Densmore responded, "I'm just so happy that the legacy of the true Doors, and Jim Morrison in particular, has been preserved by this decision."

"Not for Rent"

In an October 5, 2005, *Los Angeles Times* article titled "Drummer Nixes Doors Song for TV Ad," Densmore commented, "People lost their virginity to this music, got high for the first time to this music. I've had people say kids died in Vietnam listening to this music, other people say they know someone who didn't commit suicide because of this music. Onstage, when we played these songs, they felt mysterious and magic. That's not for rent." In 2007, Densmore remarked that he would only rejoin the Doors for the 40th Anniversary Tour if it was fronted by Eddie Vedder, the lead singer of Pearl Jam who had performed three songs with the surviving band members during the 1993 Rock and Roll Hall of Fame induction ceremony. According to Densmore, "I play with Jim. If there's someone of that level, OK. I'm not gonna join them with Ian. That's not to diss Ian, he's a good singer—but he's no Jim Morrison. Eddie Vedder? My God, there's a singer."

Manzarek-Krieger

In August 2008, the California Supreme Court decided not to review the lower court's decision, so the judgment against Manzarek and Krieger still stands. Meanwhile, Astbury had quit Riders on the Storm in 2007 in order to reunite with the Cult and was replaced by Brett Scallions, the former lead singer of Fuel. In 2010, Miljenko Matijevic briefly became the lead singer of the band, followed by Dave Brock of Hawkwind. Manzarek and Krieger continue to tour under the name "Manzarek-Krieger" or "Ray Manzarek and Robby Krieger of The Doors." In 2011, they scheduled tour dates in Mexico, Bolivia, and Russia with a lineup that included Mark Farner of Grand Funk Railroad on vocals, Phil Chen on bass guitar, and Ty Dennis on drums.

The fight over the Doors' legacy continues to this day. For example, Densmore reportedly is set to publish a new book called *The Doors Unhinged: Rock 'n' Roll on Trial* in 2011. However, due to Densmore's dispute with the publisher, it is uncertain if this new biography will ever see the light of day.

48

Can We Resolve the Past

The Most Essential (and Least Essential) Doors Biographies

I think it is one of those rites of passage books. The continuing new readership is a youthful one, just as the majority of the recordings are sold to young people who are just discovering Jim Morrison.
                    —*Jerry Hopkins on* No One Here Gets Out Alive

A sked which Doors biographies he had read in a 1993 interview that appeared in *The Doors Collectors Magazine*, Ray Manzarek responded, "[I]t's hard to read a lot of Doors books because I lived the Doors, and after *No One Here Gets Out Alive* and then *The Illustrated History*, that pretty well takes care of my need to read Doors books." Two essential Doors biographies that belong on any true fan's bookshelf include John Densmore's *Riders on the Storm* (1990) and Manzarek's *Light My Fire* (1998).

Several of Morrison's many love interests have also written about their relationship with the Lizard King (many of the books contain dubious claims, to say the least!). They include Judy Huddleston, *This Is the End . . . My Only Friend: Living and Dying with Jim Morrison* (1991); Patricia Kennealy, *Strange Days: My Life With and Without Jim Morrison* (1992), and Linda Ashcroft, *Wild Child: Life with Jim Morrison* (1997). Other recommended Doors biographies and memoirs in addition to the ones listed below include *Angels Dance and Angels Die: The Tragic Romance of Jim Morrison* (1998) by Patricia Butler, *The Lizard King Was Here: The Life and Times of Jim Morrison in Alexandria, Virginia* (2006) by Mark Opsasnick, and *The Jim Morrison Scrapbook* (2007) by James Henke. In addition, Jac Holzman's *Follow the Music* (1998) provides a great oral history of Elektra Records along with many classic Jim Morrison anecdotes. Last but not least, Danny Sugerman's autobiography, *Wonderland Avenue* (1989), subtitled *Tales of Glamour and Excess*, provides a fascinating and terrifying glimpse of Morrison's self-destructiveness.

Jim Morrison and the Doors: An Unauthorized Book (1969) by Mike Jahn

Considered the first biography of the Doors, *Jim Morrison and the Doors* was published in 1969 and sold for $1. Billed as "An Unauthorized Book," the slim, ninety-five-page book with black-and-white illustrations is essentially a colorful, hyperbolic, and highly entertaining description of the Doors' legendary performance at the then-new Fillmore East in New York City on March 22, 1968. For example, at one point the author refers to Morrison as "the Sex-Death, Acid-Evangelist of Rock, a sort of Hell's Angel of the groin."

The book was written by Mike Jahn, a rock critic for the *New York Times* who turned to mystery writing in the mid-1970s as "Michael Jahn" and received an Edgar Award for his first mystery novel, *The Quark Maneuver*. He began his popular "Bill Donovan" mystery series in 1982 with *Night Rituals*. As with most Doors biographies, the Jahn book focuses mainly on Morrison and features images of the Lizard King on the front and back covers. It's a true artifact of the era. *Rolling Stone* magazine wrote the whole enterprise off as "endless piles of super-naturally repetitious prose."

No One Here Gets Out Alive (1980) by Jerry Hopkins and Danny Sugerman

A highly sensational, phenomenally successful pioneer biography of Jim Morrison that frequently digresses into pure hero worship, *No One Here Gets Out Alive* was published in 1980. It was the first biography of Jim Morrison, spent nine months on the *New York Times* bestseller list, and helped (along with the use of "The End" in *Apocalypse Now*) to revive the popularity of the Doors nearly a decade after Jim Morrison's death.

Hopkins, who had done an extensive interview with Morrison before his death, shopped the biography around for years, and it was rejected by dozens of major publishers. According to Hopkins, it was Sugerman's "devotion and dedication that moved *No One Here Gets Out Alive* from my closet of unpublished manuscripts to the public eye." It was finally published by Warner Books, which had initially rejected it. Taking its title from the Doors song "Five to One," which appeared on the *Waiting for the Sun* album, *No One Here Gets Out Alive* is divided into three sections: "The Bow Is Drawn," "The Arrow Flies," and "The Arrow Falls." It also features a bare-chested image of the "Lizard King" on the front and back covers.

In the book's almost absurdly hyperbolic foreword, Sugerman remarks, "Jim Morrison was well on his way to becoming a mythic hero while he was still alive—he was, few will dispute, a living legend. His death, shrouded in mystery and continuing speculation, completed the consecration, assuring him a place in the pantheon of wounded, gifted artists who felt life too intensely to bear living it: Arthur Rimbaud, Charles Baudelaire, Lenny Bruce, Dylan Thomas,

James Dean, Jimi Hendrix, and so on." *No One Here Gets Out Alive* also served to perpetuate the "Morrison-Is-Still-Alive" myth: "It would be perfectly in keeping with his unpredictable character for him to stage his own death as a means to escape his public life." In fact, Hopkins initially intended to release two versions of the book: one where Morrison dies in Paris and the other where he fakes his death and disappears. A companion video was made in 1981 featuring interviews with the three surviving Doors band members, as well as Hopkins, Sugerman, and Paul Rothchild, among others. Hopkins published a sequel of sorts, *The Lizard King* (original title: *Ride the Snake: The Essential Jim Morrison*), in 1992.

Riders on the Storm: My Life with Jim Morrison and the Doors (1990) by John Densmore

Riders on the Storm served as an entertaining autobiography by John Densmore, who chronicled all the ups and downs during his stint as the Doors' drummer. Essentially, the memoir details his often cantankerous relationship with Jim Morrison, whom he refers to as "mentor, nemesis, friend." In several italicized sections throughout the book, Densmore even addresses the dead Morrison. The origins of *Riders on the Storm* can be traced to Densmore's 1975 visit to Morrison's grave at Pere Lachaise Cemetery in Paris. When he returned to his hotel room, Densmore started writing a letter to Morrison that consisted of all the issues he had failed to confront the lead singer with while he was still alive. In fact, Densmore quit the band several times due to Morrison's drunken antics in the recording studio and onstage. Densmore dedicated the book to John Lennon "who inspired me to put my personal life on the line."

One of the problems with *Riders on the Storm* is Densmore's casual approach to the facts. For instance, he places the demo recording session in July 1965 when it was actually on September 2, 1965. He also makes the claim that Morrison was from Jacksonville, Florida, when in fact he only lived in the Florida cities of Melbourne, Clearwater, and Tallahassee. In addition, he lists the New Haven Arena concert as occurring on December 5, 1967, when it actually took place on December 9, 1967. Finally, he places the notorious University of Michigan concert in 1969 when it was actually on October 20, 1967.

Break on Through: The Life and Death of Jim Morrison (1994) by James Riordan and Jerry Prochnicky

A rather straightforward, comprehensive biography of Jim Morrison presented in the form of a conventional narrative, *Break on Through* is not as entertaining as *No One Here Gets Out Alive* but more objective and less sensationalistic. At over 500 pages, *Break on Through* covers everything from Morrison's family background to the rise of Doors tribute bands in the 1980s and 1990s, with a particular emphasis on the Lizard King's influences, ranging from Nietzsche and Rimbaud to shamanism, surrealism, and the Living Theatre.

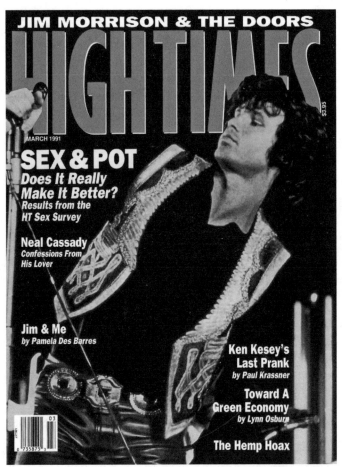

A variety of rock 'n' roll groupies, hangers-on, and "girlfriends" have come forward over the years with their outrageous Jim Morrison stories in the form of interviews and highly questionable memoirs. In this issue of *High Times*, groupie Pamela Des Barres, the author of *I'm with the Band* (1987), detailed her sexual encounters with Morrison.

Courtesy of Ida Miller/idafan.com

Rimbaud and Jim Morrison: The Rebel as Poet (1994) by Wallace Fowlie

A unique work of scholarly criticism, *The Rebel as Poet* primarily focuses on the influence of Rimbaud's poetry in Jim Morrison's lyrics. Author Wallace Fowlie (1908–98), who was James B. Duke Professor of French Literature at Duke University, received acclaim for his translations of Rimbaud. Morrison actually corresponded with Fowlie in 1968, complimenting him on his translation of Rimbaud's work: "Just wanted to say thanks for doing the Rimbaud translation.

I needed it because I don't read French that easily. I am a rock singer and your book travels around with me."

Fowlie (1908–98) was, from 1964, the James B. Duke Professor of French Literature at Duke University. In addition to his translations of Rimbaud, Fowlie was noted for his critical studies of French poetry and drama, and his late study of Morrison as a rock-poet. He also spent six decades teaching at universities in the United States, including Yale, Bennington, Holy Cross, University of Colorado-Boulder, and Duke. Fowlie corresponded with literary figures such as Henry Miller, Rene Char, Jean Cocteau, Andre Gide, Alexis Leger (Saint-John Perse), Marianne Moore, and Anais Nin. In 1990, Fowlie served as a consultant with director Oliver Stone on the film *The Doors*.

On his book *Rimbaud and Jim Morrison*, Fowlie once stated: "Most of the readers know Morrison, but many have discovered Rimbaud thanks to Morrison. This pleased me. Those two rebels make a fine couple."

The Doors on the Road (1997) by Greg Shaw

Inexplicably out of print (new copies are selling on Amazon for more than $100), this in-depth chronological history of the Doors highlights all of their live performances. It reportedly took five years of research and belongs on every Doors fan's bookshelf. *The Doors on the Road* includes a comprehensive chronicle of performance locations, dates, and set lists, as well as trivia, anecdotes, eyewitness accounts, memorabilia, and even Morrison's dialogue with the audience. *The Doors Collectors Magazine* called *The Doors on the Road* is "the ultimate guide to the Doors' live shows as well as a chronicle of their entire history."

Light My Fire: My Life with the Doors (1998) by Ray Manzarek

Notable for its lively anecdotes and outrageous hyperbole ("We ascended Olympus. We drank the nectar of the gods and became one of the elite . . .") and weird psychedelic ramblings, Manzarek's autobiography is highly entertaining and eminently readable. Although subtitled *My Life with the Doors*, the book really focuses primarily on Manzarek's friendship with Morrison, who shares the cover with him. Curiously, Manzarek devotes the first 277 pages to the early days of the band up until the end of 1967 and then rushes through the period 1968–71 in just 75 pages! Manzarek also slams Oliver Stone's *The Doors* at every opportunity. Curiously, *Light My Fire* ends with the death of Morrison and fails to even mention the Doors' last two studio albums, *Other Voices* and *Full Circle*—nor does Manzarek bother to discuss any post-Doors activities.

The Doors: When the Music's Over: The Stories Behind Every Song (2000) by Chuck Crisafulli

A comprehensive resource, *When the Music's Over* analyzes each Doors song, from their debut album to the last two post-Morrison albums, *Other Voices* (1971) and *Full Circle* (1972), as well as *An American Prayer* (1978). The book also provides a concise history of the band from their early Venice Beach days to their final breakup in 1973.

Jim Morrison: Life, Death, Legend (2004) by Stephen Davis

Another conventional and rather derivative Jim Morrison biography, *Life, Death, Legend* is full of some sensational and unsubstantiated material such as implying that he was bisexual and focusing primarily on his self-destructiveness. The author, Stephen Davis, is a rock biographer who has published *Hammer of the Gods: The Led Zeppelin Saga* (1985), *Bob Marley: Conquering Lion of Reggae* (1994), and *Watch You Bleed: The Saga of Guns N' Roses* (2008), among others. In the end, *Life, Death, Legend* is strictly for masochists.

The Doors by the Doors (2006) with Ben Fong-Torres

A well-conceived coffee-table book, *The Doors by the Doors* presents "the complete story of the Doors as told by the Doors themselves" with the assistance of esteemed journalist Ben Fong-Torres, who had interviewed Morrison for *Rolling Stone* magazine in the spring of 1971 right before he left for Paris. For *The Doors by the Doors*, Fong-Torres interviewed the three surviving Doors, as well as Morrison's and Pamela Courson's families. In addition, he compiled all known Morrison interviews that were conducted during his lifetime and interspersed them within the chronological biography, which also contains many never-before-published photos. Musicians Perry Farrell, Henry Rollins, and Chester Bennington all wrote forewords to the book.

49

You Might Recall All of the Rest

The Unique Qualities of the Documentary *When You're Strange*

In this movie, the Doors will never get old.

—*Tom DiCillo*

Written and directed by Tom DiCillo and narrated by Johnny Depp, *When You're Strange* (subtitled *A Film About the Doors*) features "the true story of The Doors," according to Ray Manzarek, who also described the documentary as "the anti-Oliver Stone." DiCillo referred to the story of the Doors as "one of the most compelling in the history of American rock music; three hugely talented musicians and a lead singer whose commitment to artistic freedom was so intense he rocketed them to a success that always hovered on the edge of chaos." DiCillo set out to utilize original footage of the band rather than retrospective interviews as had been done frequently in past Doors documentaries such as *No One Here Gets Out Alive* (1981). According to DiCillo, "To me, there is nothing more powerful and riveting than seeing Robby Krieger, Ray Manzarek, John Densmore, and Jim Morrison leap into life on the screen." DiCillo was determined not to make the mistake of breaking "the spell of this incredible footage that shows the Doors in their prime" and "cutting away to old farts talking about the significance of 'The End.'"

The film's soundtrack, which blends original studio recordings, live performances, poems read by Depp, and interviews with Morrison, was produced, mixed, and mastered by Bruce Botnick, the Doors' recording engineer and coproducer of *L.A. Woman*, the Doors' sixth studio album and last album with Jim Morrison.

Tom DiCillo

DiCillo began his film career as cinematographer for Jim Jarmusch's offbeat 1984 comedy *Stranger Than Paradise*. He also worked on the production of films such as *Johnny Suede* (1991) and *Living in Oblivion* (1995), and directed episodes

Portions of Jim Morrison's film project, *HWY*, were incorporated with the 2010 documentary, *When You're Strange*.   *Author's Collection*

of TV shows such as *Law and Order*. As the son of a colonel in the Marine Corps who grew up in a strict disciplinary environment, DiCillo was well suited to take on the Doors project. He became a Doors fan at the age of fourteen after hearing the full-length version of "Light My Fire." Regarding the 1991 film *The Doors*, DiCillo remarked, "I think that Stone made a movie about four guys, it just so happens that none of them are The Doors. Even in five frames of the real footage, Morrison is infinitely more interesting and complex than he is in the 2 and half hours of the Doors film."

Sundance Film Festival

The documentary first screened at the Sundance Film Festival on January 17, 2009. Although the film received positive reviews, DiCillo's monotonic narration was heavily criticized. DiCillo decided to hire actor Johnny Depp, a longtime Doors fan, to redub the narration. Depp later referred to *When You're Strange* as "a meticulously crafted, exhilarating ode to one of music's greatest, most exciting ensembles" and called Morrison "one of the most significant frontmen/poets/shamans to ever grace a stage."

Los Angeles Film Festival

The revised eighty-six-minute film made its debut to rave reviews at the Los Angeles Film Festival on June 21, 2009, and was also screened at the London Film Festival, which took place October 16–18, 2009. The film (rated R for "some sexual content including references, nudity, drug material, and language) was released in select theaters on April 9, 2010. The movie poster featured an early shot of the four band members strolling in front of Venice Beach. In addition, PBS showed the film as part of its *American Masters* series on May 12, 2010. Released on DVD on June 29, 2010, *When You're Strange* was nominated for a Grammy Award in the category of Best Long Form Music Video.

"Jim Morrison Alive"

Manzarek was ecstatic about the finished product, remarking in an interview in the *Dallas Morning News* (April 9, 2010), "I liked seeing Jim Morrison alive . . . That's my buddy. That was my pal. I haven't seen him alive since 1971, and he was alive in the film as he could be in this stage of our existence. It was great seeing us as young, vibrant, vital men seeking our musical destiny."

Overall, Robby Krieger felt "really happy" about how the film turned out, crediting in particular the editing work. Krieger compared the documentary favorably to Oliver Stone's biopic: "I think when you see the Oliver Stone movie—I'm amazed how good Val Kilmer did—but, you know, the problem with that movie is that the script was kind of stupid. It doesn't really capture how Jim was at all. This gives you a much better insight into how his mind worked, I think."

In an interview with the *San Francisco Examiner* (April 11, 2010), John Densmore commented, "This documentary gives you a little more feel for the time period, which pleases me . . . You get to see the self-destructive side of Jim, which you saw in the Stone movie, but you also get to see a younger, more humorous side of him."

Critical Reaction

Reviewing *When You're Strange* for *Empire* magazine, Kim Newman remarked that the film was "essential for Doors fans but enlightening to the uninitiated" and a "tantalizing study of a troubled creator whose charisma still borders on the supernatural." David Gitten of the *Daily Telegraph* stated, "This is far better than Oliver Stone's ghastly Doors movie." Steven Rea of the *Philadelphia Inquirer* said the film "offers a worshipful but insightful portrait of the group." Owen Gleiberman in *Entertainment Weekly* commented, "*When You're Strange* does have one major idiosyncrasy. There are no interviews—at all. The movie is stitched together with a narration, spoken by Johnny Depp, that sounds like a highly enlightened Wikipedia entry." David Edwards of the *UK Daily Mirror* called Morrison a "pretentious drunk" and remarked that the documentary is "unlikely to light your fire or anyone else's."

Grammy Award

During the pre-televised portion of the 53rd annual Grammy Awards on February 13, 2011, *When You're Strange* won the Grammy Award for Music Video/ Long Form. The other nominees in the category were *No Distance Left to Run* (Blur), *The Greatest Ears in Town: The Arif Mardin Story*, *Rush: Beyond the Light Stage*, and *Under Great White Northern Lights* (The White Stripes). Among the group accepting the award, Krieger commented, "Well, we finally have a great video for the Doors. This one captures the real Jim Morrison and how we reacted together."

50

I'm Going, but I Need a Little Time

Whatever Happened to . . .

Curtis Amy

Known for his saxophone solo on "Touch Me" and his appearance with the Doors on *The Smothers Brothers Comedy Hour* on December 4, 1968, Amy played on several other albums, including Carole King's *Tapestry* and Lou Rawls's *Black and Blue*. He died from complications of pancreatic cancer in 2002 at the age of seventy-two.

Tom Baker

An actor who appeared in Andy Warhol's *I, A Man* in 1967, Baker was a longtime drinking buddy of Jim Morrison and lover of Pamela Courson. After a notorious flight from Los Angeles to Phoenix on November 11, 1969, both Baker and Morrison were arrested for "drunk and disorderly conduct" and "interference with a flight crew" (the charges were later dropped). Baker, who wrote a memoir, *Blue Centre Light* (an extract of which was published in *High Times* in 1981), died of a drug overdose in a "seedy junk-house for heroin addicts" on New York City's Lower East Side in 1982 just a little over a week after his forty-second birthday.

Julian Beck

Beck cofounded the Living Theatre, a highly experimental theater troupe, along with his wife, Judith Malina, in 1947. Morrison was in attendance every night for a week-long engagement of the Living Theatre in February 1969, enthralled by the revolutionary context of the performance. Fueled by alcohol and ideas from the Living Theatre, Morrison took the stage at the Dinner Key Auditorium in Miami, Florida, on March 1, 1969, with disastrous results. Beck died of stomach cancer in 1985 at the age of sixty.

Marc Benno

A legendary guitarist, Benno was hired by the Doors to play guitar during record-ing sessions for the band's sixth studio album, *L.A. Woman*. Benno and Morrison developed a strong bond and hung out together frequently during breaks from the sessions. He currently lives in Texas, has self-released several albums, and occasionally performs in gigs throughout the Lone Star State.

Bruce Botnick

Botnick, who served as audio engineer for the Doors' first five studio albums and coproducer of *L.A. Woman*, later worked as an assistant on the Rolling Stones' *Let It Bleed* album and produced Eddie Money's first two albums, *Eddie Money* in 1977 and *Life for the Taking* in 1978. He also has engineered scores for films by Steven Spielberg and James Cameron.

Pamela Courson

Morrison's "cosmic mate" died of a heroin overdose in her Los Angeles apart-ment on April 25, 1974, at the age of twenty-seven. She was buried at Fairhaven Memorial Park in Santa Ana, California, under the name "Pamela Susan Morrison." After her death, her parents—Columbus and Penny Courson—inherited Morrison's fortune, but in the wake of several legal battles ended up sharing the estate with Morrison's parents.

John Densmore

Densmore, who published his autobiography, *Riders on the Storm*, in 1990, has filed numerous injunctions over the years to prevent his former bandmates, Ray Manzarek and Robby Krieger, from using the Doors' name during their performances. In 2006, he formed a jazz band called Tribaljazz.

Henry Diltz

The legendary rock photographer responsible for the famous *Morrison Hotel* album cover, Diltz is cofounder of the "Morrison Hotel" galleries in New York City and La Jolla, California, that specialize in rock 'n' roll photography.

Paul Ferrara

Morrison's friend took the photograph for the Doors' *Waiting for the Sun* album cover, directed Morrison's experimental film, *HWY*, and worked on a documentary of the band called *Feast of Friends*. He published his memoirs, *Flash of Eden*, in 2007. Ferrara still works as an independent photographer.

Danny Fields

A former publicist for Elektra Records, one of Fields' first responsibilities was to promote the Doors, although he never got along with Morrison. Fields was instrumental in recommending that Elektra also sign two proto-punk bands from Detroit, MC5 and the Stooges (led by Iggy Pop). In the mid-'70s, Fields discovered the Ramones at CBGB's in New York City, became their co-manager, and helped get them signed to Sire Records. The song "Danny Says," from the Ramones' 1980 album, *End of the Century*, refers to Fields. In 1990, Fields became singer-songwriter Paleface's manager and helped him get signed to Polygram Records. Fields also has written several biographies, including *Dream On* about Cyrinda Foxe and *Linda McCartney: A Portrait*.

Michael C. Ford

A celebrated poet, playwright, and recording artist, Ford first read his poetry before an audience at a fundraiser for Norman Mailer's New York mayoral campaign in 1969 along with Morrison and poets Michael McClure, Jack Hirschman, and others. He has done several collaborative recordings with Manzarek and Densmore.

Wallace Fowlie

The James B. Duke Professor of French Literature at Duke University, Fowlie published *Rimbaud and Jim Morrison: The Rebel as Poet*, which compared the poetry (and destructive lifestyle!) of Rimbaud and Morrison. Fowlie died of heart complications in 1998 at the age of eighty-nine.

Bill Gazzarri

The legendary cigar-chomping, white-hatted "Godfather of Rock 'n' Roll," Gazzarri booked the Doors, then just another up-and-coming band, at his Sunset Boulevard nightclub, Gazzarri's, in 1967. Gazzarri died of natural causes in his West Hollywood home in 1991.

Robert Gover

A bestselling novelist whose first book, *One Hundred Dollar Misunderstanding*, is a cult classic, Gover got arrested with Morrison on January 29, 1968, outside the Pussycat A Go Go in Las Vegas for "public intoxication," "vagrancy," and "failure

In addition to selling nearly 100 million albums worldwide over the years, the Doors have branched out into all forms of memorabilia, from bumper stickers and T-shirts to Converse Chuck Taylor All Star Doors Hi Retro Shoes.   *Courtesy of Ida Miller/idafan.com*

to possess adequate identification." Gover, who published his ninth novel, *On the Run with Dick and Jane*, in 2007, now lives in Rehoboth Beach, Delaware.

Bill Graham

The famous rock concert promoter who booked the Doors at the Fillmore Auditorium in San Francisco in January 1967, Graham later served as a producer on the 1991 biopic *The Doors*. Graham died in October of that year in a helicopter crash near Vallejo, California, while returning from a Huey Lewis and the News concert. Also killed in the crash were pilot Steve Kahn and Graham's girlfriend, Melissa Gold, the ex-wife of author Herbert Gold.

Tim Hardin

The singer/songwriter, who hung out with Morrison at the Chateau Marmont and penned such classics as "If I Were a Carpenter" and "Reason to Believe," died of a heroin/morphine overdose in a Hollywood apartment in 1980 at the age of thirty-nine.

Jac Holzman

The founder of Elektra Records, who signed the Doors to a contract in the fall of 1966, received the prestigious Ahmet Ertegun Award by the Rock and Roll Hall of Fame in 2011.

Jerry Hopkins

The coauthor, with Danny Sugerman, of the 1980 Morrison biography *No One Here Gets Out Alive*, Hopkins has published more than 1,000 magazine articles and thirty-three books, including *Elvis: A Biography* (1971), which was dedicated to Morrison. Known as the "Dean of the Pop Biography," Hopkins moved to Thailand in 1993 and published a collection of stories and essays called *Thailand Confidential* in 2005.

Judy Huddleston

The author of the 1991 memoir *This Is the End . . . My Only Friend: Living & Dying with Jim Morrison*, which details her relationship with Morrison, Huddleston has recently completed a second memoir, along with her first collection of poetry. She currently teaches literature, writing, film, and composition at California State University.

Dennis Jakob

Morrison's UCLA film school buddy, Jakob later became a creative consultant on *Apocalypse Now*, reportedly convincing director Francis Ford Coppola to base the movie on Joseph Conrad's 1902 novella *Heart of Darkness*. His current whereabouts are unknown.

Billy James

James, who helped the Doors get signed to their first contract to Columbia Records in 1965 and later worked for Elektra Records, left the record business in the early 1980s and worked as an advocate at the National Academy of Songwriters. He also served as a publicist for high-tech companies during the 1990s. Semi-retired, James currently lives with his wife and family in Redwood City, California.

Robby Krieger

In 2010, Krieger was nominated for a Grammy Award for his solo album, *Singularity*, in the category of Best Pop Instrumental Album.

Arthur Lee

The lead singer of Love was imprisoned under California's "three strikes law" in 1996 for the illegal possession of a firearm. Released in 2001, Lee formed a new incarnation of the band and embarked on a successful tour under the name "Love with Arthur Lee" that thrilled audiences and critics alike. In 2006, he died of acute myeloid leukemia at the age of sixty-one.

Frank Lisciandro

A skilled photographer who served as cinematographer and editor on Morrison's experimental film, *HWY*, Lisciandro later coproduced *An American Prayer*, a 1978 album of Morrison's poetry along with background music by the surviving Doors. He also published a memoir called *Jim Morrison: One Hour for Magic* in 1982. His photographs have been displayed at many galleries.

Lonnie Mack

A well-known rock and blues guitarist, Mack played in recording sessions for the Doors' fifth studio album, *Morrison Hotel*, and received credit on the songs "Roadhouse Blues" and "Maggie M'Gill." Mack lives in Tennessee and occasionally performs at special events and benefit concerts. In 2008, he was a featured performer at the Rock and Roll Hall of Fame's 13th annual Masters Tribute Concert that honored guitar pioneer Les Paul.

Ray Manzarek

Manzarek published his autobiography, *Light My Fire*, in 1998, followed by two novels: *The Poet in Exile*, a fictional account of Morrison faking his death, in 2001, and *Snake Moon*, a ghost story set during the Civil War, in 2006. Manzarek, who frequently tours with Krieger under the band name Manzarek-Krieger, lives in Napa County, California, with his wife Dorothy.

Michael McClure

A poet, playwright, and songwriter, McClure was a close friend and mentor to Morrison, and instrumental in helping promote his poetry. He also wrote the afterword to the first and most influential Morrison biography, *No One Here Gets Out Alive*. McClure still occasionally performs spoken-word poetry concerts with Manzarek, and they have released several CDs. He currently lives in San Francisco.

Clara Morrison

After a long illness, Morrison's mother died in 2005 at the age of eighty-six, surrounded by her husband Steve, daughter Anne, son Andy, and grandson Dylan at her side.

Jim Morrison

On December 9, 2010, nearly forty years after his death in Paris at the age of twenty-seven, Morrison received a full pardon for two misdemeanor convictions that stemmed from the notorious Miami concert on March 1, 1969, from Florida's Clemency Board (following a request by outgoing Governor Charlie Crist).

Patricia Kennealy Morrison

A music journalist and author who served as the editor in chief of *Jazz and Pop* magazine, Kennealy "married" Morrison in a Celtic handfasting ceremony in June 1970. In 1992, she published a memoir called *Strange Days: My Life With and*

With the amazing success of the Doors, Elektra Records evolved from a small folk label in the 1950s to a rock powerhouse that celebrated its sixtieth anniversary in 2010.

Courtesy of Kerry Humpherys/doors.com

Without Jim Morrison. In 2007, Kennealy started her own publishing company, Lizard Queen Press.

Steve Morrison

Promoted to Rear Admiral of the U.S. Navy, Morrison's father served as commander of the U.S. naval forces during the infamous Gulf of Tonkin Incident in August 1964. He died after a fall in a hospital in Coronado, California, in 2008, at the age of eighty-nine, and his ashes were scattered at sea.

Van Morrison

Legendary Northern Irish singer-songwriter Van Morrison once shared the stage with the Doors when his band, Them, performed at the Whisky A Go Go during the summer of 1966. He later embarked on a highly successful solo career that included classic albums such as *Astral Weeks* (1968), *Moondance* (1970), *Saint Dominic's Preview* (1972), *Veedon Fleece* (1974), and others. Morrison was inducted into the Rock and Roll Hall of Fame in 1993, the same year as the Doors.

Nico

A onetime lover of Morrison, who also hung out with Andy Warhol and sang with the Velvet Underground, Nico died of a cerebral brain hemorrhage in 1988 after getting injured in a bicycle accident in Ibiza, Spain.

John Rechy

One of Morrison's favorite authors ("L.A. Woman" was inspired by Rechy's cult classic, *City of Night*), Rechy lives in Los Angeles, where he teaches literature and film courses at the University of Southern California.

Paul Rothchild

The "fifth Door" produced the Doors' first five studio albums, as well as Janis Joplin's last album, *Pearl,* and the soundtrack for Oliver Stone's *The Doors.* He died of lung cancer in 1995 at the age of fifty-nine.

Jerry Scheff

A highly talented bass guitarist who worked on *L.A. Woman,* Scheff also toured with Elvis Presley as a member of his TCB Band in the early 1970s. Scheff still tours with former members of the TCB Band.

John Sebastian

One of the founders of the Lovin' Spoonful ("Summer in the City"), Sebastian played harmonica on "Roadhouse Blues" during recording sessions for the Doors' fifth studio album, *Morrison Hotel*. The Lovin' Spoonful was inducted into the Rock and Roll Hall of Fame in 2000.

Bill Siddons

The Doors' manager during the years 1968–72, Siddons also has managed or co-managed Crosby, Stills, and Nash; Poco; America; Van Morrison; Pat Benatar; and others. He later cofounded a professional management firm called Core Entertainment and represented Alice in Chains. Siddons is married to comedian Elayne Boosler.

Gloria Stavers

The editor in chief of *16 Magazine*, Stavers photographed Morrison for the legendary "Alexander the Great" photo shoot. She died of lung cancer in 1983 at the age of fifty-six.

Danny Sugerman

No. 1 Doors fan and later the band's co-manager, Sugerman died of lung cancer on January 5, 2005, and is buried at Westwood Village Park Cemetery in Los Angeles. His epitaph reads, "There are things known and things unknown and in between are the doors."

Elmer Valentine

Cofounder of two famous Sunset Strip nightclubs, the Whisky A Go Go and the Roxy Theatre, Valentine died in 2008 at the age of eighty-five.

Mary Werbelow

Morrison's ex-girlfriend from Clearwater, Florida, and the original inspiration for "The End" (which at one time was a simple goodbye song), the twice-divorced Werbelow is reportedly unemployed and lives in a mobile home park in California. In a 2005 interview with the *St. Petersburg Times*, she remarked, "I can't find anybody to replace Jim. We definitely have a soul connection so deep. I've never had anything like that again, and I don't expect I ever will."

Selected Bibliography

Bangs, Lester. *Psychotic Reactions and Carburetor Dung*. New York: Anchor Books, 2003.

Berelian, Essi. *The Rough Guide to Heavy Metal*. London: Rough Guides, 2005.

Bogdanov, Vladimir, Woodstra, Chris, and Erlewine, Stephen Thomas. *All Music Guide to Rock*. San Francisco: Backbeat Books, 2002.

Bronson, Fred. *The Billboard Book of Number One Hits*. New York: Billboard Publications, 1985.

Butler, Patricia. *Angels Dance and Angels Die: The Tragic Romance of Pamela and Jim Morrison*. New York: Omnibus Press, 1998.

Cameron, B. Douglas. *Inside the Fire: My Strange Days with the Doors*. Bloomington, IN: AuthorHouse, 2009.

Cogan, Brian. *The Encyclopedia of Punk*. New York: Sterling Publishing, 2008.

Cogan, Jim, and Clark, William. *Temples of Sound: Inside the Great Recording Studios*. San Francisco: Chronicle Books, 2003.

Constantine, Alex. *The Covert War Against Rock*. Los Angeles: Feral House, 2000.

Cook, Bruce. *The Beat Generation*. New York: Charles Scribner's Sons, 1971.

Cowie, Peter. *The Apocalypse Now Book*. Cambridge, UK: Da Capo Press, 2000.

Crisafulli, Chuck. *When the Music's Over: The Stories Behind Every Song*. New York: Thunder's Mouth Press, 2000.

Cross, Charles R. *Room Full of Mirrors: A Biography of Jimi Hendrix*. New York: Hyperion, 2005.

Dalton, David. *Mr. Mojo Risin': Jim Morrison, the Last Holy Fool*. New York: St. Martin's Press, 1991.

Davis, Stephen. *Jim Morrison: Life, Death, Legend*. New York: Gotham Books, 2004.

DeCurtis, Anthony, and Henke, James. *The Rolling Stone Album Guide*. New York: Random House, 1992.

Densmore, John. *Riders on the Storm: My Life with Jim Morrison and The Doors*. New York: Delacorte Press, 1990.

Doe, Andrew, and Tobler, John. *The Doors in Their Own Words*. New York: Penguin Books, 1991.

Doggett, Peter. *There's a Riot Going On: Revolutionaries, Rock Stars, and the Rise and Fall of the '60s*. New York: Canongate, 2007.

Doors, The, and Fong-Torres, Ben. *The Doors by the Doors*. New York: Hyperion, 2006.

Evans, Mike. *The Beats*. London: Running Press, 2007.

Fein, Art. *The L.A. Musical History Tour: A Guide to the Rock and Roll Landmarks of Los Angeles*. Los Angeles: 2.13.61 Publications, 1998.

Ferris, William. *Give My Poor Heart Ease: Voices of the Mississippi Blues*. Chapel Hill: University of North Carolina Press, 2009.

Fowlie, Wallace. *Rimbaud and Jim Morrison: The Rebel as Poet*. Durham, NC: Duke University Press, 1993.

Gilmore, Mikal. *Stories Done: Writings on the 1960s and Its Discontents*. New York: Free Press, 2008.

Goldstein, Richard. *US #1: A Paperback Magazine*. New York: Bantam Books, 1969.

Graham, Bill. *Bill Graham Presents: My Life Inside Rock and Out*. Cambridge: Da Capo Press, 2004.

Halperin, Shirley, and Bloom, Steve. *Reefer Movie Madness: The Ultimate Stoner Film Guide*. New York: Abrams Image, 2010.

Henke, James. *The Jim Morrison Scrapbook*. San Francisco: Chronicle Books, 2007.

Herman, Gary. *Rock 'n' Roll Babylon*. London: Plexus Publishing Limited, 2002.

Herme, Will, and Michel, Sia. *SPIN: 20 Years of Alternative Music*. New York: Three Rivers Press, 2005.

Heylin, Clinton. *From the Velvets to the Voidoids: The Birth of American Punk Rock*. Chicago: A Cappela Books, 2005.

Holzman, Jac. *Follow the Music: The Life and High Times of Elektra Records in the Great Years of American Pop Culture*. Santa Monica: FirstMedia Books, 2000.

Hopkins, Jerry. *The Lizard King: The Essential Jim Morrison*. London: Plexus Publishing, 2010.

Hopkins, Jerry, and Sugerman, Danny. *No One Here Gets Out Alive*. New York: Warner Books, 1980.

Hoskyns, Barney. *Waiting for the Sun: A Rock 'N' Roll History of Los Angeles*. Milwaukee: Backbeat Books, 2009.

Huddleston, Judy. *This Is the End . . . My Only Friend: Living and Dying with Jim Morrison*. New York: Shapolsky Publishers, 1991.

Irvin, Jim, and McLear, Colin. *The MOJO Collection: The Ultimate Music Companion*. New York: Canongate, 2003.

Jahn, Mike. *Jim Morrison and the Doors: An Unauthorized Book*. New York: Grosset & Dunlap, 1969.

Jones, Dylan. *Jim Morrison: Dark Star*. New York: Viking Studio Books, 1990.

Kaufman, Alan, Ortenberg, Neil, and Rosset, Barney. *The Outlaw Bible of American Literature*. New York: Thunder's Mouth Press, 2004.

Kennealy, Patricia. *Strange Days: My Life With and Without Jim Morrison*. New York: Plume, 1993.

Konow, David. *Bang Your Head: The Rise and Fall of Heavy Metal*. New York: Three Rivers Press, 2002.

Kubernik, Harvey. *Canyon of Dreams*. New York: Sterling Publishing, 2009.

Kunz, Don, ed. *The Films of Oliver Stone*. New York: Scarecrow Press, 1997.

Lisciandro, Frank. *Jim Morrison: An Hour for Magic*. New York: Putnam Publishing Group, 1982.

Manzarek, Ray. *Light My Fire: My Life with the Doors*. New York: Berkeley Boulevard, 1998.

————. *The Poet in Exile: A Novel.* New York: Thunder's Mouth Press, 2001.

McNeil, Legs, and Gillian McCain. *Please Kill Me: The Uncensored Oral History of Punk.* New York: Penguin Books, 1997.

Miller, Jim, ed. *The Rolling Stone Illustrated History of Rock & Roll.* New York: Rolling Stone Press, 1980.

Moench, Doug. *The Big Book of Conspiracies.* New York: Paradox Press, 1995.

Morrison, Jim. *The American Night.* New York: Villard Books, 1990.

————. *The Lords and the New Creatures.* New York: Fireside, 1987.

————. *Wilderness.* New York: Villard Books, 1988.

Opsasnick, Mark. *The Lizard King Was Here: The Life and Times of Jim Morrison in Alexandria, Virginia.* Bloomington, IN: Xlibris Corporation, 2006.

Priore, Domenic. *Riot on Sunset Strip: Rock 'n' Roll's Last Stand in Hollywood.* London: Jawbone Press, 2007.

Quisling, Erik, and Williams, Austin. *Straight Whisky: A Living History of Sex, Drugs, and Rock 'n' Roll on the Sunset Strip.* Chicago: Bonus Books, 2003.

Reed, J. D., and Miller, Maddy. *Stairway to Heaven: The Final Resting Places of Rock's Legends.* New York: Wenner Books, 2005.

Riordan, James, and Prochnicky, Jerry. *Break on Through: The Life and Death of Jim Morrison.* New York: HarperCollins Publishers, 1991.

Rocco, John, ed. *The Doors Companion: Four Decades of Commentary.* New York: Schirmer Books, 1997.

Sarig, Roni. *The Secret History of Rock.* New York: Billboard Books. 1998.

Schinder, Scott. *Rolling Stone's Alt-Rock-A Rama.* New York: Delta, 1996.

Segalstad, Eric, and Hunter, Josh. *The 27s: The Greatest Myth of Rock & Roll.* Berkeley, CA: Lake: Samadhi Creations, 2008.

Shaw, Greg. *The Doors on the Road: Complete Live Performances of The Doors.* London: Omnibus Press, 1997.

Silet, Charles L.P., ed. *Oliver Stone Interviews.* Jackson: University Press of Mississippi, 2001.

Sirius, R. U. *Everybody Must Get Stoned: Rock Stars on Drugs.* New York: Citadel Press, 2009.

Stanton, Scott. *The Tombstone Tourist: Musicians.* New York: Pocket Books, 2003.

Sugerman, Danny. *Appetite for Destruction: The Days of Guns N' Roses.* New York: St. Martin's Press, 1991.

————. *The Doors: The Complete Illustrated Lyrics.* New York: Hyperion, 2006.

————. *The Doors: An Illustrated History.* New York: William Morrow and Company, 1983.

————. *Wonderland Avenue: Tales of Glamour and Excess.* London: Abacus, 1989.

Sundling, Doug. *The Ultimate Doors Companion.* London: Sanctuary Publishing, 2000.

Szatmary, David P. *Rockin' in Time: A Social History of Rock-and-Roll.* Englewood Cliffs, NJ: New Jersey: Prentice-Hall, 2000.

Williams, Paul. *Outlaw Blues: A Book of Rock Music.* New York, Pocket Books, 1970.

Wilson, Colin. *The Outsider.* New York: Penguin, 1982.

Index